Hiking Oregon

HELP US KEEP THIS GUIDE UP TO DATE

Every effort has been made by the author and editors to make this guide as accurate and useful as possible. However, many things can change after a guide is published—trails are rerouted, regulations change, techniques evolve, facilities come under new management, and so on.

We would appreciate hearing from you concerning your experiences with this guide and how you feel it could be improved and kept up to date. While we may not be able to respond to all comments and suggestions, we'll take them to heart, and we'll also make certain to share them with the author. Please send your comments and suggestions to the following address:

Globe Pequot Press
Reader Response/Editorial Department
P.O. Box 480
Guilford, CT 06437

Or you may e-mail us at: editorial@GlobePequot.com

Thanks for your input, and happy trails!

Hiking
Oregon

Third edition

Lizann Dunegan

FALCONGUIDES

GUILFORD, CONNECTICUT
HELENA, MONTANA
AN IMPRINT OF GLOBE PEQUOT PRESS

To buy books in quantity for corporate use
or incentives, call **(800) 962-0973**
or e-mail **premiums@GlobePequot.com.**

FALCONGUIDES®

FalconGuides is an imprint of Globe Pequot Press
Falcon, FalconGuides, and Outfit Your Mind are registered trademarks of Morris Book Publishing, LLC.

Project editor: Ellen Urban
Layout: Sue Murray

Unless otherwise noted, all interior photos are by the author.
Maps revised by Ryan Mitchell © Morris Book Publishing, LLC

Library of Congress Cataloging-in-Publication Data is available on file.
ISBN 978-0-7627-8089-1

Printed in the United States of America
10 9 8 7 6 5 4 3 2 1

The author and Globe Pequot Press assume no liability for accidents happening to, or injuries sustained by, readers who engage in the activities described in this book.

Contents

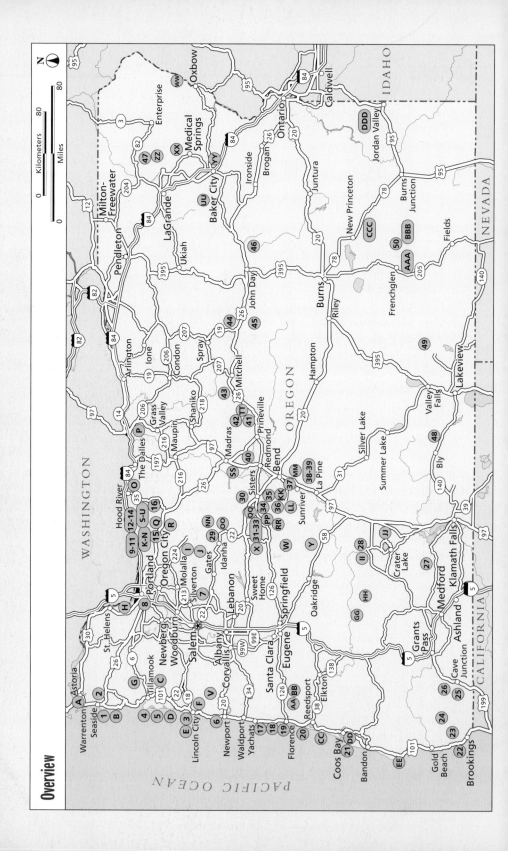

Overview

Introduction

Welcome to the adventure of hiking in Oregon! Like no other activity, hiking allows people of all ages and ability levels to experience the outdoors. This guidebook is designed to let you take your own walk into Oregon's wild places. The trails found here will take you to some of the state's most scenic locales, including rugged, rocky coast; high alpine forests, lakes, and volcanic peaks; high desert sagebrush plains; and rivers and waterfalls. You'll find trails in this guidebook for hikers of all levels, and most of the hikes listed are canine friendly.

Oregon Weather

Oregon's climate is as diverse as its landscapes. The cool, moist marine air that rises off the Pacific Ocean on the west side of the Cascade Mountains contributes to a very wet, seasonal weather pattern. While rainfall averages about 40 inches per year in Portland and other parts of the Willamette Valley, the coastal regions can receive up to 100 inches. Fog and drizzle are common in winter, spring, and late fall, and trails above 3,000 feet are generally snowed in during winter. Temperatures are fairly mild in the west, usually hovering between thirty and fifty degrees Fahrenheit in winter; freezing temperatures don't generally occur except at higher elevations. Summer temperatures usually fall between sixty-five and eighty-five degrees Fahrenheit during the day, but things can cool off significantly at night. Fall can often be dry and sunny, while spring can be unpredictable and rainy.

The Cascade Mountains create a rain shadow in the eastern half of the state, halting the moist Pacific air and making the climate on the east side of the mountains much drier and sunnier than the west. The rainfall on the east side of the mountains varies widely: As little as 4 inches of rain can fall annually in some sections of southeastern Oregon's high desert; the mountain regions receive heavy annual rainfall. Heavy snowfall blankets most mountain ranges in winter—high mountain trails are often snowed in until mid-July. Since the climate of the east isn't tempered by the Pacific Ocean, it's more extreme than in the west. Temperatures can range from lows of zero in winter to one-hundred-plus degrees Fahrenheit in summer.

Flora and Fauna

Drastically different precipitation patterns yield dramatically different ecosystems. Naturally, the eastern and western halves of Oregon support very different vegetation and wildlife.

The forests on Oregon's west side are primarily dense stands of Douglas fir. In the coastal regions expect to find Sitka spruce, red cedar, western hemlock, maple, and oak trees mixed in as well. In the southwest portion of the state, madrone and white oak trees dominate the landscape. Other distinctive forest-floor plants include the purple-fruited Oregon grape, brightly flowered rhododendrons, vine maple, salmonberries,

1

and a variety of mosses and ferns. When you're on the trail, keep an eye out for juicy marionberries, thorny blackberries, and bright-red huckleberries as they make a tasty treat while hiking. Be sure you are familiar with a type of berry before you pop one in your mouth—don't mistake a poisonous berry for a harmless snack. In the spring and summer, go wildflower hunting for the likes of trillium, bleeding hearts, white bunchberry, phlox, columbine, Indian paintbrush, and purple lupine.

If wildlife is more your thing, western Oregon offers a distinct blend of birds, small mammals, and aquatic life. Look up to catch glimpses of some of the birds native to the Oregon coast, including gulls, cormorants, pelicans, and puffins. In coastal tide pools it's common to see mussels, barnacles, sea anemones, starfish, and hermit crabs. Sea lions and seals frequent the rocky headlands and mouths of the coastal rivers, where they feast on salmon and steelhead. Majestic gray whales can be seen during their semiannual migration from December through June. Along streams and marshes blue herons, mallard ducks, belted kingfishers, and black-necked loons can be seen feeding. Mammals roaming the coastal forests include mule deer and black bears.

On the drier, eastern side of the Cascade Mountains, the forests are mainly filled with ponderosa pine, lodgepole pine, and Douglas fir. The stately ponderosa pine forms parklike stands on the sunny mountain slopes and plateaus. The first written accounts of these trees are from the Lewis and Clark expedition in 1804–06. Botanical explorer David Douglas named the trees *ponderosa* because of their magnificent size—they average 3 feet in diameter, can grow to heights of more than 120 feet, and can live 400 to 500 years. Their yellowish bark and large, cylindrical cones are easily distinguishable features. In contrast, the lodgepole pine is a tall, slender tree that grows in crowded clusters.

On the savannas and plateaus of eastern Oregon, the dominant tree species is the western juniper. (The central part of the state is home to the second-largest juniper forest in the world.) This hardy tree grows well in the hot sun and can thrive on less than 8 inches of rain per year. Stands of western juniper are interspersed throughout the mixed landscape of sagebrush, rabbitbrush, and native grasses. Poplars and cottonwoods flourish along the rivers and streams. These fast-growing trees are a common sight on farms and ranches, where they provide shade and serve as windbreakers. Wildflowers like purple lupine, Indian paintbrush, yarrow, and yellow balsamroot add splashes of color to the landscape.

Many species of raptors can be seen soaring in the skies in the eastern part of the state. Red-tailed hawks are common, and you may see osprey and bald eagles along streams and near lakes. Coyotes thrive on the eastern side of the mountains, and their distinct, haunting calls can often be heard in the late evening. Mule deer, black bears, jackrabbits, chipmunks, and squirrels are also abundant in this region. In the Blue Mountains you can find the majestic Rocky Mountain elk—listen for its bugling call in the fall mating season. A small population of about 200 mountain goats live on the windswept ridges of the Wallowa Mountains in the Eagle Cap Wilderness and in some parts of the Elkhorn Mountains in the northeastern part of the state. These tough characters were reintroduced into the area in the 1950s and are currently thriving. Bighorn sheep have also been reintroduced to some of the remote mountain areas. Pronghorn antelope—the fastest land mammals in North America—roam the hills and valleys in the central and southeastern parts of the state. Be on the lookout for rattlesnakes, as they're common in the area. They can often be seen sunning themselves on ledges and rock outcroppings.

Wilderness Restrictions/Regulations

Oregon's national forests and wilderness areas provide a magical retreat for hikers wanting to visit unadulterated nature. The Bureau of Land Management and the USDA Forest Service manage most of the public lands in Oregon. These organizations have the difficult responsibility of trying to balance the public urge to get outdoors and the need to keep these areas wild. With more and more people heading into the Oregon wilds each year, many of our popular national forests and wilderness areas are finding it necessary to issue wilderness permits and charge usage fees at trailheads.

Fees in 2012 were $5 per day at select trailheads, or $30 for an annual Northwest Forest Pass—good at all participating national forests and scenic areas in Oregon and Washington. For information on participating national forests and locations for purchasing a Northwest Forest Pass, visit www.fs.usda.gov/main/r6/passes-permits/recreation or call (800) 270-7504. If you are spending several days on the Oregon coast or you visit the Oregon coast often, you may want to purchase an Oregon Coast Passport, a multiagency (Forest Service, National Parks Service, Bureau of Land Management, and the Oregon Parks and Recreation Department) day-use passport. A five-day or annual vehicle passport covers entry, vehicle parking, and day-use fees at all state and federal fee sites along the entire Oregon Coast. You can purchase the Oregon Coast Passport at all Forest Service and Oregon Parks and Recreation offices along the Oregon Coast.

Before you head into the backcountry, find out what type of permits and restrictions are in place for the area you're going to visit. Trail park passes can be purchased at local ranger stations, participating outdoor outlets, and some trailheads. Most permits for day hikers are self-issued at wilderness trailheads. If you're planning an overnight trip into a wilderness area, call ahead to the local ranger station to see if a permit is required.

How to Use This Book

Hiking Oregon was designed to be highly visual and easily referenced. This book is divided into five regions: Northwest Oregon, Southwest Oregon, Central Oregon, Northeast Oregon, and Southeast Oregon. Each region begins with an introduction that provides a sweeping look at the lay of the land. Following the introduction are the hikes featured within that region.

To aid in quick decision making, each hike chapter begins with a summary of the hike. This short summary gives you a taste of the hiking adventure to follow. You'll learn about the trail terrain and what surprises the route has to offer. If your interest is piqued, read on and learn more about what the hike has to offer. If not, skip to the next chapter.

At the beginning of each hike chapter, you'll find the quick, nitty-gritty details of the hike: where the trailhead is located, hike distance, approximate hiking time, difficulty rating, best hiking season, the nearest town, what other trail users you may encounter, whether dogs are permitted on the trail, use fees, trail schedules, and trail contacts (for updates on trail conditions). "Finding the trailhead" gives you dependable directions from a nearby city right down to where you'll want to park. "The Hike" is the meat of the chapter. Detailed and honest, it's the author's carefully researched impression of the trail. Although it's impossible to cover everything, you can rest assured that what's important won't be missed. "Miles and Directions" provides mileage cues to identify all turns and trail name changes, as well as points of interest. The "Hike Information" section at the end of each hike will give you some ideas on where to get more information about the hike and what else to see while you are in the area.

The "Honorable Mentions" detail additional hikes that will inspire you to get out and explore.

How to Use the Maps

Don't feel restricted to just the routes and trails that are mapped here. Be adventurous and use this guide as a platform to explore Oregon and discover new routes for yourself.

You may wish to copy the directions for the route onto a small sheet of paper to help you while hiking. Otherwise, just slip the whole book in your pack and take it with you. Or if you have the electronic version of this hiking guide, you can reference the hike directions from your mobile device. Enjoy your time in the outdoors—and remember to pack out what you pack in.

Elevation Profile

This helpful profile gives you a cross-sectional look at the hike's ups and downs. Elevation is labeled on the left; mileage is indicated across the top. Road and trail names and points of interest are shown along the route. Hikes with insignificant elevation change do not have profiles.

Route Map

This is your primary guide to each hike. It shows the accessible roads and trails, points of interest, water, towns, landmarks, and geographical features. It also distinguishes trails from roads and paved roads from unpaved roads. The selected route is highlighted, and directional arrows point the way.

Map Legend

Transportation

25 Interstate Highway

40 US Highway

119 State Highway

94 Local/ County/Forest Road

Unpaved Road

Featured Trail

Trail

Railroad

Power Line

Water Features

Body of Water

River/Creek

Intermittent Creek

Waterfall

Spring

Rapids

Land Management

National Park/Forest

State/Local/Open Space Park

Wilderness/National Monument

Physical Features

Dunes

Glacier

Lava

Symbols

Boardwalk

Boat Ramp

Bridge

Bus Stop

Campground

Campsite

Cave

Direction Arrow

Gate

Lighthouse

Parking

Peak/Summit

Picnic Area

Point of Interest/Structure

Ranger Station

Restroom

Tower

Town

Trailhead

Viewpoint/Overlook

Visitor Center/Information Center

Trail Finder

Hikes for Backpackers
Hike 14: Eagle Creek to High Bridge
Hike 21: Sunset Bay, Shore Acres, and Cape Arago State Parks
Hike 22: Cape Ferrelo to Whalehead Beach
Hike 31: Three Fingered Jack
Hike 33: Little Belknap Crater
Hike 35: Tam McArthur Rim
Hike 36: South Sister
Hike 42: Twin Pillars
Hike 45: Black Canyon Trail
Hike 46: Strawberry Lakes Trail
Hike 47: Lakes Basin
Hike 49: Poker Jim Ridge
Hike 50: Steens Mountain Trails

Hikes for Beach/Coast Lovers
Hike 1: Ecola State Park to Indian Beach
Hike 3: Harts Cove
Hike 4: Cape Meares State Park
Hike 5: Cape Lookout
Hike 6: Yaquina Head Outstanding Natural Area
Hike 17: Cape Perpetua Trails
Hike 18: Heceta Head Lighthouse
Hike 19: Sutton Creek Recreation Area
Hike 20: Tahkenitch Creek
Hike 21: Sunset Bay, Shore Acres, and Cape Arago State Parks
Hike 22: Cape Ferrelo to Whalehead Beach

Hikes for Children and Beginning Hikers
Hike 4: Cape Meares State Park
Hike 6: Yaquina Head Outstanding Natural Area
Hike 8: Hoyt Arboretum
Hike 13: Wahclella Falls
Hike 15: Salmon River
Hike 17: Cape Perpetua Trails
Hike 18: Heceta Head Lighthouse
Hike 19: Sutton Creek Recreation Area
Hike 20: Tahkenitch Creek
Hike 23: Alfred A. Loeb State Park Nature Trails

Hikes for Geology Lovers

Hikes for Creek/River Lovers

Northwest Oregon

Northwest Oregon is host to some of the most scenic and varied landscapes in the state. The center of activity for this region is Portland. The largest city in Oregon, Portland has been called an urban nirvana. Forest Park, one of the world's largest city parks, rests right in the heart of the city limits. This hiking-friendly city has miles of scenic trails that wind through a cool forest of big-leaf maple and Douglas fir, including Wildwood Trail, which runs for 26 miles through the heart of Forest Park. Portland is also home to Hoyt Arboretum, which harbors more than 5,000 labeled plants and trees that represent more than 1,100 different species.

Just 90 minutes west of Portland, you can explore the rocky coast and view pounding surf on trails accessible off US 101, the main north–south artery along Oregon's coastline. Luckily for all of us, Oregon passed two Beach Bills in 1967 and 1972 that allow public access to beaches and headlands along the entire Oregon Coast.

When you visit the coast, you can expect a multitude of hiking experiences. You can hike to a historic lighthouse, explore rocky tide pools filled with colorful sea creatures, walk through a rare grove of old-growth trees, climb to the summit of a coastal peak, or stroll along a river estuary rich with wildlife. You'll find hikes located in state parks, in the vast 630,000-acre Siuslaw National Forest, which is host to wilderness areas, and in protected research areas that harbor plants and animals that are found nowhere else. In addition, there are hikes that explore amazing dune environments in the Oregon Dunes National Recreation Area, which protects more than 50 square miles of magnificent sand dunes between Florence and Coos Bay.

As you travel south along US 101, your first stop should be the artsy seaside town of Cannon Beach, which swells with tourists during the summer months. Here the nearby beach boasts prominent rocky sea stacks—including 235-foot Haystack Rock. Take a walk along the beach and view tide pools at the base of this rock. Located about 2 miles north of Cannon Beach, Ecola State Park has hiking trails leading to

Shepperds Dale Falls

scenic viewpoints on rocky headlands and secluded beaches, and the Clatsop Loop Trail interpretive loop trail gives you a scenic 2.5-mile tour through a Sitka spruce forest ecosystem.

Located 10 miles south of Cannon Beach is Oswald West State Park. Within it you'll have access to Arch Cape, Cape Falcon, Neahkahnie Mountain, Smugglers Cove, and Short Sand Beach. To get a bird's-eye view of the area, hike to the top of Neahkahnie Mountain. To explore another coastal mountain, head east of Cannon Beach on US 26 to the Saddle Mountain trailhead. Here you can begin a strenuous 5-mile expedition to the top of Saddle Mountain, the highest point in the northern Coast Range.

As you continue south on US 101, be sure to tour some of the scenic, rocky capes by driving the Three Capes Scenic Route, which heads southwest from US 101 at Tillamook. Your first stop should be Cape Meares State Park, which features a historic lighthouse and many cliffside viewpoints where you can watch for migrating gray whales and observe large colonies of nesting seabirds. As you continue south on the Three Capes Scenic Route, your next destination should be Cape Lookout. This spectacular headland takes you through an ancient old-growth Sitka spruce forest to a gorgeous viewpoint where you'll have the opportunity to view gray whales on their semiannual migration from December through June. You'll finish your tour of the Three Capes Scenic Route at Cape Kiwanda State Natural Area, located in Pacific City. This natural area features an inviting sandy beach and huge sand dune that kids love to climb. Harts Cove, located just north of Lincoln City, is another recommended hike. This hike travels through a mystical coastal forest to a magnificent viewpoint of wild, rocky coastline that is haven to herds of sea lions.

A quick 30-minute drive east of Portland on I-84 takes you into the scenic Columbia River Gorge. This magnificent gorge is carved by the mile-wide Columbia River, the dividing line between Oregon and Washington. Thanks to legislation passed in 1986, the Columbia River Gorge is a designated national scenic area. It will remain undeveloped for all to enjoy. Filled with more than seventy-five cascading waterfalls, windswept forests and ridges, wildflower meadows, and bubbling creeks, this special destination has hundreds of miles of hiking trails. If you're a waterfall lover, you'll enjoy Eagle Creek, Wahclella Falls, Elowah Falls, Horsetail Falls, Larch Mountain, Latourell Falls, and Bridal Veil Falls. If you're into vistas, check out the rugged Munra Point hike and the Angels Rest hike.

Travel another hour east on I-84 to reach the community of Hood River, gateway to the Hood River Valley, Mount Hood, and Mount Hood National Forest. At the center of this national forest is 11,235-foot Mount Hood—Oregon's tallest peak. This expansive forest boasts 189,200 acres of designated wilderness and countless miles of trails. To get a close-up view of Mount Hood's impressive glaciers and snowcapped peak, try the Cooper Spur Trail. For a pristine river hike, check out the Salmon River Trail as it traipses along the Salmon River through the Salmon-Huckleberry Wilderness. **Take note:** Trails at elevations up to 4,000 feet are usually snow-free by

Scenic Crown Point in the Columbia River Gorge

June 1; trails at 7,000 feet are usually open by mid-July. Remember, there is a chance for snow at any time—always be prepared for cold weather when you are hiking at higher elevations.

Don't miss Silver Falls State Park—Oregon's largest. The park features a classic 6.9-mile loop trail that takes you on a one-of-a-kind tour of ten cascading waterfalls. It is recommended that you try this hike during September and October, when the leaves are turning golden yellow and burnt orange and the summer crowds have thinned. Note that dogs are not allowed on this waterfall hike but are allowed on other trails in Silver Falls State Park.

1 Ecola State Park to Indian Beach

Located in scenic Ecola State Park, this classic coastal route offers a winding single-track trail through a dense coastal forest with awesome ocean views and a picturesque beach for a finale. This is one of many trails you can explore in Ecola State Park.

Start: The trailhead is located on the north side of the main parking lot in Ecola State Park, about 2.5 miles north of Cannon Beach.
Distance: 3.0 miles out and back
Hiking time: 1 to 1.5 hours
Difficulty: Easy, well-graded trail
Best season: July through Oct
Other trail users: Hikers only
Canine compatibility: Leashed dogs permitted
Land status: State park
Nearest town: Cannon Beach

Fees and permits: Day-use fee required and can be obtained at park entrance booth
Schedule: Year-round, but trail can be muddy during winter months
Maps: Maptech CD: Newport/Portland/Mount Hood/The Dalles, OR; USGS: Tillamook Head, OR
Trail contact: Oregon State Parks and Recreation, 725 Summer St. NE, Suite C, Salem, OR 97301; (800) 551-6949; oregonstateparks.org/park_188.php

Finding the trailhead: From US 101 at the north end of Cannon Beach, exit west at the Ecola State Park sign. Travel about 0.25 mile and turn right at a small sign for the park. Go 2.3 miles on a narrow, windy road to a large parking area and the trailhead. *DeLorme: Oregon Atlas & Gazetteer:* Page 64 A1. GPS: N45 55.167 / W123 58.359.

The Hike

Ecola State Park covers 1,304 acres and offers breathtaking views from several viewpoints. For a warm-up, be sure to head toward the ocean on a short, paved trail that leads to expansive viewpoints looking south toward Cannon Beach and Haystack Rock. From this vantage point you may see the spouts of gray whales during their semiannual migration. These amazing marine mammals migrate south during December and January, north during March and April. During Whale Watch Weeks—the last week in December and the last week in March—trained volunteers can help you spot the whales (see the "Hike Information" section below).

This route begins on the north side of the main parking area and follows the Oregon Coast Trail north for 1.5 miles through mystical coastal forest of Sitka spruce and western hemlock to Indian Beach.

On this route you'll pass three spectacular viewpoints. Once you reach Indian Beach, you can beachcomb and watch surfers and boogie boarders catching waves offshore. From Indian Beach you'll have great views of the 62-foot-high Tillamook Rock Lighthouse, which rests on a large chunk of basalt rock located more than a mile offshore from Tillamook Head. This lighthouse was built in 1881 and acted as

A gorgeous rocky coastline from Ecola State Park

a lifesaving beacon for ships headed for the Columbia River. Nicknamed "Terrible Tilly," this lighthouse is privately owned and does not allow public access. From Indian Beach you have the option of continuing north on the Oregon Coast Trail for about another 6 miles as it weaves through coastal forest and travels over Tillamook Head to Seaside. If you are backpacking this section of the Oregon Coast, there is a backpackers' camping area located 1.5 miles north of Indian Beach. To leave a vehicle at the northern trailhead in Seaside, travel about 10 miles north on US 101. In Seaside turn left (west) onto U Avenue; go 0.1 mile and turn left onto Edgewood Avenue. Continue for about 1.1 miles (this becomes Sunset Avenue) to the end of the road and the trailhead.

There are also other trail options in this state park. You can hike down to Crescent Beach on a trail that can be accessed on the south side of the parking lot next to the restrooms. If you want to hike the 2.5-mile Clatsop Loop Interpretive Trail, continue north on Ecola Park Road to the Indian Beach parking lot to access the trailhead.

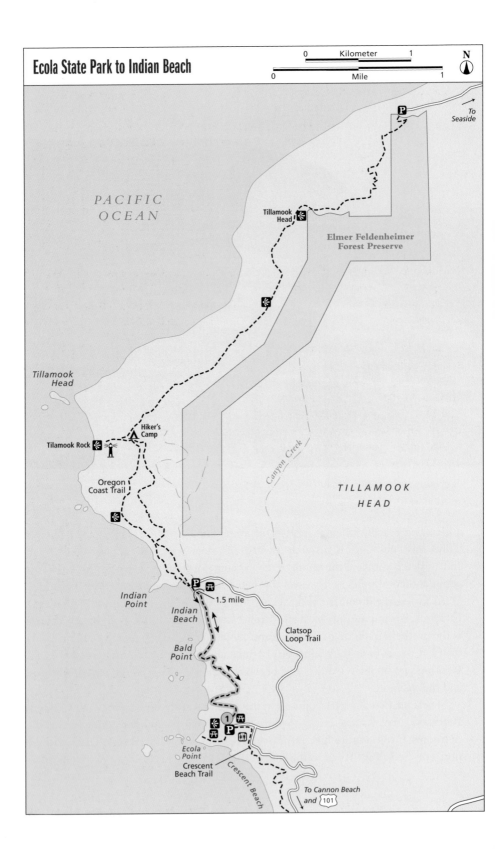

To Seaside

PACIFIC OCEAN

Tillamook Head

Elmer Feldenheimer Forest Preserve

Tillamook Head

Hiker's Camp

Tilamook Rock

Canyon Creek

Oregon Coast Trail

TILLAMOOK HEAD

1.5 mile

Indian Point

Indian Beach

Clatsop Loop Trail

Bald Point

1

Ecola Point

Crescent Beach Trail

Crescent Beach

To Cannon Beach and 101

Miles and Directions

0.0 Look for a small trailhead sign on the north side of the parking lot. Pick up the singletrack trail as it winds through a dense forest.

1.5 Turn left at the fork and continue to secluded Indian Beach (your turnaround point). From here retrace the same route back to the starting point. **Option:** Continue 6 miles north on the Oregon Coast Trail to Seaside. Look for the trailhead on the right side of the Indian Beach day-use parking area.

3.0 Arrive back at the trailhead.

Hike Information

Local Information

Cannon Beach Chamber of Commerce and Information Center, 207 N. Spruce St., Cannon Beach, OR 97138; (503) 436-2623; cannonbeach.org

Local Events and Attractions

Sandcastle Day, Cannon Beach; (503) 436-2623. This annual event is held in June.
Whale Watch Weeks, Cannon Beach; (541) 765-3407; whalespoken.org. This event is held the last week in December and the last week in March at designated locations along the entire Oregon coast.

Restaurants

Bill's Tavern and Brewhouse, 188 N. Hemlock, Cannon Beach; (503) 436-2202
Cannon Beach Bakery, 240 N. Hemlock, Cannon Beach; (503) 436-0399

2 Saddle Mountain

This trail to the top of 3,283-foot Saddle Mountain, the highest point in the northern Coastal Mountains, begins in a thickly wooded expanse of alder forest. It then climbs through a beautiful Douglas fir forest with a thick understory of wood sorrel, trillium, western columbine, coast penstemon, and many other beautiful wildflowers. Eventually, the trail becomes rocky and eroded and necessitates some careful navigation, but the effort is worth it, for those who make it to the top are rewarded with magnificent views.

Start: From the Saddle Mountain State Park trailhead located about 65 miles west of Portland (and 17 miles northeast of Cannon Beach) off US 26
Distance: 5.2 miles out and back
Hiking time: 3 to 4 hours
Difficulty: Difficult; loose rocks and dirt on steep terrain. In winter the trail can be very icy and treacherous.
Best season: July through Oct
Other trail users: Hikers only

Canine compatibility: Leashed dogs permitted
Land status: State park
Nearest town: Cannon Beach
Fees and permits: None
Schedule: Year-round
Maps: Maptech CD: Newport/Portland/Mount Hood/The Dalles, OR; USGS: Saddle Mountain, OR
Trail contact: Oregon State Parks and Recreation, 725 Summer St. NE, Suite C, Salem, OR 97301; (800) 551-6949; oregonstateparks.org/park_197.php

Finding the trailhead: From Portland travel 65 miles west on US 26 to a sign for Saddle Mountain State Park. Turn right (north) onto Saddle Mountain Road and continue 7 miles to the trailhead.

From Cannon Beach travel 10 miles east on US 26; turn left (north) onto Saddle Mountain Road and continue 7 miles to the trailhead. *DeLorme: Oregon Atlas & Gazetteer:* Page 64 A3. GPS: N45 57.773 / W123 41.391.

The Hike

One of the highest peaks in Oregon's northern Coastal Mountain range, Saddle Mountain rises 3,283 feet above sea level. The gray monolith juts its basalt head above its neighbors and stands testament to its volcanic beginnings. The peak is the eroded remnant of the Columbia basalt flows that poured through the area approximately fifteen million years ago. The massive flows originated more than 250 miles away in eastern Washington. When the lava came into contact with an ancient sea that once covered the area, it cooled rapidly and formed fragmented layers. When North America pushed

Hikers descend the Saddle Mountain Trail. ▶

The author takes a lunch break at the summit of Saddle Mountain. PHOTO KEN SKEEN

its way under the old Pacific seafloor, Saddle Mountain was born. Eventually, soft sedimentary rock eroded to reveal the dark basalt mountaintop visible today.

To see Saddle Mountain up close, try this strenuous 5.2-mile out-and-back trek to the summit. The trailhead is located at the base of the mountain, as are water, restroom facilities, and ten primitive campsites. The trail's first mile slips through a thick, secondary-growth forest of red alder that thrives in the moist environment. Red alders can be found at elevations up to 3,000 feet and are easily identified by their grayish-white bark. They're often covered with a mottled coat of moss and lichen. Coastal Indian tribes steeped the tree's bark in hot water to cure rheumatic fever. (It contains salicin, which even today is used in prescription medication for treatment of this disease.) The wood of the tree was used to make utensils and other tools.

The lower section of this route is a haven for wildflowers. The cloverlike leaves and delicate white flowers of wood sorrel carpet the forest floor. You'll also find triangular trillium, pink western columbine, and blue coast penstemon. Other botanical delights scattered throughout the woods include the hairy-stemmed checker-mallow, a high-stemmed plant with large, daisy-like purple flowers; the tooth-leafed monkey flower, a yellow, tubular flower with toothlike petals; and goat's beard, recognizable by its white, feathery flowers.

Soon the trail becomes steeper and the forest canopy thins to reveal many great views around almost every bend. The path also becomes more eroded and precipitous

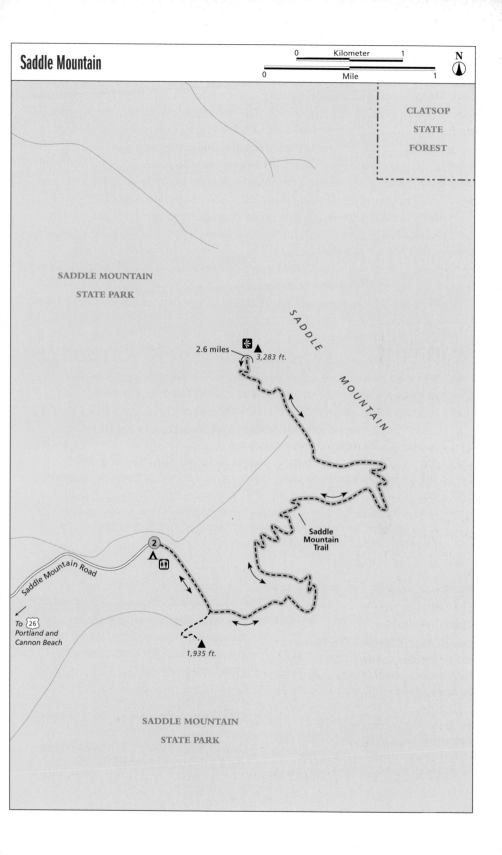

Saddle Mountain

CLATSOP

STATE

FOREST

SADDLE MOUNTAIN

STATE PARK

SADDLE

2.6 miles
3,283 ft.

MOUNTAIN

Saddle
Mountain
Trail

2

Saddle Mountain Road

To 26
Portland and
Cannon Beach

1,935 ft.

SADDLE MOUNTAIN

STATE PARK

and requires some careful footwork over rocky ledges. (Notice the firm grasp the thick, red stems of Oregon stonecrop have on the ledges—and wish you had the same.) In an attempt to make navigating easier, stairs and walkways have been built over the more difficult sections of trail. The walkways also protect the wildflower meadows of blue iris, Indian paintbrush, meadow chickweed, phlox, and larkspur.

After about 2 miles the trail crosses a narrow saddle, then climbs to the domelike summit. The push to the top is somewhat treacherous. The trail is steep and filled with loose rocks. Fortunately, stairs and cables are in place to make things easier. Still, these devices are not always reliable—some are loose and can be dangerous.

At the broad, flat summit, there are grand views of Nehalem Bay to the southwest, the Columbia River to the northwest, and the snowcapped Cascade peaks of Mount Jefferson and Mount Hood to the east.

Summertime crowds on this popular trek can be fierce—especially at the summit. If you want solitude, come here on a weekday or off-season weekend in spring or fall. This park also has a campground with primitive campsites that is open from March 1 through October 31.

Miles and Directions

0.0 Start at the trailhead at the Saddle Mountain State Park parking lot. (**Note:** There are restrooms and water here.) The trail begins with a climb through an alder forest.

1.5 The trail becomes steeper and, in parts, rocky and eroded.

1.7 Several bridges cross an alpinelike landscape of wildflowers. Look for blue iris, Indian paintbrush, white meadow chickweed, chocolate lily, phlox, and larkspur.

2.2 Hike across a narrow saddle before climbing to the summit. (**Note:** The final stretch includes loose rocks and is very steep—use the stairs, walkways, and cables to ensure that you don't slip.)

2.6 Arrive at the 3,283-foot summit, where you'll enjoy magnificent views of Nehalem Bay to the southwest, the Columbia River to the northwest, and other snowcapped Cascade peaks to the east. Retrace the same route back to the trailhead.

5.2 Arrive back at the trailhead.

Hike Information

Local Information

Cannon Beach Chamber of Commerce and Information Center, 207 N. Spruce St., Cannon Beach, OR 97138; (503) 436-2623; cannonbeach.org.

Local Events and Attractions

Sandcastle Day, Cannon Beach; (503) 436-2623. This annual event is held in June.

Whale Watch Weeks, Cannon Beach; (541) 563-2002; whalespoken.org. This event is held the last week in December and the last week in March at designated locations along the entire Oregon coast.

Restaurants

Bill's Tavern and Brewhouse, 188 N. Hemlock, Cannon Beach; (503) 436-2202

Cannon Beach Bakery, 240 N. Hemlock, Cannon Beach; (503) 436-0399

3 Harts Cove

This forest trail travels through a western hemlock and old-growth Sitka spruce forest to a dramatic cliff-top viewpoint overlooking Harts Cove. From this high perch you can view sea lions offshore and watch magnificent waves crashing into offshore rocks.

Start: The trailhead is located about 8.5 miles northwest of Lincoln City off US 101.

Distance: 5.4 miles out and back

Hiking time: 2.5 to 3.5 hours

Difficulty: Moderate due to elevation gain

Best season: Late July through Oct

Other trail users: Hikers only

Canine compatibility: Leashed dogs permitted

Land status: National forest

Nearest town: Lincoln City

Fees and permits: None

Schedule: Open July 16 through Dec 31

Maps: Maptech CD: Newport/Portland/Mount Hood/The Dalles, OR; USGS: Neskowin, OR

Trail contact: Siuslaw National Forest, 31525 Hwy. 22, Hebo, OR 97122; (503) 392-5100; www.fs.usda.gov/recarea/siuslaw/recreation/hiking/recarea/?recid=42721&actid=50

Finding the trailhead: From the junction of OR 18 and US 101 in Lincoln City, head north on US 101 for 4.1 miles to the junction with gravel FR 1861. Go left and continue 4.3 miles (after 3.3 miles you'll pass the upper trailhead to the Nature Conservancy Preserve on the left) to the road's end and the trailhead. *DeLorme: Oregon Atlas & Gazetteer:* Page 58 D1. GPS: N45 04.490 / W124 00.074.

The Hike

This forest trail begins by descending on a series of switchbacks through a monochrome stand of western hemlock. After 0.7 mile you'll cross a wooden footbridge over picturesque Cliff Creek. The soothing sounds of this bubbling creek mixed with the far-off sounds of sea lions and ocean wind blowing through the trees give you a sense of anticipation as you continue your descent toward Harts Cove. After this creek crossing the forest opens up and comes alive with giant Sitka spruce trees at center stage. These rare gentle giants thrive in coastal areas and feature stout trunks with dozens of limbs that shoot outward from the base of the tree. This tree can grow more than 200 feet tall and can have a 12-foot-thick trunk. It is one of the Northwest's largest trees, along with the western red cedar and the Douglas fir. You can easily identify these trees from other coastal species by their reddish-brown to purplish-colored bark, which is patterned in large, loose scales. The needles are also flat and prickly and do not roll easily between your fingers. Mixed in with the Sitka giants are large western hemlock trees. These trees are very prolific because the seedlings have the ability to grow in dense shady areas. You can recognize this tree by its short, blunt needles that are unequal in length. The branches of the tree also have a delicate, fanlike appearance. The cones are about an inch long and grow in large clusters. The tops of smaller western hemlock trees also tend to droop.

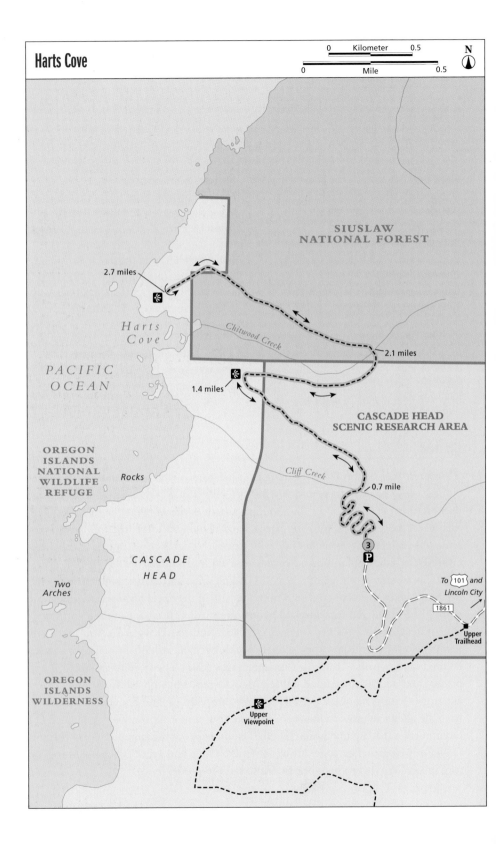

Harts Cove

0   Kilometer   0.5

0   Mile   0.5

N

SIUSLAW
NATIONAL FOREST

2.7 miles

*Harts
Cove*

Chitwood Creek

2.1 miles

PACIFIC
OCEAN

1.4 miles

CASCADE HEAD
SCENIC RESEARCH AREA

OREGON
ISLANDS
NATIONAL
WILDLIFE
REFUGE

Rocks

Cliff Creek

0.7 mile

3
P

CASCADE
HEAD

*Two
Arches*

To 101 and
Lincoln City

1861

Upper
Trailhead

OREGON
ISLANDS
WILDERNESS

Upper
Viewpoint

As you continue your journey, you'll pass a rest bench at 1.4 miles with a viewpoint of the distant headland. As you continue to descend, the sounds of crashing waves and the raucous calls of sea lions beckon you through a maze of green filled with wood sorrel, sword fern, lady fern, and candy flower. You'll also notice mushrooms of all shapes and sizes clinging to the bases of trees and old logs. After 2.1 miles you'll cross charming Chitwood Creek, and in another 0.4 mile you'll exit the trees and enter an open grassy meadow atop a dramatic bluff. Continue as the trail descends through a beautiful meadow made up of red fescue, wild rye, coastal paintbrush, wild iris, yarrow, and goldenrod. You'll arrive at a dramatic viewpoint overlooking Harts Cove to the south (your turnaround point). From here look for pods of sea lions riding the waves offshore and watch huge breakers crash into rocky cliffs.

Miles and Directions

0.0   Begin walking on the dirt path as it heads down a set of steep switchbacks.

0.7   Cross Cliff Creek on a wooden footbridge.

1.4   Pass a rest bench and viewpoint on the left. Continue your descent on the main trail.

2.1   Cross Chitwood Creek on a wooden footbridge.

2.5   Exit the trees and enter an open grassy meadow atop a dramatic bluff above Harts Cove.

2.7   Arrive at a spectacular viewpoint above Harts Cove (your turnaround point). Retrace the same route back to the trailhead. (**Note:** Don't be tempted to head down to the exposed rocks above the shoreline. Nothing grows here because waves routinely break in this region.)

5.4   Arrive back at the trailhead.

Hike Information

Local Information

Lincoln City Visitor and Convention Bureau, 540 NE Highway 101, Lincoln City, OR 97367; (541) 994-3302; oregoncoast.org

Local Events and Attractions

Fall Kite Festival, held in October, D-River State Wayside, Lincoln City; (800) 452-2151 **North Lincoln County Museum,** 4907 SW Highway 101, Lincoln City; (541) 996-6614

4 Cape Meares State Park

Cape Meares, located in Cape Meares State Park, is one of three scenic capes along the Three Capes Scenic Highway—the other two are Cape Lookout and Cape Kiwanda. A hike here includes numerous opportunities to view seabirds and migrating gray whales. Other attractions include the Cape Meares Lighthouse, which was built in 1890; old-growth Sitka spruce trees; spectacular ocean views; and abundant wildlife and coastal forestland. Plan on spending the better part of a day here—and be sure to bring your binoculars.

Start: From the state park parking area, approximately 11 miles west of Tillamook off the Three Capes Scenic Highway

Distance: Varies depending on the trails selected

Hiking time: 30 minutes to 1 hour

Difficulty: Easy; flat terrain and well-maintained trails

Best season: June through Oct

Other trail users: Hikers only

Canine compatibility: Leashed dogs permitted

Land status: State park

Nearest town: Tillamook

Fees and permits: None

Schedule: Year-round

Maps: Maptech CD: Newport/Portland/Mount Hood/The Dalles, OR; USGS Netarts, OR

Trail contact: Oregon State Parks and Recreation, 725 Summer St. NE, Suite C, Salem, OR 97301; (800) 551-6949; oregonstateparks .org/park_181.php

Finding the trailhead: From US 101 in Tillamook, follow the signs to Cape Lookout Loop Road (the Three Capes Scenic Highway). Drive approximately 10 miles west on the Three Capes Scenic Highway to the CAPE MEARES STATE PARK sign. To proceed to the main parking area in the park, turn right (west) onto the Park Road and drive 0.6 mile to the parking area.

From Pacific City drive 26 miles north on Cape Lookout Road (the Three Capes Scenic Highway) to the CAPE MEARES STATE PARK sign. Turn left (west) and drive 0.6 mile on the Park Road to the parking area.

If you want to view the Big Spruce Tree, turn right into a pullout right before the Cape Meares State Park turnoff. A short loop trail will take you by the Big Spruce Tree. *DeLorme: Oregon Atlas & Gazetteer:* Page 58 A1. GPS: N45 29.133 / W123 58.464.

The Hike

The 233-acre Cape Meares State Park is a must-see stop for anyone traveling along the north Oregon coast. This scenic cape is well known for its large concentration of nesting seabirds and its historic lighthouse.

You can start your exploration by walking down the 0.4-mile out-and-back paved Cape Meares Lighthouse Trail to the 38-foot-tall Cape Meares Lighthouse. Along the

The 38-foot-tall Cape Meares Lighthouse was built in 1890 ▷
and is the shortest lighthouse tower on the Oregon coast.

way you'll pass seabird colonies nesting on the sheer, 200-foot rocky cliffs. Bring binoculars for close-up views of these feathered cape residents, which include double-crested, Brandt's, and pelagic cormorants, pigeon guillemots, common murres, and tufted puffins. Bald eagles and peregrine falcons also have been spotted in the area.

In 1886 the US Army Corps of Engineers sent a representative to survey Cape Meares and Cape Lookout, located south of Cape Meares, to see which would be more suitable for a lighthouse. After several days of surveying, the engineers picked the Cape Meares site because of its lower elevation, which would allow light to travel farther in foggy weather. Additionally, it had a nearby spring that could provide freshwater and was more accessible than the Cape Lookout site.

In 1887 Congress passed a bill that provided funding to begin construction on the lighthouse. A road was built to the site, and construction finally commenced in spring 1889. The interior walls were built with bricks made at the construction site, the exterior walls from sheet iron shipped in from Portland. The lighthouse was completed in November 1889. At the time, the light consisted of a five-wick oil lamp turned by a 200-pound lead weight. The current lens is a first-order Fresnel lens that was shipped from Paris via Cape Horn and up the West Coast to Cape Meares. The lens has eight sides, four primary lenses, and four bull's-eye lenses covered with red panels.

To view the intricate Fresnel lens, climb a series of steps to the top of the lighthouse tower. A gift shop in the lower section of the lighthouse is open daily May through September and on weekends in March, April, and October.

If visiting the lighthouse isn't enough, check out another amazing attraction at this park: the Octopus Tree. A 0.2-mile out-and-back, wheelchair-accessible trail leads

BIRD IDENTIFICATION 101

Many bird species live along the Cliffs Road and offshore islands of this scenic cape. Following are descriptions of just a few.

- Pelagic cormorants are solid black with a white patch on their flank during breeding season. These birds nest predominantly on the south side of the cape.
- Brandt's cormorants have a buff-colored patch adjacent to a blue throat patch and solid black coloring with a sprinkling of fine white feathers on the back and neck.
- Double-crested cormorants have bright-yellow and orange markings on their throat and face and a crooked neck in flight.
- Tufted puffins have a stocky black body, white facial mask, yellow feather tufts on their head, and bright-orange feet.
- Common murres are dark brown on the head, back, and wings and have a white breast patch and dark-yellow feet. They nest on the cliff faces on the north side of the cape.

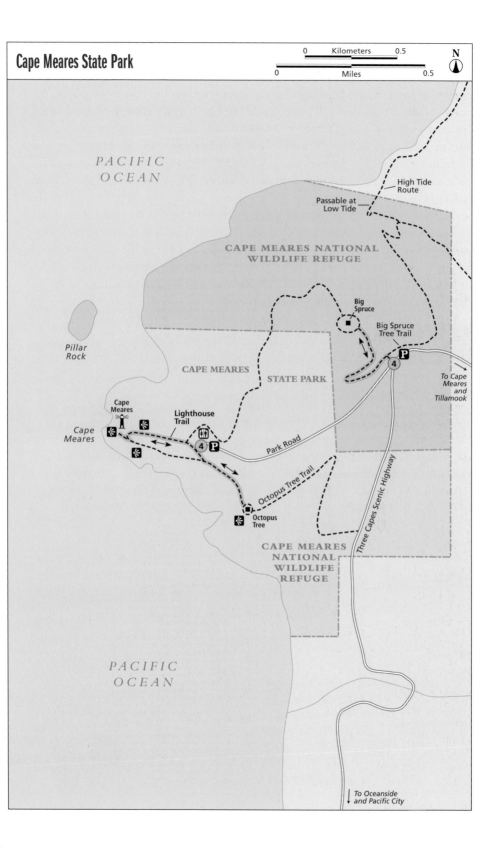

Cape Meares State Park

0 Kilometers 0.5

0 Miles 0.5

N

PACIFIC
OCEAN

High Tide
Route

Passable at
Low Tide

CAPE MEARES NATIONAL
WILDLIFE REFUGE

Big
Spruce

Big Spruce
Tree Trail

Pillar
Rock

P

4

CAPE MEARES

STATE PARK

To Cape
Meares
and
Tillamook

Cape
Meares

Cape
Meares

Lighthouse
Trail

4 P

Park Road

Octopus Tree Trail

Octopus
Tree

CAPE MEARES
NATIONAL
WILDLIFE
REFUGE

Three Capes Scenic Highway

PACIFIC
OCEAN

To Oceanside
and Pacific City

from the main parking area to an ancient Sitka spruce, whose low-slung branches truly resemble an octopus. The spruce was used as a burial tree in Native American ceremonies, and its octopus-shaped arms held the canoes in which were placed the bodies of the tribe's dead. It's speculated that Native Americans, who lived along the north Oregon coast for nearly 30,000 years, bent the young tree's more pliable branches outward into a horizontal position. Eventually the tree's branches took shape and continued to grow in that position. The Octopus Tree is thought to have endured this ritual when it was very young, surviving to grow old and maintain its odd shape.

To view another old-growth Sitka spruce, drive 0.6 mile to the park entrance and park in a dirt pullout on the north side of the road. A 0.4-mile out-and-back loop trail leads to a magnificent 400-year-old tree. As you walk the path, be on the lookout for odd-looking banana slugs. These interesting, slow-moving creatures eat plant matter and recycle the material back to the soil. They also secrete a thin coat of mucus that helps them travel over the forest floor.

Miles and Directions

The Cape Meares Lighthouse Trail and the Octopus Tree Trail start from the main parking area. The Big Spruce Tree Trail begins in a dirt pullout on the north side of the park road just before the entrance to the park.

Hike Information

Local Information

Tillamook Chamber of Commerce, 3705 Highway 101 N., Tillamook, OR 97141; (503) 842-7525; gotillamook.com

Local Events and Attractions

Tillamook Cheese Factory, 4175 Highway 101 N., Tillamook; (503) 815-1300 or (800) 542-7290; tillamook.com/cheesefactory/index.html

5 Cape Lookout

This ramble through a lush coastal forest of rare old-growth Sitka spruce leads to the end of scenic Cape Lookout in Cape Lookout State Park. Along the way there are magnificent views of Cape Meares to the north and Cape Kiwanda to the south. Gray whales can be seen in December, January, March, and April as they near the cape on their semiannual migrations. The trail can be muddy during the winter and spring months.

Start: The trailhead is located 13 miles southwest of Tillamook and 16 miles north of Pacific City on the Three Capes Scenic Highway.
Distance: 5.0 miles out and back
Hiking time: 2 to 3 hours
Difficulty: Moderate due to elevation gain
Best season: June through Oct
Other trail users: Hikers only
Canine compatibility: Leashed dogs permitted
Land status: State park
Nearest town: Tillamook

Fees and permits: Day-use pass required (small fee)
Schedule: Year-round
Maps: Maptech CD: Newport/Portland/Mount Hood/The Dalles, OR; USGS: Sand Lake, OR
Trail contact: Oregon State Parks and Recreation, 725 Summer St. NE, Suite C, Salem, OR 97301; (800) 551-6949; oregonstateparks .org/park_186.php. If you are looking for camping reservations at Cape Lookout State Park campground, call (800) 452-5687.

Finding the trailhead: From US 101 in Tillamook, head 15.5 miles southwest on the Three Capes Scenic Highway to the signed Cape Lookout trailhead on the right side of the highway.

From the intersection of OR 18 and US 101 in Lincoln City, turn north onto US 101. Travel 14.6 miles north and turn left (west) onto Brooten Road at the CAPE KIWANDA RECREATION AREA/PACIFIC CITY sign. Go 2.8 miles west and then turn left onto Pacific Avenue toward Netarts/Oceanside. Continue 0.3 mile and then turn right onto Kiwanda Drive. Go 15.3 miles to the signed Cape Lookout trailhead on the left side of the highway. *DeLorme: Oregon Atlas & Gazetteer:* Page 58 B1. GPS: N45 21.241 / W123 58.277.

The Hike

Cape Lookout, part of 2,000-acre Cape Lookout State Park (host to a campground, scenic Netarts Spit, and a variety of plants and animals), is a spectacular headland made up of a series of lava flows fifteen million to twenty million years old. Jutting into the ocean like an arrowhead, its 400-foot cliffs are regularly pounded and carved by rhythmic waves and currents.

The scenic cape is popular among whale watchers, who come to observe gray whales during their semiannual migrations—epic 10,000-mile round-trip journeys from breeding lagoons in Baja California, Mexico, to the food-rich Arctic Ocean and back again. The whales migrate south during December and January and north from March through April. Mature gray whales are 35 to 45 feet long and weigh

The author hikes with her Australian shepherd Tiz. PHOTO KEN SKEEN

from twenty-two to thirty-five tons. Females are larger than males and can live for fifty years—some males reach the ripe old age of sixty. The gentle giants feed on shrimplike amphipods by scraping mud from the ocean bottom and then filtering unwanted material through their baleen.

To reach the tip of the cape, take the trail that heads left just past the trailhead sign. The path begins by descending a series of switchbacks through a thick grove of Sitka spruce. These tough, stout trees are often referred to as "tideland spruce," and they thrive in the moist, cool temperatures that are characteristic of their coastal home. The Sitka spruce ranks with the Douglas fir and western red cedar as one of the largest tree species in the Northwest—only redwoods and sequoias are bigger.

Just over a half a mile from the trailhead, the path arrives at a commemorative marker (located on the right side of the trail) honoring an Air Force crew that perished in a nearby plane crash in August 1943. From here there are also views of Cape Kiwanda and Cascade Head to the south.

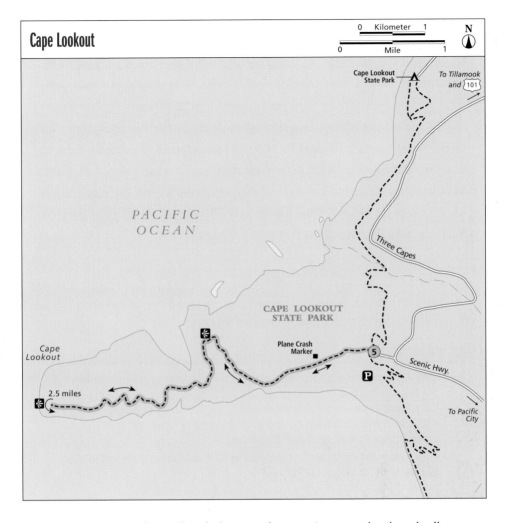

Continuing on, the trail includes several convenient wooden boardwalks over the seemingly endless mire of mud that can be present during the winter and spring months. Up to 90 inches of rain falls annually along this stretch of the coast. The resulting foliage is striking—notice the bright-green leaves of salal and salmonberry and the feathery fans of sword and maidenhair fern that cover the forest floor. After a while the trail reveals views of Netarts Bay, Three Arch Rocks, and Cape Meares. The sandy, flat bottom of Netarts Bay makes it a perfect environment for shellfish such as oysters, razor clams, butter clams, and crabs. The last half mile of the path is lined with Indian paintbrush, delicate wild iris, white yarrow, and bushy thimbleberry. The trail ends at a sharp point; if you look off the edge, you'll see the frothy Pacific pounding its huge swells against the rocky cliffs below. A convenient wooden bench has been placed at this classic viewpoint. Stay for a while and admire the view before turning back to the trailhead. If you want to explore the park more, you can camp at the Cape

CHEESE, PLEASE!

The wet climate (approximately 90 inches precipitation per year) and rich soils in the Tillamook Valley provide an excellent environment for raising dairy cattle. The Tillamook Valley is home to more than 150 dairy farms that raise more than 26,000 dairy cattle and produce over $85 million worth of cheese and other dairy products per year. You can experience the cheese-making process firsthand at the Tillamook Cheese Factory visitor center, located 2 miles north of Tillamook on US 101. At the visitor center you can watch workers make cheese, view educational videos, and tour many different interpretive displays. The cheese factory also has a cafe and gift store where you can taste different cheeses, ice cream, and other tantalizing items. The visitor center is open daily; admission is free.

Lookout State Park campground, which can be reached by driving north from the trailhead. The campground has tent sites, deluxe cabins, a hiker/biker camp, and yurts and is open year-round. They also have one rustic yurt and one deluxe cabin that are pet friendly (dogs and cats). There is a limit of two pets.

Miles and Directions

0.0 Start at the trailhead in the southwest corner of the Cape Lookout parking area. Take the trail that goes left. (The North Trail heads right and takes you 2.3 miles to Cape Lookout Campground.) After about 250 feet, bear right at the junction. (A left here will take you on the South Trail, which takes you on a 1.8-mile journey to a secluded beach.) Descend through a thick grove of statuesque spruce trees.

0.6 A commemorative marker honors the crew of an Air Force plane that crashed 500 feet west of this site on August 1, 1943.

1.4 Enjoy a picturesque view of the northern coastline and Cape Meares.

2.5 Arrive at the end of the official trail and your turnaround point. Retrace the same route back to the trailhead.

5.0 Arrive back at the trailhead.

Hike Information

Local Information

Tillamook Chamber of Commerce, 3705 Highway 101 N., Tillamook, OR 97141; (503) 842-7525; gotillamook.com

Local Events and Attractions

Tillamook Cheese Factory, 4175 Highway 101 N., Tillamook; (503) 815-1300 or (800) 542-7290; tillamook.com/cheesefactory/index.html

6 Yaquina Head Outstanding Natural Area

The trails in the Yaquina Head Outstanding Natural Area take you through a rich coastal ecosystem, giving visitors an excellent opportunity to view seabirds, tide-pool creatures, harbor seals, and migrating gray whales. The other main attraction of this special ocean oasis is the 93-foot Yaquina Head Lighthouse—the tallest lighthouse in Oregon. Bring a good pair of binoculars in order to get a close-up view of the abundant wildlife this unique area has to offer.

Start: Trails at this natural area are located about 3 miles north of Newport off US 101.
Distance: Trails vary from 0.2 mile to 1.0 mile in length.
A. Cobble Beach Access: 0.2 mile out and back
B. Communications Hill Trail: 1.0 mile out and back
C. Lighthouse Trail: 0.6 mile out and back
D. Quarry Cove Trail: 0.4 mile out and back
E. Quarry Cove Tide Pools Trail: 1.0 mile out and back
F. Salal Hill Trail: 0.8 mile out and back
G. Yaquina Head Lighthouse Trail: 0.2 mile out and back
Hiking time: 15 minutes to 1 hour, depending on the trails selected

Difficulty: Easy to moderate, depending on the trails selected
Best season: June through Oct
Other trail users: Hikers only
Canine compatibility: Dogs not permitted
Land status: Bureau of Land Management (BLM)
Nearest town: Newport
Fees and permits: Small entrance fee, which is good for 3 consecutive days. Annual permit also available.
Schedule: Year-round
Maps: Maptech CD: Newport/Portland/ Mount Hood/The Dalles, OR; USGS: Newport North, OR
Trail contact: 750 NW Lighthouse Dr., Newport, OR 97365; (541) 574-3100; www .or.blm.gov/salem/html/yaquina/index.htm

Finding the trailhead: From Newport drive 2 miles north on US 101. Turn left onto Lighthouse Drive at the park sign. Drive 1 mile to the end of the road and a parking area. *DeLorme: Oregon Atlas & Gazetteer:* Page 32 C1. GPS: N44 40.587 / W124 04.688.

The Hike

Established in 1980, the Yaquina Head Outstanding Natural Area comprises 100 acres of rocky basalt cliffs, tide pools, rocky beaches, and grassy meadows that support a multitude of animal and aquatic life.

Managed by the Bureau of Land Management, this seaside oasis has many trails that lead you through different coastal life zones. It's recommended that you begin your tour of the area at the interpretive center, located 0.7 mile from US 101 on Lighthouse Drive. The interpretive center has exhibits, video presentations, and hands-on displays about the geology and cultural and natural history of Yaquina Head. It's open

daily in summer from 10 a.m. to 6 p.m., in the fall from 10 a.m. to 5 p.m., and in winter from 10 a.m. to 4:00 p.m. Once you've filled up on facts at the interpretive center, turn right out of the interpretive center parking area and drive 0.3 mile to the end of Lighthouse Drive to the Yaquina Head Lighthouse parking area.

From the parking area take a leisurely walk over to the 93-foot-tall Yaquina Head Lighthouse, the tallest lighthouse in Oregon. Construction on the classic seacoast tower lighthouse began in fall 1871 and took two years to complete. Many of the building materials used for the lighthouse were shipped in from San Francisco and unloaded in Newport. They were then brought out to Yaquina Head by wagon over a crude, rough coastal road. It took more than 370,000 bricks to build the tower. A two-story building was also constructed next door to house the lighthouse keepers and their families. In 1872 a Fresnel lens arrived in sections from France, and on August 20, 1873, lighthouse keeper Fayette Crosby lit the lamp for the first time. In 1993 the lighthouse was refurbished by the Coast Guard and was officially named part of the Yaquina Head Outstanding Natural Area. Tours of the lighthouse are available during summer from noon to 5 p.m. Winter hours may vary depending on the weather. The lighthouse is closed on Wednesdays throughout the year. From the viewpoint at the lighthouse, you may have the opportunity to see gray whales during their winter migration, December through mid-February, or during their spring migration, March through May.

After touring the lighthouse take a walk down a long series of steps to Cobble Beach. This rocky beach and the offshore rocks and islands are all part of the Oregon Islands National Wildlife Refuge. While you're on the beach, keep your eyes peeled— you may spot black oystercatchers, easily recognized by their dark-black plumage, gold eyes, bright-red bills, and pink legs and feet. These birds feed on chitons, limpets, snails, and other shellfish by picking the shellfish off the rocks with their long, sturdy beaks. In the rocky tide pools, you may see green anemones, prickly purple sea urchins, bright-orange starfish, yellow sea lemons, oval-shelled mussels, volcano-shaped barnacles, turban snails, hermit crabs, and sculpin fish.

Looking toward the offshore islands, you may spot some of the resident harbor seals. Your best chance at seeing harbor seal pups is during April and May. And a glance toward the offshore cliffs and islands will reveal multitudes of seabirds, mainly Brandt's and pelagic cormorants, tufted puffins, common murres, and pigeon guillemots. During spring and summer more than 24,000 birds nest on the cliffs and rocky islands surrounding Yaquina Head.

Once you're back at your vehicle, drive 0.5 mile on Lighthouse Drive and turn right into the Quarry Cove parking area. The Quarry Cove Tide Pools Trail is wheelchair accessible and takes you on a tour of an area once quarried for the hard basalt rock used to build roads. Today the area has evolved into a thriving intertidal ecosystem.

◀ *Yaquina Head Lighthouse*

Yaquina Head Outstanding Natural Area

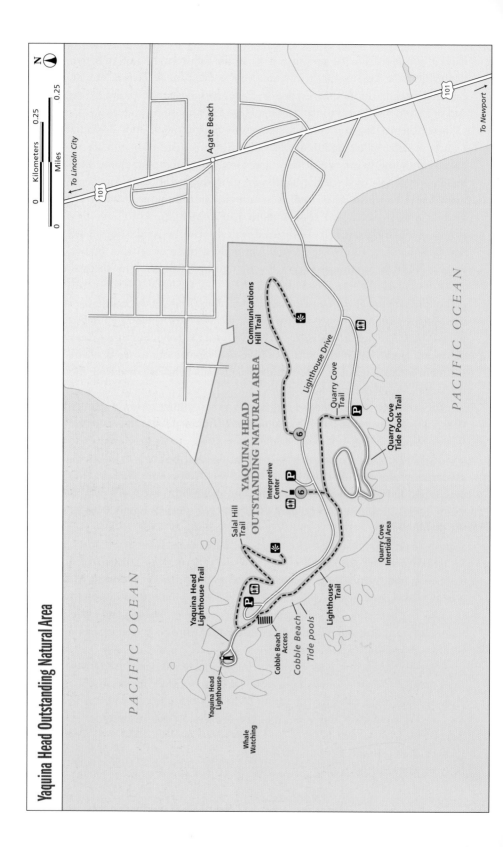

OREGON COAST AQUARIUM

If you are visiting Newport, plan on spending the day at this amazing aquarium that has natural indoor and outdoor exhibits where you can see birds and marine mammals close up. One of the most popular displays is the jellyfish tank—dozens of beautiful jellyfish swim freely in a circular tank in the middle of a large room filled with huge aquarium displays. Another favorite is the touch tank, where you can touch tidal-pool creatures such as sea anemones, starfish, and other mollusks. The outside displays are just as fascinating. You can view California sea otters, harbor seals, sea lions, and giant Pacific octopus; and you can walk through an outdoor aviary where you can watch tufted puffins, pigeon guillemots, common murres, and other seabirds swimming and feeding in a natural environment. Trails outside the aquarium lead through gardens of native plants with interpretive signs. The aquarium also has a bookstore and cafe. The aquarium is open 9 a.m. to 6 p.m. daily Memorial Day through Labor Day and 10 a.m. to 5 p.m. the rest of the year. For current admission prices, contact the Oregon Coast Aquarium, 2820 SE Ferry Slip Rd., Newport; (541) 867-3474; aquarium.org.

Miles and Directions

The Quarry Cove parking area is located on the left side of the road 0.5 mile from the intersection of Lighthouse Drive and US 101. From this parking area you can access the Quarry Cove Trail, Communications Hill Trail, and the wheelchair-accessible Quarry Cove Tide Pools Trail (see map).

The interpretive center is located on the right side of the road 0.7 mile from the intersection of Lighthouse Drive and US 101. From this parking area you can access the Lighthouse Trail and the Quarry Cove Trail (see map).

The Yaquina Head Lighthouse parking area is located 1 mile from the intersection of Lighthouse Drive and US 101. From this parking area you can access the paved trail to Yaquina Head Lighthouse, a stairway that takes you to Cobble Beach, and the Salal Hill Trail (see map).

Hike Information

Local Information

Greater Newport Chamber of Commerce, 555 SW Coast Hwy., Newport, OR 97365; (800) 262-7844; newportchamber.org

Local Events and Attractions

Newport Microbrew Festival, in October, Newport; (800) 262-7844

Newport Seafood and Wine Festival, in February, Newport; (800) 262-7844

Newport Visual Arts Center, 777 NW Beach Dr., Newport; (541) 265-6540; coastarts.org

Oregon Coast Aquarium, 2820 SE Ferry Slip Rd., Newport; (541) 867-3474; aquarium.org

7 Silver Falls State Park

This gorgeous hike weaves through Silver Creek Canyon past many spectacular water-falls in Silver Falls State Park. The trail starts next to South Falls Lodge and descends steeply into the canyon. Immediately you'll have a grand view of 177-foot South Falls—one of the park's most well-known waterfalls. Before you know it, the trail takes you behind the falls in a unique basalt cave. The cooling spray from the sweeping cascade is a welcome relief on a hot summer's day. The trail continues to travel along the South Fork of Silver Creek through a forest of big-leaf maple, sword fern, and Douglas fir. After passing several more waterfalls, the trail follows the North Fork of Silver Creek, continuing past more gorgeous canyon scenery. You'll finish the loop high up on the rim on the Ridge Trail, which takes you back to South Falls Lodge.

Start: The trailhead is located adjacent to the South Falls Lodge in Silver Falls State Park.
Distance: 6.9-mile loop
Hiking time: 2 to 3 hours
Difficulty: Moderate due to the length of hike
Best season: June through Oct
Other trail users: Hikers only
Canine compatibility: Dogs not permitted on Canyon Trail, Winter Trail, or Maple Trail but are permitted on other trails in the park
Land status: State park
Nearest town: Silverton

Fees and permits: Small day-use fee
Schedule: Year-round
Maps: Maptech CD: Newport/Portland/Mount Hood/The Dalles, OR; USGS: Drake Crossing. A trail map is available by calling Oregon State Parks at (800) 551-6949 or visiting oregonstateparks.org/images/pdf/silverfalls_trailmap.pdf.
Trail contact: Oregon State Parks and Recreation, 725 Summer St. NE, Suite C, Salem, OR 97301; (800) 551-6949; oregonstateparks.org/park_211.php

Finding the trailhead: From I-5 in Salem, turn east on OR 22 toward North Santiam Highway-Stayton-Detroit Lake. Travel 5 miles east and take exit 7 onto OR 214 toward Silver Falls State Park. At the end of the off-ramp, turn left onto OR 214 and continue 4.5 miles to a stop sign. Turn left at the stop sign and travel 12.2 miles on OR 214 to the entrance to Silver Falls State Park. After entering the park turn left at the South Falls turnoff. Proceed to the parking area and trailhead. *DeLorme: Oregon Atlas & Gazetteer:* Page 54 A3. GPS: N44 51.074 / W122 38.772.

The Hike

Silver Falls State Park—at 8,706 acres, Oregon's largest state park—is a canyon carved by the North and South Forks of Silver Creek and is loaded with waterfalls. It's thought that the creeks are named after James "Silver" Smith, who traveled to this area with his pockets full of silver coins in the 1840s. The name lived on when Silver Falls was established in the 1880s—then consisting of nothing more than

Lower South Falls ▶

a sawmill, a hotel, and several hunting lodges. The land was overzealously logged until the late 1920s, when the state considered turning the area into a national park. This ground the logging to a halt, but unfortunately national park status was never realized. Ironically, the land had been subjected to too much logging and farming and didn't pass muster for the National Park Service. The federal government did purchase the land during the Great Depression and designated it as a Recreational Demonstration Area that featured recreational facilities, hiking trails, and the South Falls Lodge. All of what you'll find here was built by the Civilian Conservation Corps during the depression.

A classic 6.9-mile loop through a forested canyon of stately Douglas fir, western hemlock, red cedar, maple, alder, and gregarious cottonwoods offers a tour of as many as ten waterfalls. In fall the maples are colored in brilliant reds, oranges, and yellows and contrast sharply with the dark green of the surrounding evergreen forest.

The trail begins at the South Falls parking area, where you'll find restrooms and the South Falls Lodge (inside is a gift shop and information on the park's plants, animals, and geology). Begin the hike by descending on a steep trail into the canyon, where you'll be greeted by a stunning view of roaring 177-foot South Falls. The trail leads behind the falls to a basalt cave. Be prepared to get wet. The large holes in the cave are formed as water trickles down through the cracks.

After the falls the trail parallels the South Fork of Silver Creek and is lined with leafy vine maple, sweeping sword fern, Oregon grape, salal, big-leaf maple, and Douglas fir trees. At 1.1 miles you'll arrive at the picturesque 93-foot Lower South Falls, and at 1.4 miles you'll arrive at a trail junction. If you turn right at this junction, you'll loop back to the starting point on the Ridge Trail.

Continue walking straight. In another mile you'll pass the 30-foot cascade of Lower North Falls. At the next intersection turn left and walk 0.1 mile to view the mesmerizing double cascade of 178-foot Double Falls. This waterfall is part of Hult Creek, which empties into the North Fork of Silver Creek. At 2.8 miles you'll arrive at 27-foot Drake Falls—namesake of June Drake, a photographer whose photos brought prominence to this area. At the 3.0-mile mark stop and investigate 103-foot Middle North Falls. Be sure to check out the side trail that leads behind the falls.

After 3.5 miles you'll come to 31-foot Twin Falls. From here the trail continues to parallel the North Fork of Silver Creek for another mile until it arrives at the thundering cascade of 136-foot North Falls. The trail leads behind the falls to large oval depressions in a basalt cave—the last signs of ancient trees that once stood here. The casts were formed when lava cooled around the trees and, over time, the trees rotted away. If you look carefully, you can see the bark ridges present in the basalt.

At this point you have two options: Continue another 0.2 mile to view 136-foot Upper North Falls, or return 2.2 miles along the Rim Trail back to the trailhead.

Silver Falls State Park

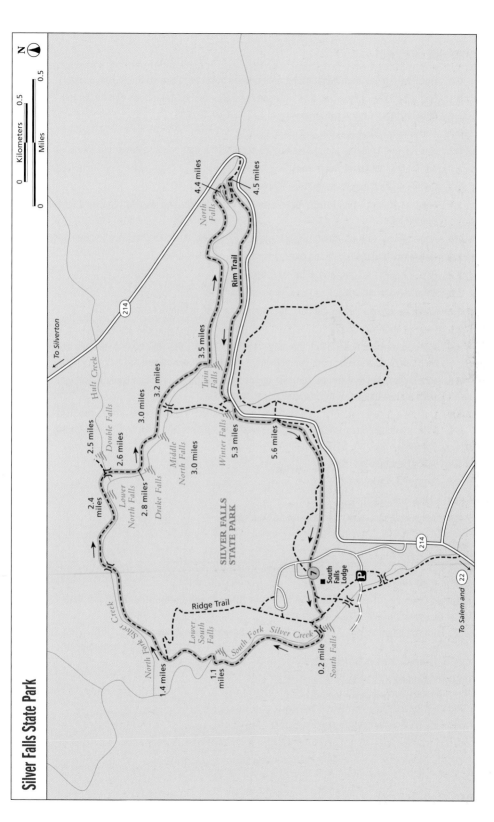

N

Kilometers
0   0.5

Miles
0   0.5

To Silverton

214

Hult Creek

2.5 miles
Double Falls

2.6 miles

2.4 miles

3.0 miles

2.8 miles
Drake Falls

Lower North Falls

Middle North Falls
3.0 miles

3.2 miles

North Fork Silver Creek

1.4 miles

Ridge Trail

Lower South Falls

1.1 miles

North Falls

4.4 miles

4.5 miles

Rim Trail

3.5 miles

Twin Falls

Winter Falls
5.3 miles

5.6 miles

SILVER FALLS STATE PARK

South Fork Silver Creek

0.2 mile

South Falls

South Falls Lodge

P

214

To Salem and 22

Miles and Directions

0.0 From the parking area begin hiking on a paved cobble path toward South Falls Lodge.

0.1 Turn left on the Canyon Trail as it descends steeply into the Silver Creek canyon. As you descend you'll have a gorgeous view of 177-foot South Falls.

0.2 Turn left and go behind the falls into a cool basalt cave.

0.3 Veer left and continue along a well-traveled path. (The path turns to dirt at this junction.)

1.1 Admire 93-foot Lower South Falls.

1.4 Continue straight (left). (The Ridge Trail heads right.)

2.4 Arrive at 30-foot Lower North Falls. Go several yards farther and head left to view 178-foot Double Falls.

2.5 Arrive at Double Falls. After viewing the falls turn around and head back to the main trail.

2.6 Turn left on the main trail and cross a footbridge over Hult Creek.

2.8 Pass the short, fat cascade of Drake Falls.

3.0 Enjoy views of 103-foot Middle North Falls.

3.2 Continue straight (left). (The trail that heads right goes to Winter Falls.)

3.5 Pass 31-foot Twin Falls.

4.4 Arrive at your last waterfall on the route—136-foot North Falls. Hike behind the falls and then power up a steep set of concrete stairs that lead to the canyon rim.

4.5 Turn sharply to the right and continue on the Rim Trail. **Option:** You can continue straight (left) and continue 0.2 mile to view Upper North Falls.

5.3 Continue straight where a sign states South Falls Trailhead 1.6 Miles. (The trail to the right leads to Winter Falls.) Walk through a paved parking area and then continue following the trail.

5.6 Turn right at the trail fork.

6.1 Turn right at the trail fork.

6.8 Cross a paved road.

6.9 Arrive at the trailhead parking area at South Falls.

Hike Information

Local Information
Silverton Chamber of Commerce, 426 S. Water St., Silverton, OR 97381; (503) 873-5615; silvertonchamber.org

Local Events and Attractions
Oregon Gardens, 879 W. Main St., Silverton; (503) 874-8100; oregongarden.org

Restaurants
Silver Creek Coffee House, 111 N. Water St., Silverton; (503) 874-9600
Seven Brides Brewing Inc., 990 N. First St., Silverton; (503) 910-8198; sevenbridesbrewing.com/index.html

8 Hoyt Arboretum

This route travels through the spectacular 185-acre tree museum of Hoyt Arboretum in Southwest Portland. The path winds through a variety of forested ecosystems, including oak woodland, redwoods, and ponderosa pine forest.

Start: The trailhead is adjacent to the arboretum visitor center, about 3 miles west of Portland off US 26.
Distance: 1.8-mile loop
Hiking time: 1 hour
Difficulty: Easy; smooth trail surface and minimal elevation gain
Best season: June through Oct
Other trail users: Hikers only
Canine compatibility: Leashed dogs permitted
Land status: City park
Nearest town: Portland
Fees and permits: None
Schedule: Year-round
Maps: Maptech CD: Newport/Portland/Mount Hood/The Dalles, OR; USGS: Portland, OR. You

can download trail maps for free from the Hoyt Arboretum website: hoytarboretum.org. You can also find the Hoyt Arboretum Trail map at the visitor center for a small fee.
Trail contact: Hoyt Arboretum, 4000 SW Fairview Blvd., Portland, OR 97221; (503) 865-8733; hoytarboretum.org. The visitor center is open 9 a.m. to 4 p.m. Mon through Fri, 11 a.m. to 3 p.m. on Sat, and it is closed on Sun and major holidays. The visitor center has restrooms and water. The visitor center and its restrooms are wheelchair accessible. Restrooms are open 6 a.m. to 10 p.m. daily. The arboretum grounds are open and free to the public from 6 a.m. to 10 p.m.

Finding the trailhead: From downtown Portland head 1.8 miles west on US 26 toward Beaverton. Take exit 72 for the Oregon Zoo and the World Forestry Center. At the end of the off-ramp, turn right onto Southwest Knights Boulevard and continue past the zoo parking lot and the Forestry Center to the intersection with Southwest Fairview Boulevard. Turn right onto Southwest Fairview and continue 0.1 mile to the arboretum visitor center and parking area on the right. *DeLorme: Oregon Atlas & Gazetteer:* Page 66 D3. GPS: N45 30.938 / W122 42.942.

The Hike

Hoyt Arboretum was founded in 1928, and the first trees were planted in the 1930s. The arboretum has more than 5,800 labeled plants and trees that represent more than 1,100 different species. Before you start the hike, be sure to stop in the visitor center. The following loop route is only one of 12 miles of trails you can explore in the arboretum. This loop route takes you past several groups of tree species that are grouped by family. You'll start off on the Oak Trail, which takes you through a sunny oak woodland filled with black oak, Japanese evergreen oak, and Konara oak. The path then travels through an immense grove of Russian elm trees and transitions into a stately stand of ponderosa pines with a thick understory of sword fern and vine maple.

After 0.5 mile you'll arrive at an amazing grove of rare dawn redwood trees. Seedlings for this ancient tree were planted here in 1951, and in 1952 the first seed-bearing

OREGON TRIVIA

- Oregon is pronounced OR-uh-gun. Many visitors pronounce it OR-ee-gone.
- Oregon's state fruit is the pear and the state nut is the hazelnut.
- The Columbia River Gorge is the country's only national scenic area.
- Oregon covers 97,073 miles and is the tenth-largest state.
- Oregon has more than 6,000 lakes, plus 112,000 miles of rivers and streams. It also has more than 7,000 bridges (fifty-one of these bridges are covered).
- Oregon's statehood was recognized on Valentine's Day, February 14, 1859.
- Oregon has sixteen hot springs.
- Nearly half of Oregon's 97,073 square miles are covered with forests.
- Mount Hood is the highest point in Oregon, at 11,235 feet.
- Portland has more microbreweries per capita than any other major city.
- Oregon has no sales tax.
- You can't pump your own gas in Oregon.

cones were produced. As you continue, the path switchbacks downhill through a thick grove of giant sequoia trees. At 0.6 mile you'll turn onto the Redwood Trail and walk past a large stand of coast redwood trees, incense cedars, and Port Orford cedars. The trail is also lined with twinflower, trillium, and starflowers in season.

After 0.9 mile you'll turn onto the White Pine Trail, which heads uphill past small groves of Swiss stone pine and Korean pine and then transitions to Douglas fir forest dotted with maidenhair fern, sword fern, and wild raspberries. After 1.4 miles you'll turn onto the Creek Trail, which parallels a small creek and takes you through dense woodland made up of spectacular coast redwood trees. At 1.6 miles you'll turn onto the Redwood Trail and follow it back to the visitor center and trailhead.

Miles and Directions

0.0 Start by walking on the paved trail paralleling Southwest Fairview Boulevard that begins next to the visitor center. The paved trail ends and joins the signed Oak Trail.

0.1 Turn left and continue descending on the Oak Trail.

0.2 Take a sharp left onto the Wildwood Trail and begin heading uphill. The trail winds through a shady grove of Russian elm trees.

0.4 Cross Southwest Fairview Boulevard and then turn right on the signed Wildwood Trail.

0.5 The trail intersects the Spruce Trail. Continue straight (right) on the Wildwood Trail. About 100 yards past the trail junction, be sure to stop and admire the magnificent dawn redwood tree on the left side of the trail. An interpretive marker in front of the tree explains its history.

Gorgeous fall colors in Hoyt Arboretum

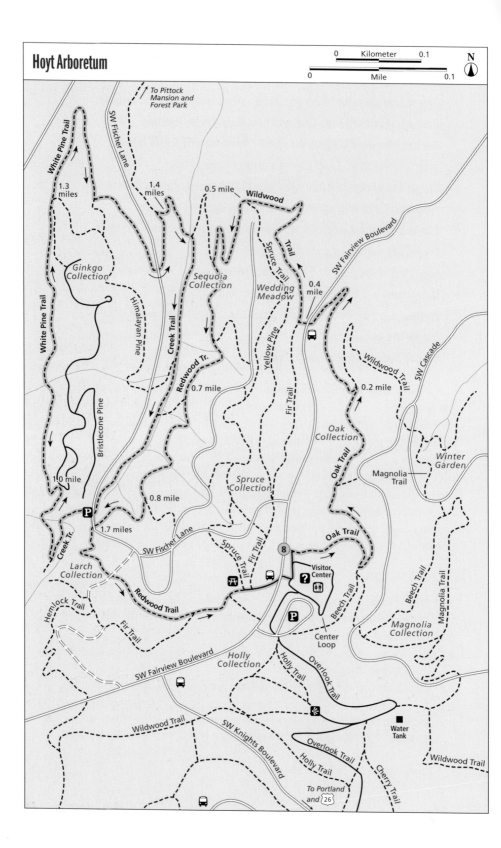

Hoyt Arboretum

Kilometer

Mile

N

To Pittock Mansion and Forest Park

SW Fischer Lane

White Pine Trail

1.3 miles

1.4 miles

0.5 mile

Wildwood

SW Fairview Boulevard

Ginkgo Collection

Himalayan Pine

Sequoia Collection

Spruce Trail

Wildwood Trail

Creek Trail

Wedding Meadow

0.4 mile

White Pine Trail

Redwood Tr.

0.7 mile

Yellow Pine

0.2 mile

SW Cascade

Bristlecone Pine

Fir Trail

Oak Collection

Winter Garden

1.0 mile

Magnolia Trail

0.8 mile

Spruce Collection

Oak Trail

P

1.7 miles

Creek Tr.

SW Fischer Lane

Spruce Trail

Fir Trail

8

Oak Trail

Larch Collection

Visitor Center

Beech Trail

Beech Trail

Magnolia Trail

Hemlock Trail

Redwood Trail

Fir Trail

P

Center Loop

Magnolia Collection

SW Fairview Boulevard

Holly Collection

Holly Trail

Overlook Trail

Wildwood Trail

SW Knights Boulevard

Water Tank

Overlook Trail

Holly Trail

Cherry Trail

Wildwood Trail

To Portland and 26

0.6 Turn left onto the signed Redwood Trail. At the next trail junction, turn right on the Redwood Trail.

0.7 Continue straight (left) on the Redwood Trail. (A spur trail leading to the Creek Trail heads right.)

0.8 Turn right on the Redwood Trail. At the next trail junction, cross Fischer Lane and then turn right. Continue a few feet until you reach a parking area. Turn left and walk through the parking area and continue on the signed Creek Trail.

0.9 Turn right onto the signed White Pine Trail. (The Creek Trail continues to the left.)

1.0 Veer sharply to the left and continue on the White Pine Trail. The route rambles beneath a shady Douglas fir canopy dotted with wildflowers and wild raspberries. Ignore the spur trail that heads right toward the Bristlecone Pine Trail.

1.2 Cross a singletrack trail and continue straight on the White Pine Trail. Go about 15 yards to another junction with the Himalayan Pine Trail. Continue straight (left) on the White Pine Trail.

1.3 Turn left on the signed White Pine Trail. (The signed Himalayan Pine Trail heads right.) The trail begins descending and then intersects Southwest Fischer Lane. Cross Southwest Fischer Lane and continue on the White Pine Trail.

1.4 At the T junction turn right onto the signed Wildwood Trail. The trail heads downhill on a series of short switchbacks. After crossing the creek you'll arrive at a T intersection. Turn right onto the signed Creek Trail. (The signed Wildwood Trail heads left.) The route heads up a creek canyon lined with spectacular coast redwood trees.

1.5 Turn left and continue on the Creek Trail. At the next trail junction, continue straight (right) on the Creek Trail. (The trail heading left crosses the creek and is signed REDWOOD TRAIL.)

1.6 The trail intersects Southwest Fischer Lane. Turn left and walk about 20 feet along the road's edge. Cross the road and continue hiking on the signed Redwood Trail.

1.7 Continue straight (left) on the Redwood Trail. (The Fir Trail joins the Redwood Trail from the left.) In a short distance the trail passes a picnic shelter on the left. Just after the shelter continue straight on the paved path that intersects Southwest Fairview Boulevard. Cross Southwest Fairview Boulevard.

1.8 Arrive back at the visitor center and trailhead.

Hike Information

Local Information

Travel Portland Visitor Information Center, 701 SW Sixth Ave., Pioneer Courthouse Square, Portland, OR 97204; (503) 275-8355 or (877) 678-5263; travelportland.com. Open Monday through Friday 8:30 a.m. to 5:30 p.m., Saturday 10 a.m. to 4 p.m., and Sunday 10 a.m. to 2 p.m. (May through Oct only).
Portland Hikers Organization is an online hiking resource found at portlandhikers.org.

Local Events and Attractions

Oregon Zoo, 4001 SW Canyon Rd., Portland; (503) 226-1561; oregonzoo.org

Restaurants

Deschutes Brewery Portland Public House, 210 NW 11th Ave., Portland; (503) 296-4906; deschutesbrewery.com

9 Angels Rest

The dramatic rock cliffs of Angels Rest, accessible from a well-maintained trail, tower 1,500 feet above the Columbia River Gorge in the Columbia River Gorge National Scenic Area. The trail is certain to test your aerobic endurance but includes enough alluring distractions to keep your mind off the elevation gain. As a reward for all your hard work, there is a first-rate view of the Columbia River Gorge from the top.

Start: The trailhead is located about 28 miles east of Portland off I-84 in the Columbia River Gorge.
Distance: 4.4 miles out and back
Hiking time: 2 to 3 hours
Difficulty: Difficult; significant elevation gain
Best season: June through Oct
Other trail users: Hikers only
Canine compatibility: Leashed dogs permitted
Land status: National scenic area

Nearest town: Portland
Fees and permits: None
Schedule: Year-round
Maps: Maptech CD: Newport/Portland/Mount Hood/The Dalles, OR; USGS: Bridal Veil, OR
Trail contact: USDA Forest Service, Columbia River Gorge National Scenic Area, 902 Wasco Ave., Suite 300, Hood River, OR 97031; (541) 308-1700; fs.usda.gov/activity/crgnsa/recreation/hiking/?recid=29872&actid=50

Finding the trailhead: From Portland travel 28 miles east on I-84 to Bridal Veil Falls (exit 28). After you exit the freeway, go 0.3 mile and turn right onto the Historic Columbia River Highway. Park your vehicle in the paved trailhead parking lot located on the right side of the road.

If you are coming from the east, take exit 35 off I-84 and travel approximately 7.3 miles west on the Historic Columbia River Highway until you reach the paved trailhead parking area on the right side of the road. *DeLorme: Oregon Atlas & Gazetteer:* Page 67 D7. GPS: N45 33.647 / W122 10.365.

The Hike

Rising almost 1,500 feet from the Historic Columbia River Highway, the rocky summit of Angels Rest offers stunning views of the Columbia Gorge. The basalt cliffs and ridges visible on this hike are the result of a thirty-million-year struggle between fire and water. The cliffs are the eroded remnants of the Columbia lava flows that poured through the region over millions of years and originated from volcanic eruptions in eastern Oregon and Washington. Approximately 15,000 years ago huge floods poured through the Columbia Gorge, widening the river channel and polishing the lofty walls visible today. This trail is one of many in the gorge leading from the Columbia River to magnificent cliff-top viewpoints.

The Angels Rest Trail begins with a steep traverse across a short hill to a forest of broadleaf maple trees. The jumble of mossy logs and rocks and the fern-covered forest floor are a masterful mosaic of Mother Nature's handiwork. In early spring you'll see a colorful carpet of white western trillium, delicate pink Barrett's penstemon, and the bluish-pink petals of the smooth-leaf Douglasia.

Ken, Lori, and Jan with Bear and Tiz on the summit of Angels Rest

Just over half a mile up the trail, there's an excellent view of Coopey Falls. The falls, which plunge over the basalt cliff in a mesmerizing cascade, are the namesake of Charles Coopey, an English tailor who owned land in the area.

The trail continues past the falls through a mostly deciduous forest to tumbling Coopey Creek. If you're hiking with a dog, stop here for a cooldown. This is the path's only watering hole.

After the creek the trail becomes steeper—gear up for a thigh-burning, heart-pumping ascent. Be sure to watch out for bald eagles that sometimes perch on the top of dead snags along the trail.

Soon the trail arrives at a boulder field, home to the cute and cuddly pika. These small gray-brown rodents, which look like rabbits, have short, rounded ears. You'll hear their distinct "cheeep" warning call as you near. During spring and summer you'll see them busily gathering grasses and seeds as they prepare for the coming winter.

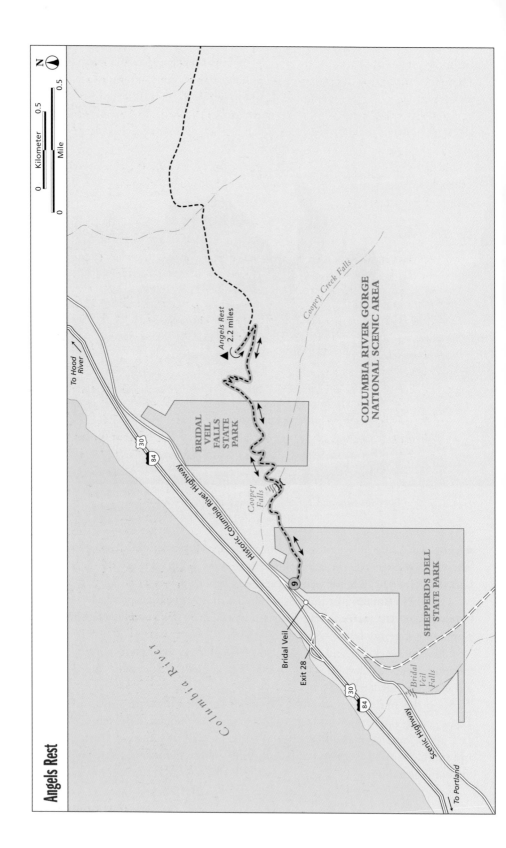

Angels Rest

Many hikers take a break to soak up the sun on the tablelike boulders on this hillside. If you choose to rest here, be sure to look for turkey vultures soaring on the air currents above. Turkey vultures are easily recognized by their dark-brown bodies, red featherless heads, and up to 6-foot wingspans. Named for their likeness to the domestic turkey, these graceful soaring birds are actually scavengers and feed on carrion of amphibians, fish, and mammals.

At the end of the boulder field, the trail forks. Follow the left branch for a short scramble to a basalt plateau—with top-notch views of the Columbia River Gorge—and the hike's turnaround point.

Miles and Directions

0.0 Start by heading to the west end of the parking lot and crossing the Historic Columbia River Highway. Hike up a short set of stone steps and continue on the signed dirt path. After approximately 100 yards you'll arrive at a T intersection. Stay to the left and continue on the main trail. (The trail going right heads toward the overflow parking lot.) The path is very rocky and steep as it takes you through a shady fern-filled forest.

0.5 **Side trip:** Stop and take a peek at the sweeping cascade of Coopey Falls from a viewpoint on your left.

0.6 Cross a wooden bridge over tumbling Coopey Creek.

2.1 The trail passes through a boulder field that is home to a colony of rabbitlike rodents called pikas. (As you walk over this rocky section, you'll no doubt hear the "cheeep cheeep" warning call made by these cute little critters.)

2.2 Turn left and climb up a short set of boulders and continue until you reach the summit viewpoint. Lounge at the summit, admire the views, and gear up for the descent on the same trail back to your starting point.

4.4 Arrive back at the trailhead.

Hike Information

Local Information

Friends of the Columbia Gorge, 522 SW Fifth Ave., Suite 720, Portland, OR 97204; (503) 241-3762; gorgefriends.org
Portland Hikers Organization is an online hiking resource found at portlandhikers.org.

Local Events and Attractions

Columbia Gorge Sternwheeler, June to September, Cascade Locks; (503) 224-3900; portlandspirit.com
Mount Hood Railroad, Hood River; (800) 872-4661; mthoodrr.com

10 Larch Mountain

Deep, mossy green forests, pristine creeks, and cascading waterfalls—the natural beauty of the Columbia River Gorge National Scenic Area is spectacular. Larch Mountain Trail 441 begins as a paved path that winds steeply up a ridge to a high point above Multnomah Falls Lodge. Here you're treated to grand views of 620-foot Multnomah Falls, one of Oregon's leading tourist attractions. Continuing past the falls, the trail parallels Multnomah Creek, traversing up the side of Larch Mountain to yet another unforgettable view, this time of several of the Cascades' major volcanic peaks.

Start: The trailhead is located at Multnomah Falls Lodge in the Columbia River Gorge, approximately 30 miles east of Portland off I-84.
Distance: 13.6 miles out and back
Hiking time: 6 to 8 hours
Difficulty: Difficult; significant elevation gain and length of hike
Best season: June through Oct
Other trail users: Hikers only
Canine compatibility: Leashed dogs permitted
Land status: National scenic area

Nearest town: Portland
Fees and permits: None
Schedule: Open mid-May through Oct
Maps: Maptech CD: Newport/Portland/Mount Hood/The Dalles, OR; USGS: Multnomah Falls, OR
Trail contact: USDA Forest Service, Columbia River Gorge National Scenic Area, 902 Wasco Ave., Suite 300, Hood River, OR 97031; (541) 308-1700; www.fs.usda.gov/activity/crgnsa/recreation/hiking/?recid=29872&actid=50

Finding the trailhead: From the intersection of I-205 and I-84 in Portland, drive 21 miles east on I-84 to exit 31 for Multnomah Falls. Park in the large paved parking area at Multnomah Falls. To reach the trailhead, go through the tunnel (under I-84) and follow the broad paved steps, which lead to the trailhead behind Multnomah Falls Lodge. *DeLorme: Oregon Atlas & Gazetteer:* Page 67 D8. GPS: N45 34.557 / W122 06.922.

The Hike

The mile-wide Columbia River carves through Columbia River Gorge as it races west to meet the Pacific Ocean at Astoria in the northwest corner of Oregon. The mighty river, made famous by Lewis and Clark, separates Oregon from Washington and has served as a major transportation route for hundreds of years.

Basalt cliffs and 2,000- to 5,000-foot-tall peaks frame this magnificent gorge. Covering these mountains and the surrounding ridges is a thick canopy of Douglas fir, red alder, big-leaf maple, and red cedar. Through it all, tumbling down the cliffs of the river gorge are Oregon's magnificent waterfalls. One of the area's most spectacular is 642-foot Multnomah Falls, the fourth-highest year-round falls in the United States and one of the top tourist attractions in Oregon. Fed by Multnomah Creek, which drains snowmelt from Larch Mountain, Multnomah Falls plunges 560 feet from the top of the cliff onto a rock ledge and then drops another 82 feet to a deep pool.

Stunning view of Mount Hood from the summit of Larch Mountain

Larch Mountain Trail 441 starts at the base of the falls at the historic Multnomah Falls Lodge. The lodge, built in 1925 and now listed on the National Register of Historic Places, was built from several kinds of rock and was originally intended to serve as a place for travelers to spend the night. Today it houses a restaurant, gift shop, and Forest Service visitor center.

Just 0.2 mile from the lodge, the trail crosses Benson Bridge, built in 1914 by Italian stonemasons. This concrete bridge offers a splendid view of the long, billowing cascade of Multnomah Falls—as well as a good mist to get you a bit wet. Continue hiking up the steep paved path another 0.8 mile to the top of a ridge above the falls. There, at a trail junction, turn right for a quick detour to a dizzying cliffside view of the falls as it plunges over the high basalt ledge.

On September 4, 1995, a tour bus–size rockslide rumbled down the upper section of the falls. The slide, weighing almost 400 tons, plunged 225 feet and sent water,

You will have many outstanding views of Multnomah Creek as you hike to the summit of Larch Mountain.

rocks, and debris more than 70 feet into the air from the valley floor. Twenty persons suffered minor injuries from flying rocks. Imagine the mayhem.

After viewing the falls, head back to the trail junction. From there continue walking on the Larch Mountain Trail. Over the next 3 miles, the trail parallels Multnomah Creek and its charming waterfalls and mossy boulders and winds through a botanical wonderland filled with ferns, wildflowers, and other forest greenery.

The last 2.8-mile section of trail is a steep climb up the side of 4,055-foot Larch Mountain. At the top you'll arrive at a picnic area and large parking lot. Walk across the parking lot and continue another 0.2 mile on a paved trail to Sherrard Point. From this high viewpoint you'll have spectacular views of Mount Hood, Mount Jefferson, Mount St. Helens, Mount Adams, Mount Rainier, the Columbia River Gorge, and the Bull Run Watershed. Soak in the scenery, and then return the way you came. Be sure to carry plenty of water with you; there is no water at the summit.

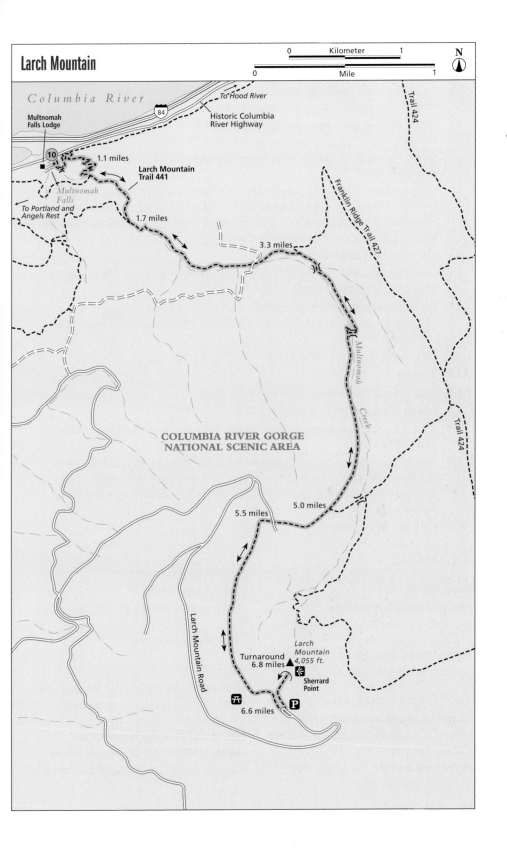

Larch Mountain

Kilometer
0   1

Mile
0   1

N

Columbia River

To Hood River

84

Historic Columbia
River Highway

Multnomah
Falls Lodge

10

1.1 miles

**Larch Mountain
Trail 441**

*Multnomah
Falls*

To Portland and
Angels Rest

1.7 miles

3.3 miles

Franklin Ridge Trail 427

Trail 424

Multnomah Creek

Trail 424

**COLUMBIA RIVER GORGE
NATIONAL SCENIC AREA**

5.0 miles

5.5 miles

Larch Mountain Road

Turnaround
6.8 miles

*Larch
Mountain*
▲ *4,055 ft.*

Sherrard
Point

P

6.6 miles

Miles and Directions

0.0 Start hiking on the paved path next to Multnomah Falls Lodge. As the trail climbs, you'll contend with a series of stairs—and crowds of people.

0.1 Pass a sign that states MULTNOMAH FALLS BRIDGE 0.2/TOP OF FALLS 1/WAHKEENAH TRAIL 1.8/LARCH MOUNTAIN 6.8.

0.2 Continue across Benson Bridge, which spans Multnomah Creek and has a striking view of Multnomah Falls.

1.0 Reach the top of the falls. The paved trail begins to descend a short distance until you arrive at a T intersection. Continue left on the dirt path. (The path that heads right leads to an overlook of the falls.) Cross a stone bridge over the creek. After you cross the creek, the trail starts climbing up scenic Multnomah Creek Canyon.

1.1 Turn left on Larch Mountain Trail 441.

1.7 Turn left on Larch Mountain Trail 441 where a sign states LARCH MOUNTAIN 5. (Wahkeenah Trail 420 heads right at this junction.)

3.0 The singletrack trail intersects a doubletrack road. Continue a short distance on the doubletrack to another trail junction. Turn right onto a singletrack trail where a sign states LARCH MOUNTAIN TRAIL 4 MILES.

3.3 Continue straight (right). (Franklin Ridge Trail 427 goes left.)

5.0 Turn right at the trail fork.

5.5 Cross a doubletrack road and continue a steep ascent.

6.5 Turn left at the trail fork.

6.6 Arrive at a paved parking area. Cross the parking area and pick up the paved trail toward Sherrard Point.

6.8 Arrive at the top of Sherrard Point. (**Note:** From this spectacular summit you'll have views—on a clear day—of Mount Rainier, Mount St. Helens, Mount Adams, Mount Hood, Mount Jefferson, and the Columbia River Gorge.) From here, retrace the same route back to the trailhead.

13.6 Arrive back at the trailhead.

Hike Information

Local Information

Friends of the Columbia Gorge, 522 SW Fifth Ave., Suite 720, Portland, OR 97204; (503) 241-3762; gorgefriends.org

Portland Hikers Organization is an online hiking resource found at portlandhikers.org.

Local Events and Attractions

Columbia Gorge Sternwheeler, June to September, Cascade Locks; (503) 224-3900; portlandspirit.com

Mount Hood Railroad, Hood River; (800) 872-4661; mthoodrr.com

Accommodations

McMenamins Edgefield, 2126 SW Halsey St., Troutdale; (503) 669-8610; mcmenamins .com/54-edgefield-home

Restaurants

McMenamins Edgefield, 2126 SW Halsey St., Troutdale; (503) 669-8610; mcmenamins .com/54-edgefield-home

Multnomah Falls Lodge Restaurant and Lounge, 50000 Historic Columbia River, Bridal Veil; (503) 695-2376; multnomahfallslodge.com

11 Horsetail, Oneonta, and Triple Falls

If you love waterfalls, this hike is for you. This route through the Columbia River Gorge National Scenic Area visits four beautiful waterfalls, offers a great view of the narrow chasm of Oneonta Gorge, and snakes through a lush, mossy forest filled with wildflowers in spring and summer. It also climbs up a ridge to the long, sweeping cascade of Horsetail Falls, passes behind the broad cascade of Ponytail Falls, parallels swift Oneonta Creek, and travels along the tall, mossy walls of Oneonta Gorge.

Start: This route starts at the Horsetail Falls trailhead, located 34.5 miles east of Portland at exit 35 off I-84.
Distance: 6.4 miles out and back
Hiking time: 2.5 to 4 hours
Difficulty: Difficult; moderate degree of elevation gain and trail length
Best season: June through Oct
Other trail users: Hikers only
Canine compatibility: Leashed dogs permitted
Land status: National scenic area
Nearest town: Portland

Fees and permits: None
Schedule: Year-round. The trail can be muddy and icy during winter.
Maps: Maptech CD: Newport/Portland/ Mount Hood/The Dalles, OR; USGS: Mult- nomah Falls, OR
Trail contact: USDA Forest Service, Columbia River Gorge National Scenic Area, 902 Wasco Ave., Suite 300, Hood River, OR 97031; (541) 308-1700; fs.usda.gov/activity/crgnsa/ recreation/hiking/?recid=29872&actid=50

Finding the trailhead: From Portland head approximately 33 miles east on I-84 to Ainsworth (exit 35). Travel 1.5 miles west on the Historic Columbia River Highway and turn right into the Horsetail Falls Parking area. *DeLorme: Oregon Atlas & Gazetteer:* Page 67 D8. GPS: N45 35.419 / W122 04.104.

The Hike

The steep and scenic Columbia River Gorge, carved by the Columbia River, is filled with miles of hiking trails, lush forest, and beautiful waterfalls. The main highway that travels through the gorge, I-84, allows easy access to many trails leading to dramatic vistas, through mossy forests, and along bubbling creeks.

In the early 1900s travel through the gorge was difficult if not impossible. Without a road, the trip was dangerous, tedious, and usually avoided. So when two Portland businessmen, Simon Lancaster and Sam Hill, convinced the government to build a highway that would match the gorge's natural beauty while allowing easy access to and through the area, many people were thankful. The resulting Columbia River Highway, which stretched 196 miles from Portland to The Dalles, was completed in 1922 at a cost of $11 million. Today drivers still travel on sections of the original highway. Old bridges, walls, and public buildings from the project are still standing, built from locally quarried basalt to last forever.

Horsetail Falls

There are dozens of waterfalls in the area, and this hike takes you to four of the best: Horsetail, Ponytail, Oneonta, and Triple Falls. The trail starts beside 176-foot Horsetail Falls. As its name implies, the plunging water mimics the swishing motion of a horse's tail. Moving on, the trail climbs a ridge along a series of steep switchbacks, past ferns clinging tightly to a hillside dotted with candy flowers and geraniums. After 0.4 mile the trail passes Ponytail Falls (also known as Upper Horsetail Falls). This quick cascade drops from a rocky cirque into a deep, rounded pool. An open, circular cave has formed in the basalt behind the falls, allowing hikers to see the action from a different angle. If you step inside the cave, be sure to check out the cave roof—fractures in the ceiling (and the blocks on the floor) are a result of water penetrating from above then freezing and expanding.

At 1.2 miles you'll cross a bridge offering excellent views of 60-foot Oneonta Falls.

At 2 miles you'll have a great view of the three-tiered cascade of Triple Falls. Like three long fingers, the triple cascade dangles over a basalt ledge and dips into the creek far below. From here hike another 0.2 mile to a wooden footbridge, a good place to enjoy a well-deserved break and admire bubbling Oneonta Creek. After taking a break continue another mile as the trail parallels the bouldery creek to another wooden footbridge and your turnaround point.

Miles and Directions

0.0 Start this route by crossing the Historic Columbia River Highway and powering uphill where a sign states UPPER HORSETAIL FALLS 0.4/VIEWPOINT 0.8/ONEONTA CREEK 1.2/ONEONTA TRAIL 1.3. You'll immediately have a grand view of the long, swerving cascade of 176-foot Horsetail Falls.

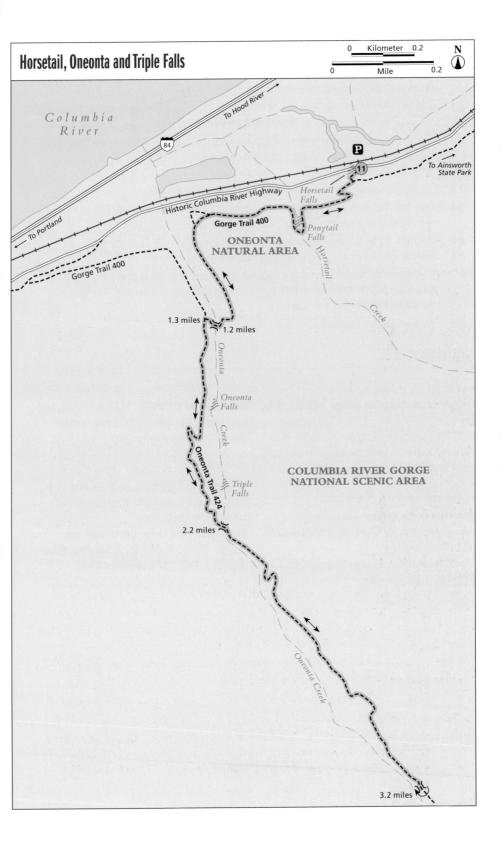

Horsetail, Oneonta and Triple Falls

Columbia River

84

To Hood River

P

11

To Ainsworth State Park

Horsetail Falls

Historic Columbia River Highway

Gorge Trail 400

Ponytail Falls

ONEONTA NATURAL AREA

To Portland

Horsetail

Gorge Trail 400

Creek

1.3 miles

1.2 miles

Oneonta

Oneonta Falls

Creek

Oneonta Trail 424

Triple Falls

COLUMBIA RIVER GORGE NATIONAL SCENIC AREA

2.2 miles

Oneonta Creek

3.2 miles

0.1 Turn right onto Gorge Trail 400 where a sign indicates Ponytail Falls 0.2/Oneonta Trail

0.8 Continue uphill on a series of steep switchbacks as the trail passes through a shady bigleaf maple forest and fern-covered hillside.

0.4 Arrive at Ponytail Falls. This shimmering cascade drops over a basalt ledge into a deep rock pool. The trail leads you behind the falls through a cool basalt cave.

1.2 Cross a metal bridge, where you can glance at the brilliant 60-foot Oneonta Falls on your left. (**Note:** Get ready to climb again on some steep switchbacks after you cross the bridge.)

1.3 Turn left where a sign indicates Oneonta Trail #424/Horsetail Creek Trail.

2.1 Gorge Trail 400 goes right at this junction. Continue hiking on Oneonta Trail 424 as it winds steeply up gorgeous Oneonta Creek Canyon.

2.2 Arrive at a log bridge above Triple Falls and scenic Oneonta Creek. Cross the bridge and continue on the trail as it travels uphill along the creek.

3.2 Arrive at another log bridge crossing Oneonta Creek (your turnaround point). Retrace the same route back to the trailhead. (**Note:** Watch your footing on the descent. The rocks on this trail can be very wet and slippery.)

6.4 Arrive back at the trailhead.

Hike Information

Local Information

Friends of the Columbia Gorge, 522 SW Fifth Ave., Suite 720, Portland, OR 97204; (503) 241-3762; gorgefriends.org

Portland Hikers Organization is an online hiking resource found at portlandhikers.org.

Local Events and Attractions

Columbia Gorge Sternwheeler, June to September, Cascade Locks; (503) 224-3900; portlandspirit.com

Mount Hood Railroad, Hood River; (800) 872-4661; mthoodrr.com

Accommodations

McMenamins Edgefield, 2126 SW Halsey St., Troutdale; (503) 669-8610; mcmenamins .com/54-edgefield-home

Restaurants

McMenamins Edgefield, 2126 SW Halsey St., Troutdale; (503) 669-8610; mcmenamins .com/54-edgefield-home

Multnomah Falls Lodge Restaurant and Lounge, 50000 Historic Columbia River, Bridal Veil; (503) 695-2376; multnomahfalls lodge.com

12 Munra Point

This hike, one of the most challenging in the Columbia River Gorge National Scenic Area, throws just about everything at you at once: dense forest; steep ascents and descents on slippery, often muddy slopes; rock scrambling; steep drop-offs; and stunning views of the gorge. The hike starts by heading west on Gorge Trail 400, a dirt path that turns into a doubletrack dirt road. After half a mile it hooks up with the relentlessly steep Munra Point Trail, which winds its way up a ridge to the dramatic summit of Munra Point.

Start: The trailhead is located approximately 40 miles east of Portland off I-84 in the Columbia River Gorge.

Distance: 2.0 miles out and back

Hiking time: 2 to 3 hours

Difficulty: Difficult; steep, loose terrain, rock scrambling, and significant elevation gain

Best season: June through Oct

Other trail users: Hikers only

Canine compatibility: Leashed dogs are permitted, however, this trail is not recommended for dogs because of steep drop-offs and technical terrain.

Land status: National scenic area

Nearest town: Cascade Locks

Fees and permits: Northwest Forest Pass (small fee) required. Purchase a pass online at www.fs.usda.gov/main/r6/passes-permits/recreation or by calling (800) 270-7504.

Schedule: Apr through Nov

Maps: Maptech CD: Newport/Portland/Mount Hood/The Dalles, OR; USGS: Bonneville Dam, OR

Trail contact: USDA Forest Service, Columbia River Gorge National Scenic Area, 902 Wasco Ave., Suite 300, Hood River, OR 97031; (541) 308-1700; fs.usda.gov/activity/crgnsa/recreation/hiking/?recid=29872&actid=50

Finding the trailhead: From Portland travel east on I-84 for approximately 40 miles, exiting at Bonneville Dam (exit 40). At the stop sign turn south (right) and pull into the gravel parking lot at the Wahclella Falls trailhead. *DeLorme: Oregon Atlas & Gazetteer:* Page 68 C1. GPS: N45 37.399 / W121 58.581

Special considerations: This hike has exposed sections and sections that require rock scrambling.

The Hike

The Columbia River Gorge stretches east from Portland and is a popular destination for those living in and visiting northwest Oregon. The mighty Columbia River flows west toward Astoria. On its banks are more than forty million years' worth of Mother Nature's forces at work. High cliff walls and ridges covered with forest greenery and magnificent waterfalls are found between Troutdale and Hood River off I-84. East from Hood River (toward the community of The Dalles) sagebrush- and oak-covered slopes prevail thanks to decreased rainfall and the resulting hotter, drier climate.

For early settlers traveling along the Oregon Trail, The Dalles was a main stopping point—a place to rest and refuel before attempting the most difficult part of their journey, a dangerous rafting trip down the rapids of the Columbia River (overland travel was, at the time, impossible). These huge rafts were built from logs up to 40 feet in length and were manned by skilled river runners. The trip downriver was slow and tiring, and the water was icy cold. Often the rafts traveled just a few miles per day, and on dangerous sections of the river, rafts, wagons, and other gear had to be portaged.

In 1845 Samuel Barlow and Joel Palmer came up with an alternative overland route that was to become known as the Barlow Road. Built in 1846, the road proved to be almost as difficult as the trip down the river, as settlers were faced with the challenge of sending wagons and gear up and down 60 percent grades. A toll was charged to users, including a $5 fee for each wagon and $1 for each head of stock. Many settlers could not afford to pay, so Barlow made them sign a note that promised payment in the future. One particularly hazardous section of the road was at Laurel Hill, located above Government Camp off present-day US 26. This stretch was so steep that it filled travelers' hearts with fear. Today nothing remains of this route but old wagon ruts. Visitors can now make the journey over Mount Hood in about an hour via US 26. While pale in comparison, the hike to the top of scenic Munra Point is physically demanding, even to experienced hikers, with its relentlessly steep grade and large, loose rocks.

The trail starts out innocently enough. Hike south from the Wahclella Falls trailhead on Gorge Trail 400 and climb up the side of a ridge. Eventually the trail flattens out and becomes a doubletrack road. You'll find juicy blackberries here during August and September.

After half a mile a side trail ascends Munra Point Ridge, but Gorge Trail 400 continues straight. The trail is lined with big-leaf maple, Oregon grape, and other forest greenery. The higher the trail goes, the steeper and more eroded it becomes. Soon the vegetation is primarily scrub oak and poison oak, but splashes of Indian paintbrush, purple lupine, and wild roses keep things cheery. At 0.7 mile some rock scrambling is required, and at 0.9 mile there's a steep, narrow, and rocky gully. Finally, after a mile the trail arrives at the small, flat summit. The reward for all your hard work: spectacular views of the Columbia River Gorge and a steep descent back to your car.

Miles and Directions

0.0 Start at the Wahclella Falls trailhead parking lot. Walk back up the paved entrance road; turn left at the Gorge Trail 400 sign and walk over the concrete bridge over Tanner Creek.

0.1 Turn left at another Gorge Trail 400 sign and begin weaving your way up the hill on the dirt footpath lined with sword fern, big-leaf maple, and cedar trees.

Shannon and Mike hiking the steep trail to the summit of Munra Point

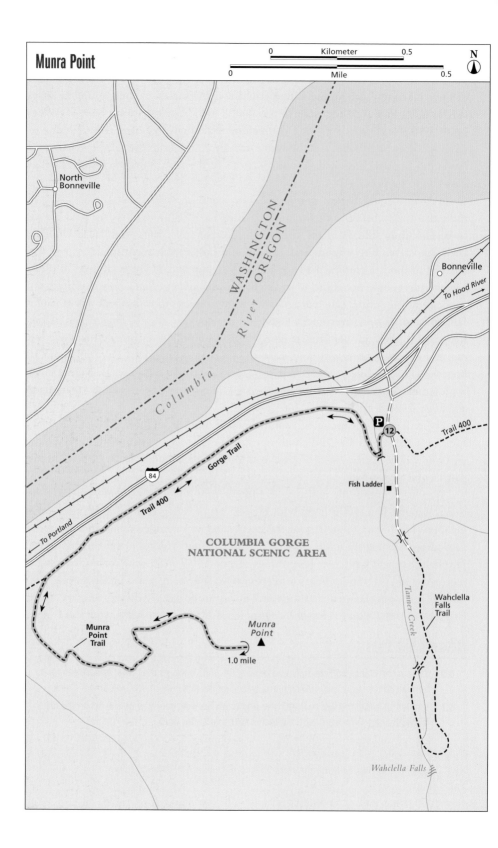

Munra Point

0 ——— Kilometer ——— 0.5

0 ——————— Mile ——————— 0.5

N

North Bonneville

WASHINGTON
OREGON

Columbia River

Bonneville

To Hood River

84

Gorge Trail

Trail 400

Trail 400

To Portland

Fish Ladder

P

12

COLUMBIA GORGE
NATIONAL SCENIC AREA

Tanner Creek

Wahclella
Falls
Trail

Munra
Point
Trail

Munra
Point

1.0 mile

Wahclella Falls

0.2 Pass through an area dominated by blackberry bushes. These hardy and prickly plants bear tasty berries starting in mid- to late August.

0.3 The trail forks; stay left.

0.5 Turn left onto an unmaintained dirt trail that begins climbing fairly steeply. There is poison oak scattered everywhere along this section of the trail. Be sure to wear long pants and Ivy Block to protect exposed skin from this obnoxious plant.

0.7 You'll scramble up two consecutive rocky sections. Watch your footing if the rocks are wet! As you scramble on these rocks, you'll see bunches of Oregon stonecrop clinging to the rocky ledges.

0.9 Scramble up a series of rocks through a narrow, steep gully.

1.0 Reach the small, flat summit and soak in the views of the magnificent Columbia River and Columbia River Gorge. Retrace the same route back to the trailhead.

2.0 Arrive back at the trailhead.

Hike Information

Local Information

Friends of the Columbia Gorge, 522 SW Fifth Ave., Suite 720, Portland, OR 97204; (503) 241-3762; gorgefriends.org

Portland Hikers Organization is an online hiking resource found at portlandhikers.org.

Local Events and Attractions

Columbia Gorge Sternwheeler, June to September, Cascade Locks; (503) 224-3900; portlandspirit.com

Mount Hood Railroad, Hood River; (800) 872-4661; mthoodrr.com

Accommodations

McMenamins Edgefield, 2126 SW Halsey St., Troutdale; (503) 669-8610; mcmenamins .com/54-edgefield-home

Restaurants

McMenamins Edgefield, 2126 SW Halsey St., Troutdale; (503) 669-8610; mcmenamins .com/54-edgefield-home

Multnomah Falls Lodge Restaurant and Lounge, 50000 Historic Columbia River, Bridal Veil; (503) 695-2376; multnomah fallslodge.com

13 Wahclella Falls

This short but sweet hike takes you along the edge of Tanner Creek to a roaring two-tiered waterfall, which plunges into a deep rocky pool. Shady maples, wild raspberries, and splashes of wildflowers decorate this fun family hike. An optional loop takes you down to the creek's edge, where you can wade in the cool, clear water on hot summer days.

Start: From the Wahclella Falls trailhead off I-84 exit 40 in the Columbia River Gorge
Distance: 2.2 miles out and back (with a loop option)
Hiking time: 1 hour
Difficulty: Easy; smooth trail surface and minimal elevation gain
Best season: May through Oct
Other trail users: Hikers only
Canine compatibility: Leashed dogs permitted
Land status: National scenic area
Nearest town: Cascade Locks

Fees and permits: Northwest Forest Pass (small fee) required. Purchase a pass online at www.fs.usda.gov/main/r6/passes-permits/recreation or by calling (800) 270-7504.
Schedule: Year-round
Maps: Maptech CD: Newport/Portland/Mount Hood/The Dalles, OR; USGS: Bonneville Dam, OR
Trail contact: USDA Forest Service, Columbia River Gorge National Scenic Area, 902 Wasco Ave., Suite 300, Hood River, OR 97031; (541) 308-1700; www.fs.usda.gov/activity/crgnsa/recreation/hiking/?recid=29872&actid=50

Finding the trailhead: From Portland travel east on I-84 for approximately 40 miles and exit at Bonneville Dam (exit 40). At the stop sign, turn south (right) and pull into the gravel parking lot at the Wahclella Falls trailhead. *DeLorme: Oregon Atlas & Gazetteer:* Page 68 C1. GPS: N45 37.860 / W121 57.240

The Hike

Head east from Portland on I-84 and you'll reach the Columbia River Gorge in about 30 minutes. The gorge is chock-full of scenic hiking trails that wind through mossy, green forests and lead to spectacular ridgetops and cascading waterfalls. The gorge has one of the highest concentrations of waterfalls in the United States. More than seventy-seven falls make a roaring dive over basalt cliffs in a 420-square-mile area. The most well-known waterfall in the Columbia Gorge is Multnomah Falls, located off exit 31 on I-84. The long, thin, two-tiered cascade of this magnificent waterfall plunges 620 feet into a deep, rocky pool.

Another magnificent river falls that could be seen in the gorge during the first part of the twentieth century is the now-extinct Celilo Falls, located 12 miles east of The Dalles on the Columbia River. This 20-foot falling torrent of water was a favorite fishing spot for local Native Americans, who seasonally congregated here to spear exhausted salmon making their way up the falls to spawn. This attractive fishing area was also a trading post of sorts. Native Americans from California, Canada, and the Rockies would assemble here to trade goods and gamble. Lewis and Clark passed through the area in 1805 and noted seeing more than 10,000 pounds of dried salmon here. This spectacular falls all but disappeared in the 1950s when The Dalles Dam was built. Today Celilo Park is all that remains of the falls. You can view pictures of Celilo Falls and learn more about its history by visiting the Columbia Gorge Discovery Center, located 3 miles west of The Dalles off I-84.

Other well-known waterfalls in the Columbia River Gorge include Horsetail, Ponytail, and Oneonta Falls (see Hike 11). This concentration of these magnificent waterfalls is due to the 2,000- to 3,000-foot basalt cliff walls that line the gorge. Huge basalt lava flows poured through the area between ten million and seventeen million years ago, creeping toward the sea. For millions of years the Columbia River has carved the beautiful gorge you see today. A few massive floods (we're talking geologic proportions) following periods of glaciation made abrupt changes in the landscape. One such flood occurred as recently as 13,000 years ago. A natural dam broke on the Clark Fork River in Montana, unleashing a massive wall of water through the narrow gorge. The enormous wave acted like a natural bulldozer, gouging out hundreds of thousands of tons of earth and rock as the water rushed to the sea.

If you're still in the mood for waterfalls, take the time to do this easy 2.2-mile out-and-back hike to the base of Wahclella Falls. The trail parallels tree-lined Tanner Creek. During July and August keep your eye out for wild raspberries along the trail. The half-sphere-shaped berries range in color from light pink to a darker red and make a sweet treat as you stroll down the trail. If it's a hot summer day, be sure to bring along some sandals so that you can wade in the creek and cool off on the way back to your car. If you still haven't had your fill of some of Oregon's most scenic waterfalls, check out Elowah Falls, which pushes its way over a high cliff wall in a long, thin cascade (see Northwest Honorable Mention Hikes for driving directions to the Elowah Falls trailhead).

Miles and Directions

0.0 Start hiking at the wooden trailhead sign at the south end of the parking lot. Begin walking on a wide, well-graded gravel path next to picturesque Tanner Creek.

0.3 Arrive at a cement fish ladder.

0.4 Cross a wooden bridge; notice the splashing falls on your left.

0.6 Walk up a flight of wooden steps.

0.8 Continue straight at the trail fork. **Option:** The right fork takes you on the optional loop section of the trail.

0.9 Cross a wooden footbridge.

1.1 Reach the roaring Wahclella Falls (your turnaround point). Retrace the same route back to the trailhead.

2.2 Arrive back at the trailhead.

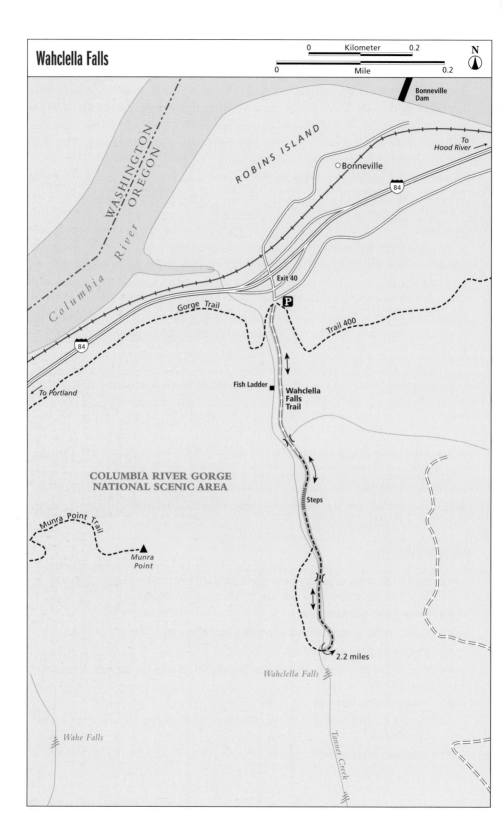

Wahclella Falls

Bonneville
Dam

To
Hood River

ROBINS ISLAND

WASHINGTON
OREGON

○ Bonneville

84

Columbia River

84

Exit 40

P

Gorge Trail

Trail 400

To Portland

Fish Ladder ■

Wahclella
Falls
Trail

COLUMBIA RIVER GORGE
NATIONAL SCENIC AREA

Steps

Munra Point Trail

▲ Munra
Point

) (

2.2 miles

Wahclella Falls

Wahe Falls

Tanner Creek

N

Hike Information

Local Information

Friends of the Columbia Gorge, 522 SW Fifth Ave., Suite 720, Portland, OR 97204; (503) 241-3762; gorgefriends.org
Portland Hikers Organization is an online hiking resource found at portlandhikers.org.

Local Events and Attractions

Columbia Gorge Sternwheeler, June to September, Cascade Locks; (503) 224-3900; portlandspirit.com
Mount Hood Railroad, Hood River; (800) 872-4661; mthoodrr.com

Accommodations

McMenamins Edgefield, 2126 SW Halsey St., Troutdale; (503) 669-8610; www.mcmenamins.com/54-edgefield-home

Restaurants

McMenamins Edgefield, 2126 SW Halsey St., Troutdale; (503) 669-8610; mcmenamins.com/54-edgefield-home
Multnomah Falls Lodge Restaurant and Lounge, 50000 Historic Columbia River, Bridal Veil; (503) 695-2376; multnomahfalls lodge.com

14 Eagle Creek to High Bridge

This trail through the Columbia River Gorge National Scenic Area leads through a deep, scenic canyon carved by bubbling Eagle Creek and shaded by a canopy of oak, big-leaf maple, and cedar. Along the route, hikers are rewarded with views of half a dozen cascading waterfalls and a creek perfectly suited for a swim during the hot summer months. Backpackers can hike in and camp at any one of four established campsites along the first 7.5 miles of the trail—but keep in mind that these sites fill up fast. For more solitude, forge ahead 13.3 miles from the Eagle Creek trailhead to Wahtum Lake and camp there.

Start: The trailhead is located off I-84 at exit 41 in the Columbia River Gorge.
Distance: 6.8 miles out and back (with longer options)
Hiking time: 3 to 4 hours
Difficulty: Moderate; trail length and an exposed, rocky section of trail
Best season: May through Oct
Other trail users: Hikers only
Canine compatibility: Leashed dogs permitted. Hang on tight to your pooch on the exposed trail section at the 0.8-mile mark.
Land status: National scenic area
Nearest town: Cascade Locks

Fees and permits: Northwest Forest Pass (small fee) required. Purchase a pass online at www.fs.usda.gov/main/r6/passes-permits/recreation or by calling (800) 270-7504.
Schedule: Year-round. The trail can be icy during the winter months.
Maps: Maptech CD: Newport/Portland/Mount Hood/The Dalles, OR; USGS: Bonneville Dam, OR; Tanner Butte, OR
Trail contact: USDA Forest Service, Columbia River Gorge National Scenic Area, 902 Wasco Ave., Suite 300, Hood River, OR 97031; (541) 308-1700; www.fs.usda.gov/activity/crgnsa/recreation/hiking/?recid=29872&actid=50.

Finding the trailhead: From Portland head east on I-84 for about 41 miles. Take exit 41, signed for EAGLE CREEK RECREATION AREA. At the stop sign, turn right and stay to the right toward the picnic area and trailhead. Continue about 0.5 mile to a paved parking area at the road's end.

From Hood River head west on I-84 and take the Bonneville (exit 40). Get back on I-84 heading east and take exit 41 for Eagle Creek Recreation Area. At the stop sign turn right and stay to the right toward the picnic area and trailhead. Continue about 0.5 mile to a paved parking area at the road's end. *DeLorme: Oregon Atlas & Gazetteer:* Page 68 C1. GPS: N45 38.220 / W121 55.140

The Hike

Eagle Creek is a classic gorge hike that should not be overlooked by hikers of any level. As you hike this trail, it's hard not to appreciate the time and effort spent creating this engineering marvel that sweeps along the high cliff walls, offering spectacular views of many of the area's waterfalls. Be forewarned, though, if you're planning on hiking Eagle Creek with children: There are many steep drop-offs along the route, and unsupervised children could be at great risk of falling from

The author backpacking on the Eagle Creek Trail

one of the trailside cliffs. If you're determined to take your child with you, be sure to keep a close eye on him or her at all times. (Of course, this same philosophy also applies to dogs. If you must take your dog with you, keep it leashed at all times.) Because of the trail's spectacular scenery and fairly easy grade, this very popular hike is often crowded—especially on sunny summer weekends—so consider making the trip on a weekday to avoid the crowds. Otherwise, be prepared to share this trail with a slew of outdoor enthusiasts.

At the start of the trail, don't pass up the opportunity to visit the Cascade Fish Hatchery (near a picnic area and a campground). Many visitors choose to explore the hatchery before setting out on the trail because of the unique role it plays in the fish supply of the Columbia River. Built in 1957 in connection with the Columbia River Fishery Development Program, the hatchery's primary purpose is to provide coho salmon for the ailing salmon fishery in the Columbia River. Adult salmon migrate upriver every year to spawn. Salmon that make it as far as the hatchery are captured and killed so that their eggs and sperm may be collected. (While this may sound harsh, adult salmon die naturally in the wild after spawning.) The eggs and sperm are mixed in a bucket, allowing the eggs to become fertilized. The fertilized eggs are then placed in trays and moved to an incubation building for twelve weeks. At

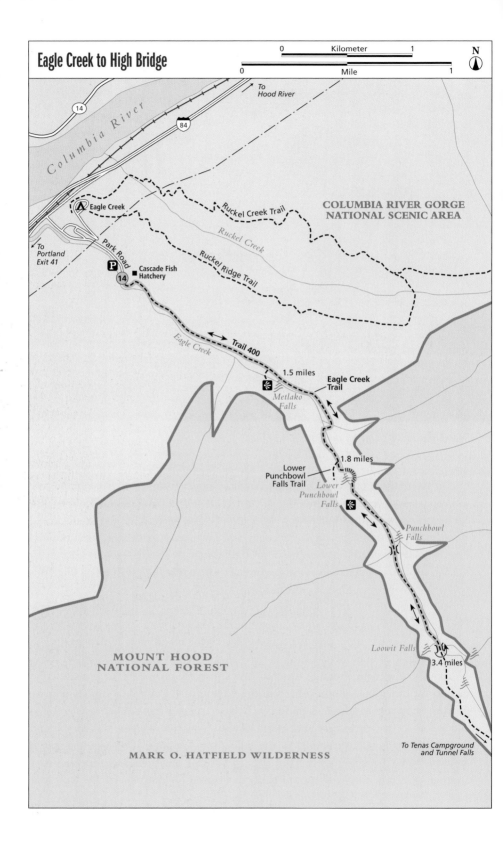

Eagle Creek to High Bridge

0   Kilometer   1
0   Mile   1

N

To
Hood River

14

Columbia River

84

Eagle Creek

COLUMBIA RIVER GORGE
NATIONAL SCENIC AREA

Ruckel Creek Trail

Ruckel Creek

To
Portland
Exit 41

Park Road

P

14   Cascade Fish
      Hatchery

Ruckel Ridge Trail

Eagle Creek

Trail 400

1.5 miles

Metlako
Falls

Eagle Creek
Trail

1.8 miles

Lower
Punchbowl
Falls Trail

Lower
Punchbowl
Falls

Punchbowl
Falls

MOUNT HOOD
NATIONAL FOREST

Loowit Falls

3.4 miles

MARK O. HATFIELD WILDERNESS

To Tenas Campground
and Tunnel Falls

that point, baby fish, or fry, hatch and are moved to starter ponds, where they are carefully monitored, fed, and raised. There are thirty raising ponds at the hatchery, and each pond is filled with 75,000 smolt (young salmon ready to migrate to the ocean). The fish are held in the raising ponds for a year, until they reach about 6 inches in length. Once the coho (also known as "silvers") are released, they migrate to the ocean. There they spend two to three years before returning to the hatchery (weighing nearly eight pounds at this point) to spawn and begin the cycle all over again.

The trail starts just above the creek and ascends very slowly over the next 3 miles to High Bridge (your turnaround point). Along the route you'll pass twisted oak trees and shady big-leaf maples. In spring and summer, wildflowers along the trail compete among one another in a show of vibrant colors for all who visit to enjoy.

At 0.8 mile there's a section of trail that often proves tricky to those unaccustomed to heights. Fortunately, cables are in place to help hikers navigate this precipitous stretch of cliffside trail. The trail is actually in good shape;

Eagle Creek runs through a deep and scenic canyon.

it's just the steep drop-off to the right that makes your brain put on the brakes.

After 1.5 miles there's a very short, optional side trail to Metlako Falls, which takes its name from the Native American goddess of salmon (in fact, the falls seem to sweep off the basalt cliff like a salmon racing to the sea). At 1.8 miles you'll arrive at Lower Punchbowl Falls Trail. Descend steeply here for 0.2 mile to the creekbed and falls, a broad cascade that tumbles into a rocky, circular bowl. If it's a hot summer day, this area will be packed with kids, dogs, and others splashing and wading in the water. Walk a short distance upstream to view the tumbling cascade of 30-foot Punchbowl Falls.

As you continue on the Eagle Creek Trail, the gorge becomes steeper and deeper until you reach High Bridge, a long, skinny expansion bridge that stretches precariously across the canyon. From the middle of the bridge you'll have a giddy downward view into the deep chasm carved by Eagle Creek. The water rushing through the canyon over mossy boulders and ledges is absolutely mesmerizing.

Following the bridge, it's time to turn around and head back the way you came. If you still have some energy left, however, consider pressing on toward Tenas Campground and Skooknichuck Falls, 0.4 mile up the trail. Two miles beyond that you'll arrive at the roaring cascade of Tunnel Falls.

Miles and Directions

0.0   Start hiking on the signed singletrack trail that is lined with oak trees and parallels tumbling Eagle Creek.

0.8   The trail becomes precipitous and drops off steeply to the canyon floor. Watch your footing here!

1.5   Arrive at a side trail on the right that leads to 100-foot Metlako Falls.

1.8   Turn right onto the Lower Punchbowl Falls Trail.

2.0   Arrive at a viewpoint of 15-foot Lower Punchbowl Falls. Walk along the creek a short distance to view 30-foot Punchbowl Falls. Once you've finished viewing the falls, head back to the main trail.

2.2   Turn right onto Eagle Creek Trail.

3.4   Arrive at High Bridge—a steel bridge that gives you an amazing view of the narrow creek canyon far below. This is your turnaround point. Retrace the route back to the trailhead.
Option: Continue 0.4 mile to Tenas Campground and Skooknichuck Falls. Two miles beyond Skooknichuck Falls, you'll arrive at the roaring cascade of Tunnel Falls. If you are backpacking you may want to continue another 10.3 miles to Wahtum Lake, which gives you a total round-trip journey of 26.6 miles.

6.8   Arrive back at the trailhead.

Hike Information

Local Information
Friends of the Columbia Gorge, 522 SW Fifth Ave., Suite 720, Portland, OR 97204; (503) 241-3762; gorgefriends.org
Portland Hikers Organization is an online hiking resource found at portlandhikers.org.

Local Events and Attractions
Columbia Gorge Sternwheeler, June to September, Cascade Locks; (503) 224-3900; portlandspirit.com.
Mount Hood Railroad, Hood River; (800) 872-4661; mthoodrr.com

Accommodations
McMenamins Edgefield, 2126 SW Halsey St., Troutdale; (503) 669-8610; mcmenamins.com/54-edgefield-home

Restaurants
McMenamins Edgefield, 2126 SW Halsey St., Troutdale; (503) 669-8610; mcmenamins.com/54-edgefield-home
Multnomah Falls Lodge Restaurant and Lounge, 50000 Historic Columbia River, Bridal Veil; (503) 695-2376; multnomahfallslodge.com

15 Salmon River

The Mount Hood National Forest's Salmon River Trail takes hikers on a journey through a mossy old-growth forest next to the wild and scenic Salmon River. The trail begins by hugging the edge of the river. It then climbs a steep ridge, ending with a short loop that offers impressive views of Salmon River Canyon and the surrounding forested ridges of the Salmon-Huckleberry Wilderness. Backpackers who follow the trail for 14.4 miles can look forward to spectacular scenery around every bend. Established campsites are available, but they fill up quickly on summer weekends.

Start: The trailhead is located on FR 2618, about 47 miles northeast of Portland off US 26.
Distance: 7.2 miles out and back
Hiking time: 3 to 4 hours
Difficulty: Moderate; moderate elevation gain and trail length
Best season: June through Oct
Other trail users: Hikers only
Canine compatibility: Dogs permitted
Land status: Wilderness
Nearest town: Zigzag

Fees and permits: Northwest Forest Pass (small fee) required. Purchase a pass online at www.fs.usda.gov/main/r6/passes-permits/recreation or by calling (800) 270-7504. A wilderness permit (free) is also required.
Schedule: Year-round (snow can be present in winter)
Maps: Maptech CD: Newport/Portland/Mount Hood/The Dalles, OR; USGS: Rhododendron, OR
Trail contact: Zigzag Ranger Station, 70220 E. Hwy. 26, Zigzag, OR 97049; (503) 622-3191; www.fs.fed.us/r6/mthood/.

Finding the trailhead: From Portland travel 42 miles east on US 26 to Zigzag. Turn right (south) onto Salmon River Road and travel 4.9 miles to the parking area and trailhead on the left side of the road. *DeLorme: Oregon Atlas & Gazetteer:* Page 62 B1. GPS: N45 16.680 / W121 56.356

The Hike

Salmon River Trail 742 traipses through the 44,560-acre Salmon-Huckleberry Wilderness, established in 1984. Located about an hour from the Portland metropolitan area, the Salmon River has carved a splendid canyon with prominent ridges, buttes, and pinnacles. Chinook and coho salmon spawn in its clear waters, and anglers enjoy casting for steelhead trout in its rushing currents.

Major landmarks in the Salmon-Huckleberry include Huckleberry Mountain to the north, 5,045-foot Devil's Peak to the east, and 4,877-foot Salmon Butte to the south. As its name implies, the wilderness is well known for its purplish, pea-size huckleberries, most abundant near Devil's Peak and Huckleberry Mountain. The enticing fruit, related to blueberries, is usually ripe by late August and makes a delicious treat if you happen across some while out along the trail.

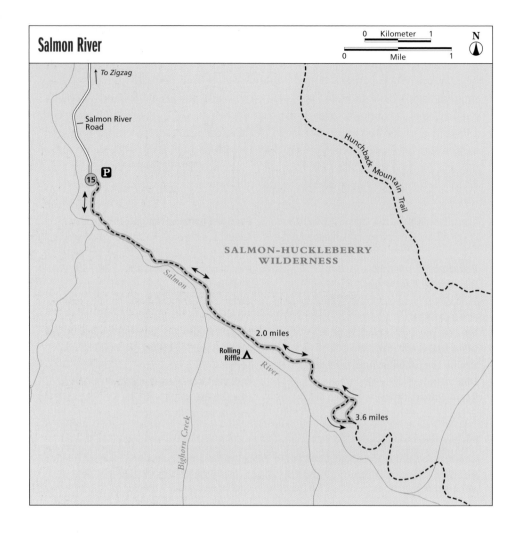

0   Kilometer   1

0   Mile   1

N

To Zigzag

Salmon River
Road

P

15

SALMON-HUCKLEBERRY
WILDERNESS

Salmon

Hunchback Mountain Trail

2.0 miles

Rolling
Riffle

River

3.6 miles

Bighorn Creek

The Salmon River trailhead is 4.9 miles south of Zigzag off Salmon River Road (FR 2618). Large red alders, Douglas firs, and western hemlocks shade the trail, and towering old-growth trees give the forest a mystical quality. Beneath these giants are broad, fan-shaped leaves of vine maple and thick bunches of raspberry bushes. Wildlife includes black bear, mule deer, cougar, badger, and marten.

The trail begins by paralleling the shallow, boulder-strewn Salmon River, which carves its way westward and eventually empties into the Sandy River near Brightwood, 4 miles west of Zigzag off US 26. The river, which flows for a total of 31 miles, receives its water as snowmelt from Mount Hood's Palmer Glacier. At 0.4 mile you'll pass a cliff where thick stems of Oregon stonecrop have a firm grasp on the rocky ledges. The bright-yellow flowers of this hardy plant thrive in the sunshine that basks the cliff walls.

At 1.5 miles you'll come to Rolling Riffle Campground, a great place to pitch a tent (the ten sites fill up fast, so come early); after 2 miles you'll cross a footbridge and enter the Salmon-Huckleberry Wilderness. The trail climbs a steep ridge at the base of Devil's Peak for the next 1.5 miles. At the top of the ridge is an unsigned trail junction. Take a right and walk a short distance to a spectacular view of the canyon and the river far below.

From here the trail makes a loop along the edge of the ridge. When you've finished the loop, return to your vehicle the way you came. If you're backpacking, it's possible to follow the Salmon River for another 10.5 miles to Trillium Lake.

To get to Trillium Lake by car (a shuttle will be necessary for a one-way backpacking trip), drive 3 miles east of Government Camp on US 26 to a road junction with FR 2656. Turn right onto FR 2656. At the junction with FR 309, continue straight 2 miles to the trailhead.

Miles and Directions

0.0 Start on the singletrack trail located on the far end of the parking area next to the bridge. The trail takes you close to the river through big old growth cedars and Douglas fir trees.

2.0 Cross a footbridge and arrive at a self-issue wilderness permit station. Fill out a wilderness permit before continuing your journey.

3.4 Turn right to begin a short loop.

3.5 You'll exit the trees onto a grassy ridge with spectacular views of the river canyon. (**Note:** Watch your footing on the trail—it can be loose and slippery.)

3.6 Turn left at a T junction.

3.8 The loop section of the trail ends. Veer right and retrace the route back to the trailhead.

7.2 Arrive back at the trailhead.

Hike Information

Local Information

Mount Hood Area Chamber of Commerce, 24403 E. Welches Rd., Suite 103, Welches, OR 97067; (503) 622-3017; mthood.org

Portland Hikers Organization is an online hiking resource found at portlandhikers.org.

Restaurants

El Burro Loco, 67211 E. Hwy. 26, Welches; (503) 622-6780

16 Cooper Spur Trail

This trek explores the high country on the east side of Mount Hood. The trail leads to the top of Cooper Spur for great views of the deep crevasses of Eliot Glacier and the snow-covered summits of Mounts Hood, Adams, and Rainier. But don't worry about climbing any snow routes—the most dangerous part of this trail is the 45-degree snowfield far beyond and high above this hike's turnaround point.

Start: The trailhead is located about 33 miles south of Hood River off OR 35.
Distance: 7.6 miles out and back
Hiking time: 4 to 5 hours
Difficulty: Difficult; significant elevation gain and trail length
Best season: July through Oct
Other trail users: Hikers only
Canine compatibility: Dogs permitted
Land status: Wilderness area
Nearest town: Hood River

Fees and permits: Northwest Forest Pass (small fee) required. Purchase a pass online at www.fs.usda.gov/main/r6/passes-permits/recreation or by calling (800) 270-7504.
Schedule: July through Sept
Maps: Maptech CD: Newport/Portland/Mount Hood/The Dalles, OR; USGS: Parkdale, OR
Trail contact: Hood River Ranger District, 6780 Highway 35, Mount Hood-Parkdale, OR 97041; (541) 352-6002; www.fs.fed.us/r6/mthood/

Finding the trailhead: From Hood River travel 22.4 miles south on OR 35 to the junction with Cooper Spur Road and a sign that reads COOPER SPUR SKI AREA. Turn right (west) and go 2.4 miles to Cloud Cap Road (FR 3512). Continue straight (stay to the right) toward Cloud Cap and Tilly Jane Campground. Drive approximately 8 miles, where you'll come to a road junction. Turn right toward Cloud Cap and drive 0.6 mile to the trailhead parking on the right. *DeLorme: Oregon Atlas & Gazetteer:* Page 62 A3. GPS: N45 24.144 / W121 39.300

The Hike

Mount Hood, a young Cascade volcano rising 11,235 feet above sea level, is the highest peak in Oregon and one of the most well-known landmarks in the Pacific Northwest. Covered with twelve glaciers and five unique ridges, Mount Hood—the second-most climbed mountain in the world after Japan's Mount Fuji—is a tantalizing quest for mountain climbers the world over. Historical records indicate that the first person reached the summit of this lofty peak in either 1845 or 1857; the first woman did so in 1867.

Today, many people reach Mount Hood's summit each year, but the climb is certainly not for novice mountaineers. Regardless of your experience, climbers will need special mountaineering equipment just to succeed. Many deaths and injuries occur every year because inexperienced or ill-equipped climbers get in over their heads, become lost when the weather turns bad, fall into crevasses, or develop frostbite when they wear improper clothing.

View of Eliot Glacier and the summit of Mount Hood

Mount Hood is located just 75 miles east of Portland in the 74-square-mile Mount Hood Wilderness. Thick forests of Douglas fir, mountain hemlock, and noble fir characterize the wilderness area. At its highest elevations, whitebark pine and high alpine meadows filled with bright splashes of white avalanche lilies, red Indian paintbrush, brilliant purple lupine, and Cascade aster make up the summer scene.

Mount Hood—thought to be less than 780,000 years old—is young compared with other peaks in the area. Classified as a stratovolcano, the mountain has had four eruptive periods over the past 15,000 years: Polallie (15,000 to 12,000 years ago), Timberline (1,800 to 1,400 years ago), Zigzag (600 to 400 years ago), and Old Maid (250 to 180 years ago). Evidence of recent volcanic activity is present at Crater Rock, a volcanic lava dome believed by geologists to be only 200 years old. The dome is located south of the summit, where you'll notice the emission of sulfur gas and steam.

Cooper Spur, located on the northeast side of the mountain, is a remnant of the massive proportions of this mountain before erosion whittled it down to its present size. The high ridge, sandwiched between Eliot and Newton Clark Glaciers, is the namesake of David Rose Cooper, an early settler who often camped on the peak's

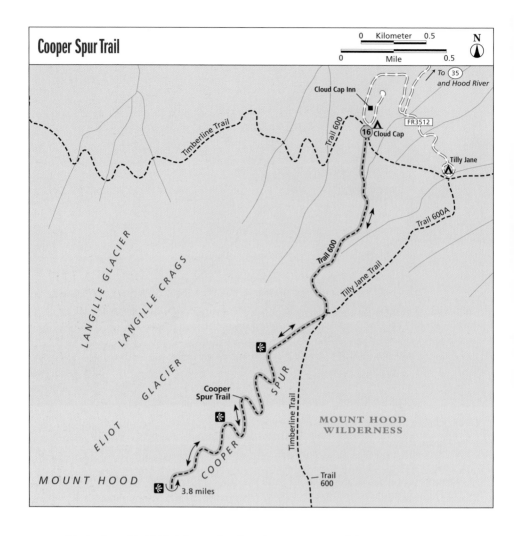

east side in the mid-1800s. The trail offers close-up views of the two glaciers and their deep crevasses and jumbled ice. During the summer months local climbers learning crevasse rescue come to Eliot Glacier, the second-largest glacier in Oregon and the largest glacier on Mount Hood, to practice rescue techniques.

The trail also includes outstanding views of Mount Hood's summit and of Mount Rainier and Mount Adams much farther north in Washington State. A plaque at the turnaround point is dedicated to climbers who have died trying to climb up this side of Hood and is a somber reminder that weather conditions on the mountain are wild and unpredictable and can be fatal to hikers and climbers who come to this mountain unprepared.

Miles and Directions

0.0 Start hiking on Trail 600. Walk 100 yards and veer to the left.

0.8 The trail starts climbing out of the trees, and you have a panoramic view of Mounts Hood, Rainier, and Adams.

1.2 Come to a junction with the Timberline Trail. Continue straight (right) on the Cooper Spur Trail as it switchbacks steeply up the ridge.

3.8 Arrive at the end of the trail and your turnaround point. A commemorative marker here is dedicated to climbers who have lost their life climbing to the summit of Mount Hood. Retrace the same route back to the trailhead.

7.6 Arrive back at the trailhead.

Hike Information

Local Information

Hood River Chamber of Commerce, 405 Portway Ave., Hood River, OR 97031; (800) 366-3530; www.gorge.net/hrccc

Local Events and Attractions

Columbia Gorge Sternwheeler, June to September, Cascade Locks; (800) 643-1354; sternwheeler.com

Mount Hood Railroad, Hood River; (800) 872-4661; mthoodrr.com

Restaurants

Big Horse Brew Pub–Horse Feathers & Co., 115 W. State St., Hood River; (541) 386-4411

Double Mountain Brewery and Taproom, 8 Fourth St., Hood River; (541) 387-0042; doublemountainbrewery.com

Full Sail Brewing, 506 Columbia St., Hood River; (541) 386-2247

Honorable Mentions

Northwest Oregon

A Cathedral Tree to Astoria Column

This moderate 3.0-mile out-and-back route explores a unique coastal forest right in the heart of Astoria. On this tour you'll get to view an over-300-year-old Sitka spruce tree and climb to the top of the historic 125-foot Astoria Column. From the top of the column, you'll have gorgeous views of downtown Astoria and the Columbia River.

To get there from US 101 in Astoria, turn south onto Sixteenth Street toward the Astoria Column. Travel 0.3 mile and turn left onto Irving Street. Continue 0.8 mile and park in a small gravel parking area on the right side of the road. Start walking on a wide gravel path. At 0.3 mile turn right and begin walking on a wooden ramp. Turn left at the next trail junction and continue a short distance to the Cathedral Tree. After viewing this impressive tree, go back to the last trail junction and continue straight up a series of stairs. Watch for blue-and-white circular trail markers placed on trees marking the route. After 1.1 miles turn right and continue toward the signed Astoria Column. At 1.5 miles you'll arrive at the historic Astoria Column. Climb the narrow spiral staircase to the top of the 125-foot tower. Enjoy the spectacular views from the top, and then retrace the same route back to your starting point.

For more information, contact the Astoria/Warrenton Chamber of Commerce, 111 W. Marine Dr., Astoria, OR 97103; (800) 875-6807. *DeLorme: Oregon Atlas & Gazetteer:* Page 70 C3.

B Neahkahnie Mountain

This difficult 3.2-mile out-and-back trail climbs through forests of Sitka spruce and open meadows to the 1,631-foot summit of Neahkahnie Mountain, where you'll have far-reaching views of the scenic Oregon coastline. Start by walking about 15 feet up the gravel road and turning left on a singletrack trail marked with a brown trail sign. You'll immediately begin climbing very steeply. After 1.5 miles you'll round a sharp bend to the right (before emerging from the trees). Look for a rough trail that heads steeply uphill to the right. Turn right and ascend on this rough, rocky trail to the summit viewpoint. Return to the trailhead on the same route.

To get there from the junction of US 26 and US 101 (just north of Cannon Beach), travel 17.2 miles south on US 101 (or 28 miles north of Tillamook) to the junction with gravel FR 38555, marked by a brown hiker sign (this turn is difficult to see!). Turn left (east) and continue on FR 38555 for 0.6 mile and park in a pullout on the left.

For more information, contact Oregon State Parks and Recreation, 725 Summer St. NE, Suite C, Salem, OR 97301; (800) 551-6949; oregonstateparks.org. *DeLorme: Oregon Atlas & Gazetteer:* Page 64 C1.

Ⓒ Munson Creek Falls

This easy 0.6-mile out-and-back route takes you on a short stroll through spectacular old-growth red cedar and Sitka spruce to a viewpoint of Munson Falls—Oregon's second-highest waterfall. To get there from the intersection of the Three Capes Scenic Highway and US 101 in Tillamook, travel 7.4 miles south on US 101 to the signed Munson Creek Falls State Natural Site turnoff on the left side of the road. Turn left (east) on Munson Creek Road and go 1.5 miles to a circular parking lot and the trailhead.

For more information, contact Oregon State Parks and Recreation, 725 Summer St. NE, Suite C, Salem, OR 97301; (800) 551-6949; oregon stateparks.org/park_245.php. *DeLorme: Oregon Atlas & Gazetteer:* Page 58 A2.

Ken Skeen hikes with Bear and Tiz on the Munson Creek Falls Trail.

Ⓓ Cape Kiwanda State Natural Area

This moderate 1.0-mile out-and-back route takes you on a beach trek and then to the top of Cape Kiwanda in Pacific City. You can explore tide pools, play in the surf, and enjoy spectacular views of Haystack Rock, Nestucca Bay to the south, and Cape Lookout to the north. To get there from Tillamook, travel 25 miles south (or 15 miles north of Lincoln City) on US 101 and turn right (west) onto Brooten Road where a sign states Cape Kiwanda Recreation Area—Pacific City. Go 2.8 miles west on Brooten Road and then turn left onto Pacific Avenue toward Netarts-Oceanside. Continue 0.3 mile on Pacific Avenue and then turn right onto Kiwanda Drive. Go 1 mile and then turn left into the Cape Kiwanda public parking area adjacent to the Pelican Pub and Brewery Restaurant.

For more information, contact Oregon State Parks and Recreation, 725 Summer St. NE, Suite C, Salem, OR 97301; (800) 551-6949; oregonstateparks.org/park_180 .php. *DeLorme: Oregon Atlas & Gazetteer:* Page 58 C1.

Ocean views from Cascade Head PHOTO KEN SKEEN

E Cascade Head

This 4.2-mile moderate route takes you on a trek through the Cascade Head National Scenic Research area, which harbors one of six remaining populations of the threatened Oregon silverspot butterfly and rare wildflowers. You'll take a journey through coastal forest, where you may see Roosevelt elk or black-tailed deer, and then arrive on the top of the open, windy summit of Cascade Head.

To get there from the junction of OR 18 and US 101, travel north on US 101 for 1.3 miles to the junction with Three Rocks Road. Turn left and continue 2.5 miles to a parking area on the left side of the road at Knight County Park.

For more information, contact Cascade Head Scenic Research Area, The Nature Conservancy of Oregon, 821 SE Fourteenth Ave., Portland, OR 97215; (503) 802-8100; www.fsl.orst.edu/chef/index.htm or nature.org. *DeLorme: Oregon Atlas & Gazetteer:* Page 58 D1.

F Drift Creek Falls

This easy 3.0-mile out-and-back forest path descends 340 feet and takes you on a fun tour through a thick coastal forest and across a magnificent suspension bridge over Drift Creek. From the bridge you'll have a grand view of the shimmering cascade of Drift Creek Falls. To get there from US 101, turn left (east) onto Drift Creek Road, just past milepost 119 in Lincoln City. Go 1.6 miles on Drift Creek Road to the junction with South Drift Creek Road and turn right. Go 0.4 mile and turn left onto Drift Creek

Camp Road. Continue 0.9 mile to another road junction, signed for the Drift Creek Falls Trail, and turn left. Continue about 9.8 miles (following signs to the Drift Creek Falls Trail) to a parking area on the right side of the road.

A Northwest Forest Pass is required for this hike. You can purchase a pass online at www.fs.usda.gov/main/r6/passes-permits/recreation or by calling (800) 270-7504. For more information, contact the Siuslaw National Forest, Hebo Ranger District, 31525 Highway 22, Hebo, OR 97122; (541) 750-7000; fs.usda.gov/main/siuslaw/home. *DeLorme: Oregon Atlas & Gazetteer:* Page 52 A1.

G King Mountain

The 4.8-mile King Mountain Trail is a difficult, strenuous trek through a red alder and spruce forest to a viewpoint atop King Mountain, with spectacular 360-degree views of the Coast Range and Cascade Mountains. This hike will turn your thighs to noodles, but the view from the top is worth the effort. To get there from Portland, drive 30 miles west on US 26 to its junction with OR 6. Exit and drive 27 miles west to a dirt pullout and the trailhead on the right (north) side of the road.

For more information, contact Oregon Department of Forestry, Tillamook State Forest, 2600 State St., Salem, OR 97310; (503) 945-7200; oregon.gov/ODF/tillamookstateforest/. *DeLorme: Oregon Atlas & Gazetteer:* Page 64 C4.

H Warrior Rock Lighthouse

This easy 6.0-mile out-and-back hike travels through a thick cottonwood forest to the northern tip of Sauvie Island along the sandy shores of the Columbia River. Large freighters, tugs, and other ships can be seen sailing up the Columbia to the Port of Portland. Wildlife abounds—from great blue herons to bald eagles—not to mention some of the bovine species. At your halfway point you can view the whitewashed beacon of Warrior Rock Lighthouse, which rests on a sandy beach at the tip of the island.

To get there from I-405 in Portland, take the NW Industrial Area/St. Helens/Highway 30 west exit, and follow the signs for St. Helens. Drive 8.8 miles north on US 30 until you see a sign indicating Sauvie Island Wildlife Area. Exit to the right and cross the bridge to the island. After crossing the bridge, continue straight (north) on Northwest Sauvie Island Road for 2.3 miles. Turn right onto Northwest Reeder Road and go 13.2 miles until it dead-ends at a gravel parking area (the last 2.2 miles of this road are gravel).

A permit (small fee) is required for this hike. Permits can be purchased at Sam's Cracker Barrel Store, located on the left after crossing the Sauvie Island Bridge. For more information, contact the Oregon Department of Fish and Wildlife, Sauvie Island Wildlife Area, 18330 NW Sauvie Island Rd., Portland, OR 97231; (503) 621-3488; dfw.state.or.us/resources/visitors/sauvie_island/index.asp. *DeLorme: Oregon Atlas & Gazetteer:* Page 66 B2.

| Clackamas River

This moderate 16.0-mile out-and-back river trail traces the contours of the Clackamas River through pockets of old-growth western red cedar and Douglas fir. Great views of the river and multiple swimming opportunities are added attractions.

To get there from I-205 in Southeast Portland, take exit 12A, signed HIGHWAY 212/HIGHWAY 224/CLACKAMAS/ESTACADA. Head east for 3.5 miles and then veer right onto OR 224 toward Estacada. You'll reach Estacada in about 14 more miles. From Estacada continue 14.7 miles east on OR 224 to the turnoff for Fish Creek Campground. Turn right onto Fish Creek Road (unsigned) and go 0.3 mile to a large parking area on the right. This is the end (or turnaround point) for the hike. If you are doing a shuttle, leave a bike or car at this trailhead.

To continue to the upper trailhead, turn left out of the parking area onto Fish Creek Road and go 0.3 mile. Turn right (east) onto OR 224 and go 6.6 miles. Turn right onto unsigned FR 4620 toward Indian Henry Campground. Travel 0.6 mile on FR 4620 and turn right into the trailhead parking area opposite the entrance to Indian Henry Campground.

A Northwest Forest Pass is required for this hike. You can purchase a Northwest Forest Pass online at www.fs.usda.gov/main/r6/passes-permits/recreation or by calling (800) 270-7504. For more information, contact the Mount Hood National Forest, Estacada Ranger Station, 595 NW Industrial Way, Estacada, OR 97023; (503) 630-6861; www.fs.fed.us/r6/mthood. *DeLorme: Oregon Atlas & Gazetteer:* Page 61 D8.

J Bagby Hot Springs

Take an easy 3.0-mile out-and-back hike through a majestic old-growth forest to a free hot springs bathhouse. Bagby Hot Springs is located along the shores of a fork of the Collawash River. Take a hot, relaxing soak in the public tubs or a private log-bath. (**Warning:** This area is very popular and probably not the best place for small children, as there's frequent nudity. Because of the number of people, taking your dog along is also not wise.) To shorten your wait time for a private bathing room, visit the springs on a weekday. Don't leave valuables in your car; they are often broken into in this parking area.

To get there from Estacada, drive south on OR 224 for 26 miles to the bridge at Ripplebrook. Proceed straight on FR 46 for 3.6 miles. Turn right onto FR 63 and drive 3.5 miles. Turn right onto FR 70 and drive 6 miles to the parking area on the left side of the road.

A Northwest Forest Pass is required for this hike. You can purchase a pass by calling (800) 270-7504 or online at www.fs.usda.gov/main/r6/passes-permits/recreation. For more information, contact the Mount Hood National Forest, Estacada Ranger Station, 595 NW Industrial Way, Estacada, OR 97023; (503) 630-6861; www.fs.fed.us/r6/mthood. *DeLorme: Oregon Atlas & Gazetteer:* Page 55 A8.

K Latourell Falls

This 2.3-mile easy loop route takes you on a tour of Upper and Lower Latourell Falls in the Columbia River Gorge National Scenic Area. The route travels through a scenic creek canyon filled with colorful wildflowers and wild berries. Additional highlights include opportunities to wade in the creek and have a picnic at a shady picnic area near the trail's end.

To get there from the intersection of I-205 and I-84 in Portland, travel about 18.3 miles east on I-84 to Bridal Veil Falls (exit 28). Continue 0.4 mile to a stop sign at the intersection with the Historic Columbia River Highway. Turn right (west) onto the Historic Columbia River Highway and travel 2.7 miles to the Latourell Falls parking area located on the left side of the highway. Start hiking on the paved trail that heads uphill from the parking area. Ascend 100 yards and arrive at a scenic viewpoint of Lower Latourell Falls. Continue on the trail as it switchbacks steeply uphill. At 0.8 mile cross a footbridge over a creek. Admire the swirling cascade of Upper Latourell Falls as it plunges into a deep rock pool. Continue on the trail as it descends paralleling the creek.

After 1.9 miles cross the Historic Columbia River Highway and continue on the paved trail on the other side. At a four-way junction, continue straight (left) and head downhill. You'll pass through a shady picnic area. At the next trail fork (before a paved road), turn right and continue walking on the paved trail as it goes underneath the highway. Soon you'll arrive at a footbridge that crosses the creek near the base of Lower Latourell Falls. Enjoy the view of the falls, and continue on the paved trail back to your starting point. At 2.3 miles arrive back at the trailhead and your starting point.

For more information, contact the USDA Forest Service, Columbia River Gorge National Scenic Area, 902 Wasco Ave., Suite 300, Hood River, OR 97031; (541) 308-1700; fs.usda.gov/recarea/crgnsa/recreation/hiking/recarea/?recid=30030&actid=50. *DeLorme: Oregon Atlas & Gazetteer:* Page 67 D7.

L Bridal Veil Falls

This 1.3-mile easy ramble takes you on a tour of two trails in Bridal Veil Falls State Park in the Columbia River Gorge. You'll begin on the Overlook Loop Trail, which offers commanding views of the Columbia River Gorge. The trail strolls through a wildflower meadow filled with the rare camas plant. The route continues on the Bridal Veil Falls Trail, which descends into a shady creek canyon and takes you to a grand viewpoint of Bridal Veil Falls. To get there from the intersection of I-205 and I-84 in Portland, travel about 18.3 miles east on I-84 to Bridal Veil Falls (exit 28). Continue 0.4 mile to a stop sign at the intersection with the Historic Columbia River Highway. Turn (right) west onto the Historic Columbia River Highway and travel 0.8 mile to Bridal Veil State Park, located on the right side of the highway.

This state park area features a picturesque picnic area and has two scenic hiking trails. Begin the hike on the Overlook Loop Trail, which passes through a thick undergrowth of wild raspberries, ferns, vine maple, bright-purple lupine, and other bright wildflowers. After 0.1 mile you'll pass an interpretive sign on the left that describes the Native Americans, who have lived here more than 10,000 years. The Columbia River allowed the Chinookan-speaking people to travel via canoe and was an important trade route between the coast and the central and eastern parts of the state. Traders gathered here from all over the Northwest at large fairlike gatherings that featured gambling, games, races, dances, and ceremonial displays. As you continue on this trail, you'll pass through one of the largest remaining meadows of camas in the western part of the Columbia River Gorge. This plant can grow 6 to 24 inches tall and can be identified by its beautiful blue flowers, which bloom from mid-April to May. This plant has a small bulb that Native Americans baked in earth ovens and then pressed into cakes. Pioneers also dined on the camas plant and took care not to confuse it with the toxic, white-flowered death camas.

As you continue on the trail, you'll pass more viewpoints of the Columbia River Gorge. The Overlook Loop Trail ends at the parking lot after 0.5 mile. The route continues on the Bridal Veil Falls Trail, which travels through thick stands of big-leaf maple, sword fern, vine maple, yarrow, wild roses, bright purple lupine, and wild raspberries. After a short distance the paved trail turns to gravel and begins descending into a creek canyon. After 0.9 mile you'll cross a bridge over a bubbling creek. From here continue up a series of stairs to a viewpoint of the billowy cascade of Bridal Veil Falls (your turnaround point). After viewing the falls, return 0.4 mile on the same trail to your starting point.

For more information, contact the USDA Forest Service, Columbia River Gorge National Scenic Area, 902 Wasco Ave., Suite 300, Hood River, OR 97031; (541) 308-1700; fs.usda.gov/recarea/crgnsa/recreation/hiking/recarea/?recid=30036&actid=50. *DeLorme: Oregon Atlas & Gazetteer:* Page 67 D7.

M Multnomah Falls-Wahkeena Falls Loop

This 4.9-mile loop starts at scenic Multnomah Falls and Multnomah Falls Lodge and hooks up with the picturesque Wahkeena Falls Trail. You will finish the loop on Trail 400, which parallels the Historic Columbia River Highway and takes you back to your starting point at Multnomah Falls. To get there from the intersection of I-205 and I-84 in Portland, head 21 miles east on I-84 to Multnomah Falls, exit 31. Park in the large paved parking area. To reach the trailhead, go through the tunnel (under I-84) and follow the broad paved steps, which lead you to the trailhead behind Multnomah Falls Lodge. Restrooms and water are available here.

From Multnomah Falls Lodge follow the paved path as it climbs steeply uphill and offers nice viewpoints of Multnomah Falls. At the top of Multnomah Falls, you'll reach the crest of the hill and then the paved trail begins to descend a short distance until you arrive at a T intersection. Continue left on the dirt path (the path that heads right leads to an overlook of Multnomah Falls). Cross the stone bridge over the creek.

After crossing the creek the route enters the gorgeous Multnomah Creek canyon, with its waterfalls, rocky outcrops, and fern-covered hillsides. At 1.1 miles you'll arrive at a T intersection. Go left on Larch Mountain Trail 441. The trail continues upward as it turns away from Multnomah Creek and winds its way across a ridge through a scenic fir forest. At 1.7 miles you'll arrive at a T intersection with a sign that indicates WAHKEENA TRAIL 420/WAHKEENA TRAILHEAD 2.7/ANGELS REST 1.2. Head right and continue your uphill journey on Wahkeena Trail 420.

At 2.7 miles the Devil's Rest Trail 420C joins the trail from the left. Continue straight. Proceed about another 100 feet to a T intersection. Turn right where a sign indicates VISTA POINT 419/WAHKEENA 1/COLUMBIA RIVER HIGHWAY 1.9. At 3.2 miles you'll cross Wahkeena Creek and continue 100 feet to a trail intersection toward the COLUMBIA RIVER HIGHWAY/WAHKEENA FALLS TRAILHEAD 1.2 sign. Turn right and continue your steep descent on multiple switchbacks next to Wahkeenah Creek. At 3.5 miles you'll pass the cascade of Upper Wahkeena Falls on

Multnomah Falls in the Columbia River Gorge

your right. At 3.7 miles you'll arrive at a T intersection. Go right and continue your descent on a series of switchbacks that skip back and forth across Wahkeenah Creek. At 4.2 miles the trail turns to a paved path. Proceed another 100 yards and soak in the views of Lower Wahkeena Falls on your left. You'll finish the loop by following Gorge Trail 400, which parallels the Columbia River Highway and takes you back to your starting point at Multnomah Falls Lodge.

For more information, contact the USDA Forest Service, Columbia River Gorge National Scenic Area, 902 Wasco Ave., Suite 300, Hood River, OR 97031; (541) 308-1700; fs.usda.gov/recarea/crgnsa/recreation/hiking/recarea/?recid=30036&actid=50. *DeLorme: Oregon Atlas & Gazetteer:* Page 67 D8.

N · Elowah Falls and Upper McCord Creek Falls

The 3.2-mile round-trip hike to Elowah Falls and McCord Creek Falls is a great introduction to some of the beautiful waterfalls in the Columbia River Gorge. To get there from the junction of I-205 and I-84 East in Portland, travel east on I-84 for 27.3 miles to exit 35 for Ainsworth State Park. At the stop sign go left (west) on the Historic Columbia River Highway toward Dodson/Warrendale/Hood River. Go 2.2 miles to the John B. Yeon State Park parking area, located on the right side of the road.

From the parking area walk 0.1 mile up the trail and turn left toward Elowah Falls. After 0.4 miles you'll arrive at a trail junction. Turn left and continue 0.4 mile to a viewpoint of the impressive cascade of Elowah Falls. From here retrace the same route 0.4 mile back to a trail junction and turn left toward McCord Creek Falls. Follow the trail as it switchbacks steeply up a fern-covered hillside and continue for 0.7 mile to a viewpoint of Upper McCord Creek Falls. There is a small section with a handrail just before you reach the falls. Enjoy the view of the falls as it splashes down a steep creek canyon, and then head back on the same trail to the parking area.

For more information, contact the USDA Forest Service, Columbia River Gorge National Scenic Area, 902 Wasco Ave., Suite 300, Hood River, OR 97031; (541) 308-1700; fs.usda.gov/activity/crgnsa/recreation/hiking/?recid=29872&actid=50. *DeLorme: Oregon Atlas & Gazetteer:* Page 68 C1.

O · Mark O. Hatfield/Twin Tunnels Trail

This fun, easy route is a favorite paved hiker-biker trail that travels for 4.6 miles between the windsurfing capital of Hood River and the small, cozy town of Mosier. This trail is part of the historic Columbia River Highway that was originally built between 1913 and 1922. A main feature of this trail is the Mosier Twin Tunnels, designed by Conde B. McCullough, a well-known state bridge engineer for the Oregon Highway Department. The tunnels were built in 1921 and were lined with timbers for extra support and finished with handcrafted stonework. The tunnels also featured viewing portals and a mesmerizing cliff walk that was built right into the cliff outside the tunnels. This hike requires an Oregon State Park day pass or annual pass. Purchase a day pass from the self-pay station at the Hood River and Mosier trailheads. You can purchase an annual pass at the visitor center at the Hood River trailhead.

This route has two trailheads:

Mark O. Hatfield West Trailhead in Hood River

From the intersection of I-205 and I-84 in Portland, go 54 miles east on I-84 toward Hood River and The Dalles. Turn off the highway at exit 64 where a sign indicates Hood River Highway 35/White Salmon/Government Camp. At the end of the off-ramp, turn right (south) toward Hood River. Continue 0.3 mile to a stop sign and a four-way intersection. Turn left (east) onto the Old Columbia River Highway.

Travel 1.3 miles on the Old Columbia River Highway until you reach a parking area, visitor center, and the Mark O. Hatfield West Trailhead on the left side of the road.

Mark O. Hatfield East Trailhead in Mosier

From Hood River go 5 miles east on I-84 to Mosier (exit 69). At the end of the off-ramp, turn right. Go 0.2 mile and then take a sharp left onto Rock Creek Road at the HISTORIC STATE PARK TRAIL sign. Continue 0.6 mile on Rock Creek Road to the Mark O. Hatfield East Trailhead located on the left side of the road.

For more information, contact Oregon State Parks and Recreation, 725 Summer St. NE, Suite C, Salem, OR 97301; (800) 551-6949; oregonstateparks.org/park_155.php. *DeLorme: Oregon Atlas & Gazetteer:* Page 68 C4, Page 69 C5.

P Deschutes River State Park

This 3.7-mile loop route follows the shores of the swift-running Deschutes River in Deschutes River State Park and then hooks up with the doubletrack rail-trail that takes you back to your starting point. The route offers great views of the river and a chance to view a variety of wildlife present in the sagebrush-scented Deschutes River Canyon. There is also an overnight campground in this state park, if you want to stay for a few days. A parking fee is required; envelopes for the parking fee are available at the campground self-pay station.

To get there from The Dalles, travel 14 miles east on I-84 to exit 97, signed HIGH-WAY 206/CELILO PARK/DESCHUTES RIVER STATE PARK. Turn right at the end of the off-ramp, and then take an immediate left onto OR 206. Head east for 3.1 miles and turn right into the entrance for Deschutes River State Park. Proceed 0.4 mile on the paved road through the campground to where it dead-ends at the trailhead sign.

For more information, contact Oregon State Parks and Recreation, 725 Summer St. NE, Suite C, Salem, OR 97301; (800) 551-6949; oregonstateparks.org/park_37.php. *DeLorme: Oregon Atlas & Gazetteer:* Page 84 B1.

Q Lost Lake

This 3.0-mile easy route takes you on a tour around picturesque Lost Lake in Mount Hood National Forest. Perks include spectacular views of Mount Hood, pockets of old-growth forest, and opportunities for swimming. Begin hiking in a counterclock-wise direction on Lakeshore Trail #656.

To get there from the intersection of I-205 and I-84 in Portland, head east 7.2 miles on I-84 to exit 13, 238th Drive/Wood Village. Turn right on 238th Drive and proceed 2.9 miles. Turn left onto Burnside Road. Travel 1 mile, then turn left (east) onto US 26. Continue 27.5 miles east to the town of Zigzag. At the Zigzag Store turn left (north) onto East Lolo Pass Road. Travel 10.9 miles to the intersection with unsigned gravel FR 1810 (McKee Creek Road), which is the first right turn after signed FR 828. Turn right onto FR 1810 and continue 7.5 miles until the road intersects FR 18. Proceed 7 miles on pavement to the intersection with FR 13. Turn left onto FR 13 and travel 6 miles to the pay booth at Lost Lake. After the entry booth stay right as the road parallels the lake. Continue past the general store to the road's end at a day-use picnic area.

From I-84 in Hood River, take exit 62 for West Hood River. Travel about a mile into Hood River and take a right onto Thirteenth Street. Travel approximately 3.5 miles to Odell. Cross a bridge and turn right past Tucker Park and travel 6.3 miles. Stay right toward Dee. From the small town of Dee, travel 14 miles, following signs to Lost Lake. After the pay booth at the lake, stay right as the road parallels the lake. Continue past the general store to the road's end at a day-use picnic area.

A Northwest Forest Pass is required on this hike. You can purchase a pass by calling (800) 270-7504 or visiting www.fs.usda.gov/main/r6/passes-permits/recreation. For more information, contact Mount Hood National Forest Headquarters Office, 16400 Champion Way, Sandy, OR 97055; (503) 668-1700; www.fs.fed.us/r6/mthood/. *DeLorme: Oregon Atlas & Gazetteer:* Page 62 A2.

R Mirror Lake

This 3.2-mile singletrack route travels through a pine-scented forest to scenic Mirror Lake. The trail loops around the lake and offers gorgeous views of Mount Hood. To get there from the intersection of I-205 and I-84 in Portland, head east for 7.2 miles on I-84 to exit 13, 238th Drive/Wood Village. Turn right onto 238th Drive and proceed 2.9 miles. Turn left onto Burnside Road. Continue about a mile and turn left (east) onto US 26. Travel east on US 26 to an unmarked trailhead between mileposts 51 and 52 on the right (south) side of the highway.

To get there from Hood River, head south on OR 35 to the junction with US 26. Turn right (west) onto US 26 and travel west to Government Camp. From Government Camp continue approximately 2 miles west on US 26 to an unmarked trailhead on the left (south) side of the highway between mileposts 51 and 52.

A Northwest Forest Pass is required on this hike. You can purchase a pass by calling (800) 270-7504 or visiting www.fs.usda.gov/main/r6/passes-permits/recreation. For more information, contact the Mount Hood National Forest Headquarters Office, 16400 Champion Way, Sandy, OR 97055; (503) 668-1700; www.fs.fed.us/r6/mthood/. *DeLorme: Oregon Atlas & Gazetteer:* Page 62 B2.

S McNeil Point

The McNeil Point Trail is a difficult 9.0-mile hike that takes you to a historic stone shelter at the base of spectacular Mount Hood. To get there from downtown Portland, drive east on US 26 for 42 miles to Zigzag. Turn left (north) onto East Lolo Pass Road (FR 18), and drive 4.2 miles to FR 1825. Turn right onto FR 1825 and drive 0.7 mile to a junction with FR 1828. Proceed straight (stay to the left) on FR 1828, and drive 5.6 miles to a road junction. Stay to the right (the road turns to gravel here) and continue driving on FR 1828 where the sign indicates TOP SPUR TRAIL 788. Drive 1.6 miles to the trailhead parking area on the left side of the road.

Start hiking on the dirt path located straight across from the parking area. After 0.5 mile come to a T junction and turn right. (Going left leads to Lolo Pass.) Walk 60 yards and come to a three-way trail junction. Proceed on the center trail where the sign reads PACIFIC CREST TRAIL 2000/TIMBERLINE TRAIL 600. Walk 30 yards, and be sure to fill out a wilderness permit at the self-registration station, located on the left side of the trail.

After 0.8 mile emerge from the forest and walk along the wildflower-filled slopes of Bald Mountain, with outstanding views of Mount Hood in front of you. At mile 1.1 look for an unmarked dirt path and turn left onto it. Climb over a small ridge to where the trail intersects unmarked Timberline Trail 600. Turn right onto Timberline Trail 600 and hike 0.2 mile to a fork. Stay to the right—a sign reads CAIRN BASIN. (Going left leads to McGee Creek Trail 625 and Ramona Road 1810-620.) After 3 miles take the left fork in the trail. Over the next 0.5 mile you'll cross several creeks. At 3.6 miles stay to the left. At mile 3.7 pass two scenic ponds. At mile 3.8 stay to the right at the trail intersection. (Mazama Trail 625 goes left.) At mile 4.2 stay to the right, and at mile 4.5 reach the McNeil Shelter, which on a clear day will offer up spectacular views of Mounts Hood, Adams, Rainier, and St. Helens. After you've admired the view, you have two options of returning the way you came proceeding down a steep, 0.5-mile rock scramble back to the Timberline Trail, where you can retrace your track to your car.

For more information, contact the Mount Hood National Forest Headquarters Office, 16400 Champion Way, Sandy, OR 97055; (503) 668-1700; www.fs.fed.us/r6/mthood/. *DeLorme: Oregon Atlas & Gazetteer:* Page 62 A2.

T East Zigzag Mountain Loop

The 7.7-mile East Zigzag Mountain Loop is a difficult hike. It begins with a 2.0-mile hike along Burnt Lake Trail to Devil's Meadow, an area bursting with wildflowers in June and July. Continue straight past the Devil's Tie Trail junction. After a series of switchbacks, the trail skirts the crest of a high ridge, affording a grand view of Mount Hood and Burnt Lake. Turn left at the next junction onto the Zigzag Mountain Trail, which climbs unrelentingly to a magnificent viewpoint at the summit of 4,941-foot East Zigzag Mountain. From this viewpoint hike downhill 0.7 mile to the Cast Creek Trail junction. Turn left and hike a short way to the Cast Lake Trail junction (you have the option here of turning right and heading 0.7 mile to view Cast Lake). Continue straight to a junction with the Devil's Tie Trail. Turn left and hike 0.4 mile on the Devil's Tie Trail to the intersection with the Burnt Lake Trail. Turn right at the Burnt Lake Trail and hike the 2.6 miles back to your car.

To get there from Rhododendron, drive east on US 26 for 1.5 miles and turn left (north) onto FR 27. Proceed 0.6 mile and turn left onto FR 207. Drive 4.5 miles to a parking area at the end of the road. Note that the last half-mile section of this route is rough.

A Northwest Forest Pass is required for this hike. You can purchase a pass by calling (800) 270-7504 or visiting www.fs.usda.gov/main/r6/passes-permits/recreation. For more information, contact the Mount Hood National Forest Headquarters Office, 16400 Champion Way, Sandy, OR 97055; (503) 668-1700; www.fs.fed.us/r6/mthood/. *DeLorme: Oregon Atlas & Gazetteer:* Page 62 A2.

Ա Elk Meadows Loop

The moderate 6.8-mile Elk Meadows loop takes you on a scenic journey on the southeast side of majestic Mount Hood. The trailhead is located at the Clark Creek Sno-Park area. To get there from Portland drive east on US 26 for about 90 minutes to the intersection with OR 35. Turn left (north) onto OR 35 and drive toward Hood River for approximately 8 miles to the CLARK CREEK SNO-PARK sign. Enter the Sno-Park and drive about a quarter mile to the ELK CREEK MEADOWS trail sign. The trail begins by paralleling clear, rocky Clark Creek.

Hike along the creek for almost a mile, then turn right at the trail junction. Cross the creek over a bridge and proceed straight for 0.6 mile to the junction with the Newton Creek Trail. Continue straight and cross rushing Newton Creek. Climb up long, wavy switchbacks through a forested area to a four-way junction. Continue straight and take a right onto the 1.2-mile Elk Meadows Perimeter Trail, which circles the delicate, high alpine landscape of Elk Meadow. At the next two trail junctions, stay to the left. After about 0.6 mile of walking on this trail, arrive at a wooden shelter. Be sure to stop here and soak in the stunning view of Mount Hood. Follow the circuit trail for another 0.6 mile as it circles Elk Meadow. Come to a trail junction for Gnarl Ridge, and stay to the left until you reach the next trail junction, where you'll turn right to return to your car.

A Northwest Forest Pass is required for this hike. You can purchase a pass by calling (800) 270-7504 or visiting www.fs.usda.gov/main/r6/passes-permits/recreation. For more information, contact the Mount Hood National Forest Headquarters Office, 16400 Champion Way, Sandy, OR 97055; (503) 668-1700; www.fs.fed.us/r6/mthood/. *DeLorme: Oregon Atlas & Gazetteer:* Page 62 B3.

Ⅴ Valley of the Giants

This 51-acre preserve is haven to a rare grove of old-growth, over-400-year-old Douglas fir and western hemlock trees, some of which have trunks that measure more than 20 feet in circumference. This area was protected as an Outstanding Natural Area by the Bureau of Land Management (BLM) in 1976. You can walk through this land of giant trees on a scenic 1.3-mile loop trail. Once on the trail you'll feel as if you're in a prehistoric place with the moss-covered giants standing as sentinels in a fog-shrouded setting filled with ferns, trillium, and oxalis.

To get there from Salem, travel west on OR 22 to the junction with OR 223. Turn south and continue to Falls City. Once in Falls City, follow Falls City Road into town. Turn south onto Bridge Street and follow it as it turns into Valsetz Road and turns to gravel. Follow this road for about 14.8 miles to the now-abandoned logging community of Valsetz. Follow the road as it veers to the left and then arrives at a T junction. Go right; continue 8.4 miles and go right at a road junction. Continue another 5.2 miles (keeping left at all junctions) to a bridge crossing the North Fork Siletz River. Travel about a mile after the bridge to a road junction and turn right; travel 0.5 mile to the signed trailhead.

For more information, contact the Bureau of Land Management, Salem District, 1717 Fabry Rd. SE, Salem, OR 97306; (503) 375-5646; blm.gov/or/districts/salem/index.php. *DeLorme: Oregon Atlas & Gazetteer:* Page 52 A3.

W French Pete Creek

This easy 3.4-mile out-and-back trek leads you through an amazing old-growth Douglas fir and red cedar forest in the Three Sisters Wilderness. The trail has only 400 feet of elevation gain and travels through thick undergrowth of Oregon grape, sword fern, and vine maple and under towering trees until you arrive at French Pete Creek at 1.7 miles. Turn around here or wade through the creek and continue on this magical trail for another 8.1 miles through a picturesque forested valley.

To get there, travel about 45 miles east of Eugene on US 126 to Blue River. Travel 4 more miles east of Blue River and turn right (south) onto FR 19 (Aufderheide Drive); continue 0.4 mile to a road junction. Bear right toward the signed Cougar Reservoir and continue another 11 miles to a signed trailhead parking area on the left side of the road.

A Northwest Forest Pass is required for this hike. You can purchase a pass by calling (800) 270-7504 or visiting www.fs.usda.gov/main/r6/passes-permits/recreation. For more information, contact the Willamette National Forest, McKenzie Ranger District, 57600 McKenzie Hwy., McKenzie Bridge, OR 97413; (541) 822-3381; www.fs.fed.us/r6/willamette. *DeLorme: Oregon Atlas & Gazetteer:* Page 49 D7.

X Sahalie and Koosah Falls

This easy 2.6-mile hike explores some of the waterfalls that tumble over dramatic lava cliffs on the McKenzie River. To get there from Eugene, drive approximately 50 miles east on OR 126 to the small community of McKenzie Bridge. From McKenzie Bridge head 19 miles east on OR 126 and turn left into a signed parking area for Sahalie Falls.

Start the hike by heading down to a viewpoint of impressive Sahalie Falls, which roars over a lava shelf into a churning spring-fed pool. From the viewpoint continue left, following signs for the Waterfall Trail. After 0.5 mile soak in the views of the splashing cascade of Koosah Falls, and then continue downstream (staying right at all trail junctions) until you reach a gravel road at 0.9 mile. Turn right onto the gravel road as it parallels Carmen Reservoir. Continue until you see a signed spur trail that leads to the McKenzie River Trail. At the McKenzie River Trail, turn right and head upstream for more great views of the churning McKenzie River. At 2.2 miles turn right and cross a footbridge over the river. After crossing the bridge bear right and continue 0.4 mile to the trailhead.

A Northwest Forest Pass is required for this hike. You can purchase a pass by calling (800) 270-7504 or visiting www.fs.usda.gov/main/r6/passes-permits/recreation. For more information, contact the Willamette National Forest, McKenzie Ranger District, 57600 McKenzie Hwy., McKenzie Bridge, OR 97413; (541) 822-3381; www.fs.fed.us/r6/willamette. *DeLorme: Oregon Atlas & Gazetteer:* Page 49 D7.

Ỵ Waldo Lake Trail

This 4.6-mile out-and-back route takes you on a scenic section of the 21-mile Waldo Lake Trail. This trail circles Waldo Lake—Oregon's second-deepest natural lake. From I-5 in Eugene take exit 188A, signed OREGON HIGHWAY 58/OAKRIDGE/KLAMATH FALLS. Head southeast on OR 58 about 36 miles to Oakridge. Continue about 24 miles east of Oakridge on OR 58, and turn left onto FR 5897. Travel on FR 5897 for 7 miles to the junction with FR 5896. Turn left onto FR 5896 and continue about 2 miles to the boat ramp parking area at Shadow Bay Campground.

Start the hike by picking up the trail on the left side of the parking area and following it as it skirts the edge of Shadow Bay and follows the lakeshore. Keep your eyes open for good swimming holes. At 1.7 miles you'll reach the South Waldo Lake Shelter. Continue right on your journey around the lake. At 2.3 miles you'll reach a trail junction, your turnaround point; or continue on the trail as far as you want.

A Northwest Forest Pass is required for this hike. You can purchase a pass by calling (800) 270-7504 or visiting www.fs.usda.gov/main/r6/passes-permits/recreation. For more information, contact the Middle Fork Ranger District, 46375 Highway 58, Westfir, OR 97492; (541) 782-2283; www.fs.fed.us/r6/willamette. *DeLorme: Oregon Atlas & Gazetteer:* Page 49 D7.

Southwest Oregon

Southwest Oregon is a collage of scenic coastline, rugged mountains, wild and remote rivers, unusual endemic plants, and, of course, the astonishing Crater Lake National Park. The renowned Rogue River plunges through its namesake valley, home to the cultured towns of Ashland and Medford. When you're tired of walking, stop by the uncommon Ashland and join thousands of tourists and performers for a taste of the Oregon Shakespeare Festival.

Ken Skeen enjoying the views of Whalehead Beach

The best-known attraction in southwest Oregon is Crater Lake National Park, host to the impossibly blue waters of the deepest lake in the United States. Surrounding the park are the mighty volcanic peaks of Mount McLoughlin and Mount Thielsen, each rising abruptly from the nearby forests. You can hike to the summit of both of these lofty peaks and get a bird's-eye view of the nearby lakes and mountains of the Sky Lakes and Mount Thielsen Wildernesses.

Highlights along the southwest coast include Cape Perpetua, the Sutton Creek Recreation Area, Tahkenitch Creek, Sunset State Park, Shore Acres State Park, Cape Arago State Park, and Alfred A. Loeb State Park. Visit the Cape Perpetua Natural Area and walk through a botanical wonderland of coastal forest, rocky tide pools, and spouting geysers; and watch the waves as they crash into Devil's Churn, a collapsed sea cave. If you want to hike a section of the Oregon Coast Trail, be sure to visit Sunset Bay State Park. It offers opportunities to view the Cape Arago Lighthouse, admire golden sandstone cliffs, tour a botanical garden at Shore Acres State Park, and observe sea lions at Cape Arago State Park. Go to Alfred A. Loeb State Park to see two rare tree species. Located about 8 miles east of Brookings, this state park has two nature trails that take you on a journey through groves of rare Oregon myrtle and coastal redwoods. The park also has a campground that serves as a good base camp for exploring the immediate area as well as other hiking trails in the Kalmiopsis Wilderness.

Moving farther east, the wild and rugged Kalmiopsis Wilderness and the Siskiyou National Forest dominate, each offering a unique array of plants and animals that call the Illinois River home. Take a tour along the Illinois River Trail to get a closer look at the deep canyon it has carved over the millennia. For a different perspective of this wilderness area, hike into Babyfoot Lake to glimpse a hard-to-find grove of old-growth Brewer's spruce. For greater variety, hike to the glacier-carved basin that is home to Vulcan Lake.

17 Cape Perpetua Trails

Take your pick of ten trails that wind through the 2,700-acre Cape Perpetua Scenic Area. Depending on the trail you select, you can experience a botanical wonderland of coastal forest, rocky tide pools, and other ocean spectacles, such as the geyser-like Spouting Horn and the narrow rock channel of Devil's Churn. While you're here, plan on spending a few hours at the Cape Perpetua Interpretive Center. The center provides a good introduction to the plants and animals that live here as well as a look into the area's rich history.

Start: Cape Perpetua is located 3 miles south of Yachats and 22.5 miles north of Florence on US 101.
Distance: Trails vary in length from 0.2 mile to 10 miles:
A. Whispering Spruce Trail: 0.25-mile loop, easy
B. Saint Perpetua Trail: 2.6 miles out and back, moderate to difficult
C. Trail of Restless Waters: 0.4-mile loop, easy
D. Cape Cove Trail: 0.3 mile out and back, easy
E. Giant Spruce Trail: 2.0 miles out and back, easy
F. Captain Cook Trail: 0.6-mile loop, easy
G. Oregon Coast Trail: 2.6 miles out and back, moderate
H. Discovery Loop Trail: 1.0-mile loop, moderate
I. Cooks Ridge to Gwynn Creek Loop Trail: 6.4-mile loop, moderate
J. Cummins Creek Loop Trail: 10.0-mile loop,

moderate to difficult
Hiking time: 30 minutes to 3 hours, depending on trail selected
Difficulty: Easy to difficult, depending on the trail selected
Best season: June through Oct
Other trail users: Hikers only
Canine compatibility: Leashed dogs permitted
Land status: National forest
Nearest town: Yachats
Fees and permits: Day-use permit (small fee) is required. Permit can be purchased from the self-pay machine in the parking area or at the visitor center.
Schedule: Year-round
Maps: Maptech CD: Coos Bay/Eugene/Bend, OR; USGS: Yachats, OR
Trail contact: Cape Perpetua Interpretive Center, 2400 Highway 101, Yachats, OR 97498; (541) 547-3289; fs.usda.gov/recarea/siuslaw/recreation/recarea/?recid=42279

Finding the trailhead: From Yachats travel 3 miles south on US 101 to the Cape Perpetua Interpretive Center, located on the left (east) side of the highway.

From Florence travel 22.5 miles north on US 101 to the Cape Perpetua Interpretive Center, located on the right (east) side of the highway. *DeLorme: Oregon Atlas & Gazetteer:* Page 32, Inset 2, B2. GPS: N44 16.861 / W124 06.530.

The Hike

If you're looking to explore the diversity of the Oregon coast, you'll want to stop by the Cape Perpetua Scenic Area, located 3 miles south of Yachats and approximately

Devil's Churn

22.5 miles north of Florence off US 101. This 2,700-acre area preserves large stands of coastal forest and rocky tide pools.

First, stop in and explore the interpretive center, where you'll receive a comprehensive overview of coastal ecology, tides and weather, whale migration, and the history of the Alsea Indian tribe. You'll find interpretive exhibits, films, naturalist lectures, and a good selection of books about coastal ecology.

Each of the ten trails in the Cape Perpetua Scenic Area has something different to offer. For craggy tide pools, sealife, and a bit of Native American culture, hit the 0.6-mile Captain Cook Trail. The trail takes you past the historic Cape Creek Camp building, used by the Civilian Conservation Corp (CCC) from 1933 to 1942 to house the workers who built many of the park's trails and structures. The trail then dips under US 101 past a shell middens site—where Native Americans discarded shells from the mussels they collected for food. The trail ultimately leads to rocky tide pools where you'll be able to view sea stars, mussels, hermit crabs, sea anemones, and purple sea urchins. Once you've finished exploring the tide pools, continue to a viewpoint where you can watch for the geyser-like spray of Spouting Horn, an old

COASTAL SEA CREATURES

Cape Perpetua is home to a number of fascinating sea creatures. The easily recognizable five-legged sea star (also known as the ochre sea star) varies in color from orange to purple and can grow to 15 inches in width. Feasting primarily on mussels and other shellfish, the sea star employs a rather curious method of consumption. It pries apart its victim's shell with its tube feet and inserts its stomach into the shell, secreting enzymes that help digest the soft tissue.

Mussels are another common tide-pool resident. You'll find mussels clinging tightly to the rocks by threadlike appendages called "byssus threads." These black, oval-shaped mollusks obtain their food by filtering microscopic organisms from the water at high tide.

You'll likely see the industrious hermit crab scurrying about the shoreline in search of shelter. These comical creatures lack a hard shell for protection, so they're constantly looking for cover, often in abandoned snail shells. It's not uncommon to see two hermit crabs fighting fiercely over the rights to a prize shell.

Another tide-pool inhabitant is the bright-green sea anemone, which resembles a shimmering sea flower. This interesting creature has long tubelike feet that wave with the rise and fall of the tide. The feet contain stinging cells that can stun small fish and other sea creatures, allowing the sea anemone to wrap itself around the victim and digest it.

Sea urchins frequent the rocky tide pools and can be identified by their purple, round bodies, which are covered with short, sharp spines. These industrious creatures eat just about anything, including seaweed, dead animal matter, and microorganisms.

sea cave with a small opening in its roof. Waves surge into this cave and shoot out of the small opening, creating a spectacular sea spray.

To see a 500-year-old spruce tree, take the easy 2.0-mile (round-trip) walk on the Giant Spruce Trail. The trail parallels Cape Creek and leads you through an old-growth forest filled with ferns, salal, thimbleberry, and skunk cabbage. At the turn-around point is the trail's prize feature, an ancient Sitka spruce tree that's about 15 feet in diameter.

Another shorter trail that gives you a feel for the diversity of the coastal forest is the 1.0-mile Discovery Loop Trail. If you love sweeping views, you'll want to hike on the 2.6-mile round-trip Saint Perpetua Trail, which ascends the south side of Cape Perpetua on a series of fairly steep switchbacks and rewards you with excellent views (on a clear day) of Cape Foulweather to the north and Cape Blanco to the south. For great views without the long hike, walk the easy, 0.25-mile Whispering Spruce Trail. This trail promises spectacular ocean views (on a clear day) and an opportunity to explore the West Shelter, a stone building built by the CCC.

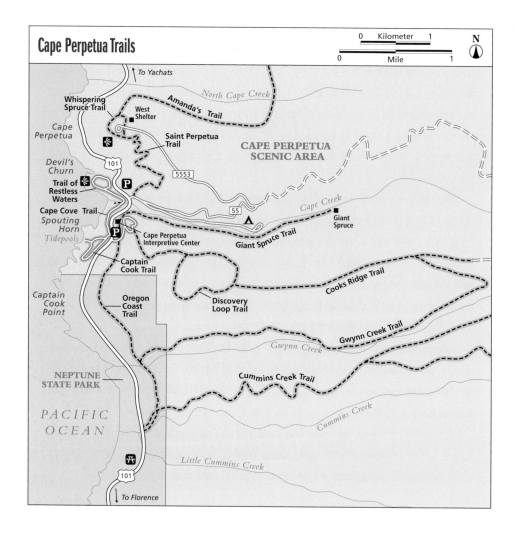

Cape Perpetua Trails

0 Kilometer 1

0 Mile 1

N

To Yachats

Whispering Spruce Trail

North Cape Creek

West Shelter

Amanda's Trail

Cape Perpetua

Saint Perpetua Trail

CAPE PERPETUA SCENIC AREA

Devil's Churn

101

5553

Trail of Restless Waters

P

Cape Cove Trail

55

Cape Creek

Spouting Horn

Giant Spruce

Tidepools

Cape Perpetua Interpretive Center

Giant Spruce Trail

Captain Cook Trail

Cooks Ridge Trail

Captain Cook Point

Oregon Coast Trail

Discovery Loop Trail

Gwynn Creek Trail

Gwynn Creek

NEPTUNE STATE PARK

Cummins Creek Trail

PACIFIC OCEAN

Cummins Creek

101

Little Cummins Creek

To Florence

If you're up to a longer hike, try the combination Cooks Ridge to Gwynn Creek Loop. This 6.4-mile loop departs from the interpretive center and winds through old-growth forests, offering up several sneak peaks at the ocean. If you're interested in similar scenery but a lengthier hike, pack a lunch and strike out on the 10.0-mile Cummins Creek Loop. From the interpretive center, the hike heads up the Cooks Ridge Trail and eventually hooks up with the Cummins Creek Trail for a return to the Oregon Coast Trail. Then it's straight back to the interpretive center.

If you love to watch the churning ocean, head down the 0.4-mile Trail of Restless Waters loop to the rocky tide pool known as Devil's Churn. The rough, porous texture of the shoreline rock here is evidence of its volcanic past. Roughly forty million years ago, offshore volcanoes deposited lava along the shoreline. As the molten rock cooled, hot gases within forced their way to the surface, creating the porous texture. The pounding surf carved into the rock to form a sea cave. At some point the roof of the cave collapsed, leaving behind the long, wide rock channel that forms Devil's Churn. The force of the waves crashing in the channel sends spectacular sprays of water dozens of feet into the air. If you're hiking with children or dogs, keep a close eye on them. The slippery surface of the rocks and sneaker waves can catch you off balance if you get too close to the edge of the channel.

Miles and Directions

The Whispering Spruce Trail is accessed 2.2 miles from the interpretive center via FR 55 and then FR 5553.

The Saint Perpetua, Cape Cove, Giant Spruce, Captain Cook, Oregon Coast, Discovery Loop, Cooks Ridge to Gwynn Creek Loop, and Cummins Creek Loop Trails can be accessed from the interpretive center. The Trail of Restless Waters starts from the Devil's Churn parking area, 0.7 mile north of the interpretive center off US 101.

Hike Information

Local Information

Florence Chamber of Commerce, 290 Highway 101, Florence, OR 97439; (541) 997-3128; florencechamber.com
Yachats Chamber of Commerce, 241 Highway 101, Yachats, OR 97498; (541) 547-3530 or (800) 929-0477; yachats.org

Local Events and Attractions

Chowder, Blues and Brews Festival, held in October, Florence; (541) 997-3128; florencechamber.com
Sea Lion Caves, 91560 Highway 101 N., Florence; (541) 547-3111; sealioncaves.com

18 Heceta Head Lighthouse

Take a picturesque walk to one of Oregon's most photographed lighthouses. Nestled on the edge of the coastal protrusion Heceta Head, the 205-foot-tall Heceta Head Lighthouse is a welcoming beacon to ships and hikers alike.

Start: The trailhead is located 12 miles north of Florence and 14 miles south of Yachats on US 101.
Distance: 1.0 mile out and back
Hiking time: 30 minutes to 1 hour
Difficulty: Easy; well-maintained gravel path and minimal elevation gain
Best season: June through Oct
Other trail users: Hikers only
Canine compatibility: Leashed dogs permitted

Land status: State park
Nearest town: Florence
Fees and permits: Small day-use fee required
Schedule: Year-round
Maps: Maptech CD: Coos Bay/Eugene/Bend, OR; USGS: Heceta Head, OR
Trail contact: Oregon State Parks and Recreation, 725 Summer St. NE, Suite C, Salem, OR 97301; (800) 551-6949; oregonstateparks .org/park_124.php

Finding the trailhead: From Florence travel 12 miles north on US 101 to the sign for Heceta Head Lighthouse State Scenic Viewpoint (also known as Devil's Elbow State Park). Turn left (west) and proceed 0.3 mile to the parking area. The hike begins on the north end of the parking lot.

From Yachats travel 14 miles south on US 101 to the sign for Heceta Head Lighthouse State Scenic Viewpoint (also known as Devil's Elbow State Park). Turn right (west) and proceed 0.3 mile to the parking area. The hike begins on the north end of the parking lot. *DeLorme: Oregon Atlas & Gazetteer:* Page 32, Inset 2, C2. GPS: N44 08.235 / W124 07.638.

The Hike

Heceta (huh-SEE-tuh) Head Lighthouse stands as a quiet sentinel on the central Oregon coast, shining its beacon 21 miles out to sea. This magnificent structure was finished in 1894 after two years and at a cost of $80,000. The stone was shipped to the site from Oregon City, and the bricks and cement were brought in from San Francisco. Local sawmills supplied the wood, and the two-ton Fresnel lens was hand-crafted and brought in by boat. The lighthouse and the scenic headland on which it sits owe their name to Captain Bruno Heceta, a Spanish captain who sailed his ship *Corvette* from Mexico to this part of the Oregon coast. George Davidson, of the Coastal Survey, officially named the point in 1862.

The whitewashed lighthouse is accessed by a 1.0-mile out-and-back trail that starts at the north end of the Heceta Head Lighthouse State Scenic Viewpoint parking lot. The wide gravel path begins climbing through a thick coastal cedar-and-fir forest dotted with sword fern, wild iris, and salal. Picnic tables have been set up so visitors can enjoy the sweeping view of the rocky shore and rugged cape, as well as the 220-foot crowning arch of the Cape Creek Bridge. This bridge

Heceta Head Lighthouse

is just one of 162 bridges designed and built by Conde McCullough, head of the bridge division for the Oregon Department of Transportation from 1920 to 1935. McCullough designed virtually all the bridges on the Oregon Coast Highway, using innovative techniques to overcome the many challenges of building coastal bridges. One of the biggest challenges he faced was how to design bridges that used materials other than steel, which doesn't hold up well in the stormy, salty air of the Oregon coast. He also needed a material that was strong enough to span the region's wide estuaries. His solution was to use the Freyssinet method, developed in France, to build bridges that used arches made of prestressed concrete. Construction on this scenic highway began in 1927, and the final bridges were finished in 1936.

At mile 0.2 you pass the immaculately maintained light keeper's house. Built in 1893, this lovely Queen Anne–style house is now being used by the USDA Forest Service as an interpretive center, gift shop, and B&B. In spring you may spot the teardrop-shaped petals of white lilies scattered along this section of trail. A white picket fence surrounds the Victorian house and its three upper-story rooms. Picture

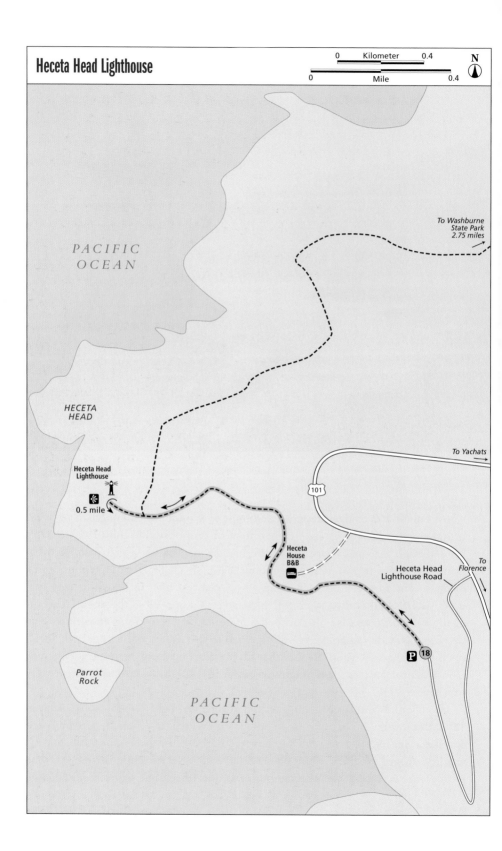

Heceta Head Lighthouse

0 Kilometer 0.4
0 Mile 0.4

N

PACIFIC
OCEAN

To Washburne
State Park
2.75 miles

HECETA
HEAD

To Yachats

101

Heceta Head
Lighthouse
0.5 mile

Heceta
House
B&B

Heceta Head
Lighthouse Road

To
Florence

Parrot
Rock

PACIFIC
OCEAN

P 18

windows offer a grand view of the rocky coast and lighthouse, and everything is topped off with a bright-red roof.

Continue another 0.3 mile to reach the lighthouse and your turnaround point. After you've soaked in the views of the lighthouse, glance offshore to the rocky promontory called Parrot Rock, which is an important nesting area for Brandt's cormorants. Tours of the lighthouse are offered daily in the spring and summer months.

Miles and Directions

0.0   Start at the north end of the parking area. (**Note:** Before you begin, check out the interpretive signs that give you an in-depth view of the history of the lighthouse and light keeper's house.)

0.2   Pass the light keeper's house on your right.

0.5   Reach 205-foot Heceta Head Lighthouse, your turnaround point.

1.0   Arrive back at the parking area.

Hike Information

Local Information

Florence Chamber of Commerce, 290 Highway 101, Florence, OR 97439; (541) 997-3128; florencechamber.com

Yachats Chamber of Commerce, 241 Highway 101, Yachats, OR 97498; (541) 547-3530 or (800) 929-0477; yachats.org

Local Events and Attractions

Sea Lion Caves, 91560 Highway 101 N., Florence; (541) 547-3111; sealioncaves.com

Accommodations

Heceta Head Lighthouse Bed and Breakfast, 92072 Highway 101 S., Yachats; (866) 547-3696, hecetalighthouse.com/bed-breakfast

19 Sutton Creek Recreation Area

The Sutton Creek Recreation Area has more than 6 miles of trails to explore, giving you a close-up view of a diverse coastal ecosystem made up of sand dunes, coastal forest, freshwater lakes, a coastal stream, and a sandy beach. The Sutton Creek Campground has a short walk through a wet bog, where you can view the interesting, insect-eating cobra lily.

Start: The trailhead is located approximately 5 miles north of Florence off US 101.

Distance: Varies depending on the trails selected

Hiking time: 1 to 4 hours

Difficulty: Easy to moderate. The trail through the sand dunes is moderately difficult. The hike to Sutton Beach requires that you ford Sutton Creek.

Best season: June through Oct

Other trail users: Hikers only

Canine compatibility: Leashed dogs permitted. Dogs are not allowed off their leash from Mar 15 to Sept 30 because they might

disturb the nesting of rare birds. Restricted areas are posted.

Land status: National forest

Nearest town: Florence

Fees and permits: Small day-use fee, payable at the self-pay station at the Holman Vista parking area

Schedule: Year-round

Maps: Maptech CD: Coos Bay/Eugene/Bend, OR; USGS: Mercer Lake, OR

Trail contact: Siuslaw National Forest, 4480 Highway 101, Bldg. G, Florence, OR 97439; (541) 902-8526; www.fs.fed.us/r6/siuslaw/

Finding the trailhead: For the Sutton Creek Campground trailhead, drive 4.2 miles north of Florence on US 101 to Sutton Beach Road and turn left (west) at the SUTTON RECREATION sign. Proceed 0.7 mile and turn right into the Sutton Creek Campground. At the T intersection, turn left (toward the A loop of campsites) and drive approximately 0.2 mile to the Sutton Group Camp parking area, located between campsites A18 and A19. The trailhead is located on the right side of the Sutton Group Camp parking area.

For the Holman Vista day-use parking area, drive 4.2 miles north of Florence on US 101 to Sutton Beach Road and turn left (west) at the SUTTON RECREATION sign. Drive 2 miles west to the day-use parking area. *DeLorme: Oregon Atlas & Gazetteer:* Page 32, Inset 2, D2. GPS: N44 03.524 / W124 06.969

The Hike

The roughly 2,700-acre Sutton Creek Recreation Area preserves a unique coastal environment within Oregon's Siuslaw National Forest. Protected within the recreation area are fragile coastal forests and freshwater lakes, not to mention the region's trademark dunes. If you're of the mind that a sand dune is a sand dune is a sand dune, you're missing out on some interesting distinctions. The Sutton Creek area contains a variety of sand dunes including fore-, traverse, oblique, and parabola dunes.

You begin with the foredune. As you move inland you find hummocks, a deflation plain, transverse dunes, tree islands, oblique dunes, parabola dunes, and transition

A scenic sand dune in the Sutton Creek Recreation Area

forest. Foredunes parallel the ocean and can reach heights of 20 to 30 feet. Nowadays you'll find these dunes covered with European beach grass, a nonnative plant species introduced by settlers in the early 1900s to stabilize the soil. The European beach grass has spread rapidly, interrupting the natural movement of sand—the mark of an active dune—and altering the landscape.

Following the foredunes are hummocks, which form when sand collects around vegetation. In winter you may notice these as small sand islands, the result of the water table rising to fill the depressions around the hummocks. Farther inland from the hummocks is the deflation plain. You can recognize a deflation plain by its fairly flat landscape. As the foredunes block new sand from moving inland, the wind carries off the remaining dry sand, leaving only wet sand behind—thus deflating the area. The wet sand is a great environment for such plants as bush lupine, Scotch broom, yarrow, and a variety of scented grasses such as large-headed sage, salt rush, and the invasive European beach grass. Farther inland are traverse dunes, created when the northwesterly winds of summer sculpt wavy crests into 5- to 20-foot sandhills. Traverse dunes are perpendicular to the wind direction, and during winter the southwesterly winds tend to flatten out the crests.

WESTERN SNOWY PLOVERS

The Pacific Coast breeding colonies of western snowy plovers can be found from southern Washington to Baja California. Snowy plovers are sparrow-size birds with a dusty, sand-colored back and a white underside with a black chest band. They like to nest in open sandy areas next to the water. The plovers' nesting season is from mid-March through mid-September. They usually lay two to three greenish-brown eggs in a sandy depression above the beach. In 2001 110 nesting adults were counted along the southern Oregon coast. Out of 110 nests, only thirty-four were successful, producing ninety-four hatchlings. Study areas include Necanicum Spit, Bayocean Spit, Sutton Beach, Siltcoos, Dunes Overlook, Tahkenitch, Tenmile, Coos Bay North Spit, Bandon State Natural Area, New River, and Floras Lake.

The western snowy plover's rapid decline is due to several different factors. The encroachment of European beach grass has caused a large amount of habitat loss. The grass stabilizes dunes and reduces the amount of unvegetated area above the tide line, making the sandy beach narrower and steeper, and ultimately making the nesting area less suitable for the birds. Predators are another major reason for the decline of snowy plover populations. Major predators include gulls, crows, ravens, skunks, dogs, coyotes, foxes, cats, opossums, raccoons, hawks, and owls. The most preventable factor is human impact on nesting habitat. Off-road vehicle use, loose dogs, walking and running on the beach, and beach raking have all taken their toll.

Unfortunately, the nesting season for the snowy plover coincides with the highest beach-going traffic season. Measures have been introduced to help protect the snowy plover. Nesting sites are now fenced off to minimize human impact, and nest enclosures have been introduced to protect the birds from predators. After you reach the beach, keep a lookout for these quick birds as they run up and down the beach feeding on crabs, marine worms, beetles, sand hoppers, shore flies, and other insects.

The next transition zone is the tree island. These small stands of trees are remnants of a prior coastal forest that was buried by the moving sand. Tree islands have steep, unstable slopes, which are highly susceptible to erosion. Even farther inland are oblique dunes. These sloped dunes can reach a height of 180 feet and can be up to a mile long. The west face of an oblique dune is long and gentle, and the east side is steep—this is due to the winds hitting the dunes from the northwest and southwest. The constant pushing of the sand from the west side creates a longer, gentler west face. Because of the winds that are constantly shaping oblique dunes—and their instability—plants do not grow on this type of dune.

Sutton Creek Recreation Area

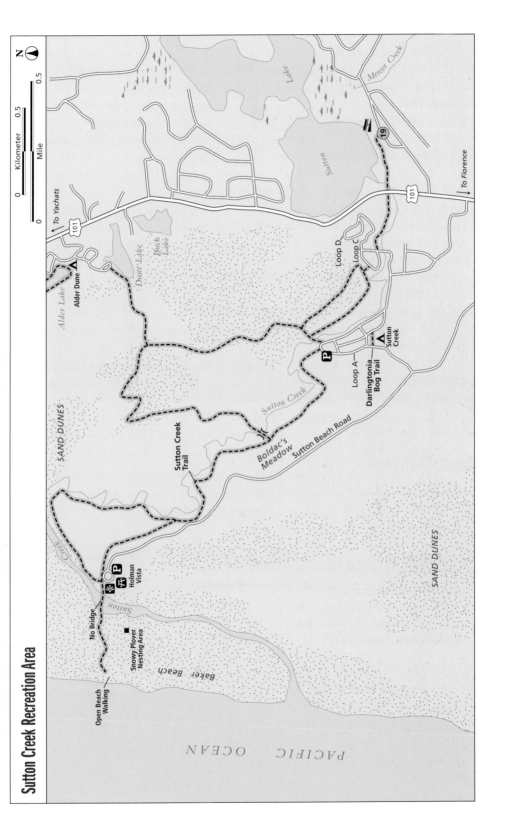

The transition forest zone is where the sand dune environment meets up with the land environment. This type of forest is filled with a variety of plants that thrive in the windy, sandy environment, such as shore pines, rhododendrons, salal, and thimbleberry. The large, sandy, U-shaped ridge in the middle of the coastal forest is the parabola dune. Constant wind erodes the soil so that plants can live here.

The Sutton Creek Recreation Area is filled with a variety of trail options to explore this diverse community. From Sutton Creek Campground you can hike the 2.25-mile trail to scenic Baker Beach, breeding ground for the endangered western snowy plover. Along the way you get a taste of ever-changing sand dunes and lush coastal forests of shore pine, rhododendrons, thimbleberry, salal, and spruce trees. You might even see otter swimming in Sutton Creek or osprey fishing along its banks. Other trail options from Sutton Creek Campground include hiking 1.75 miles to Alder Dune Campground, where you can hike to Dune Lake and Alder Lake.

To see the rare insect-eating cobra lily plant, hike the wheelchair-accessible Darlingtonia Bog Trail, located just to the right of the Sutton Creek Campground entrance. These unique plants lure insects into their slow-but-sure traps and digest them even more slowly. The insects provide the much-needed nutrients that are lacking in the nutrient-poor coastal soil.

If you park at the Holman Vista day-use parking area, walk up the wheelchair-accessible walkway to Holman Vista, where you have far-reaching views of the rolling sand dunes, scenic beach, and rambling Sutton Creek. Notice the bent and twisted shore pine trees. These rugged trees are called krummholzes, and their irregular shape is caused by the constant wind and salt air that batter them on the windward side.

Miles and Directions

You can access the trails in the Sutton Creek Area from the Sutton Creek Campground and the Holman Vista day-use parking area trailhead. Refer to the map for individual trails.

Hike Information

Local Information

Florence Chamber of Commerce, 290 Highway 101, Florence, OR 97439; (541) 997-3128; florencechamber.com

Local Events and Attractions

Chowder, Blues and Brews Festival, held in October, Florence; (541) 997-3128; florencechamber.com

Oregon Dune Mushers Mail Run, held in March, Florence; (541) 677-8393; oregondunemushers.com

Rhododendron Festival, held in May, Florence; (541) 997-3128; florencechamber.com

20 Tahkenitch Creek

This pleasant loop takes you through a coastal dune environment along picturesque Tahkenitch Creek in the Oregon Dunes National Recreation Area.

Start: The trailhead is located 9.2 miles north of Reedsport (or 12 miles south of Florence) off US 101.

Distance: 1.5-mile lollipop (with longer options)

Hiking time: 45 minutes to 1 hour

Difficulty: Easy; smooth trail surface and minimal elevation gain

Best season: June through Oct

Other trail users: Hikers only

Canine compatibility: Leashed dogs permitted

Land status: National recreation area

Nearest town: Reedsport

Fees and permits: Northwest Forest Pass (small fee) required. Purchase a pass online at www.fs.usda.gov/main/r6/passes-permits/recreation or by calling (800) 270-7504.

Schedule: Year-round

Maps: Maptech CD: Coos Bay/Eugene/Bend, OR; USGS: Tahkenitch Creek, OR

Trail contact: Oregon Dunes National Recreation Area, 855 Highway Ave., Reedsport, OR 97467; (541) 271-3611; www.fs.fed.us/r6/siuslaw/

Finding the trailhead: From the junction of OR 38 and US 101 in Reedsport, travel 9.2 miles north (or 12 miles south of Florence) on US 101 to the Tahkenitch Creek trailhead, located on the left side of the highway. *DeLorme: Oregon Atlas & Gazetteer:* Page 32, Inset 3, B4. GPS: N43 48.800 / W124 09.245

The Hike

This short loop hike is one of three loop hikes that you can try from the Tahkenitch trailhead. This route covers 1.5 miles; the other optional routes are 2.5 and 4.0 miles long. You can also hike to the beach and hook up with the Tahkenitch Dunes Trail (see the trail map).

You'll start this route by walking through thick coastal woodland dotted with pink-flowered rhododendrons and blue-berried salal. Soon you'll arrive at a nice viewpoint of smooth-flowing Tahkenitch Creek at a footbridge spanning the creek. Look for minks, otters, ducks, and geese. After 0.4 mile you'll begin the loop portion of the hike. Here the landscape changes to a dune environment characterized by small transitional islands dotted with shore pine trees; grassy meadows; and small sand dunes covered with European beach grass, yellow-flowered Scotch broom, and yarrow. As you continue you can hear the distant roar of waves crashing on the beach. Western snowy plovers nest in the sandy areas at the mouth of Tahkenitch Creek as well as on the beach. The nesting season lasts from March 15 to September 15. If you decide to head to the beach, watch for signs marking protected areas. If you have a canine hiking partner with you, be sure to keep your dog on a leash so he doesn't disturb these endangered birds.

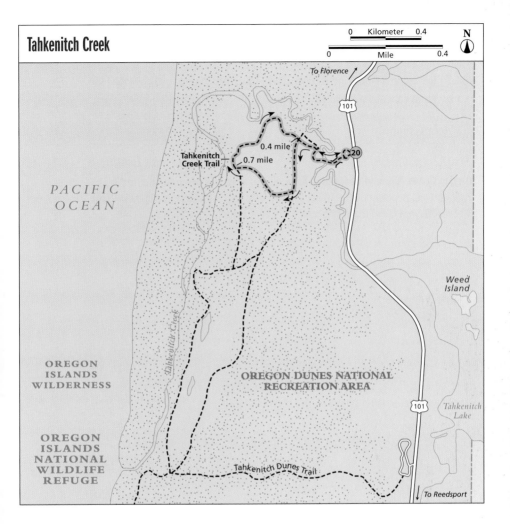

Tahkenitch Creek

0   Kilometer   0.4

0   Mile   0.4

N

To Florence

101

0.4 mile

Tahkenitch
Creek Trail

0.7 mile

20

PACIFIC
OCEAN

Weed
Island

Tahkenitch Creek

OREGON
ISLANDS
WILDERNESS

OREGON DUNES NATIONAL
RECREATION AREA

101

*Tahkenitch
Lake*

OREGON
ISLANDS
NATIONAL
WILDLIFE
REFUGE

Tahkenitch Dunes Trail

To Reedsport

Near the end of the loop portion of the hike, you'll be able to view the lazy curves of the creek and have another good opportunity to watch for wildlife.

Miles and Directions

0.0   Start walking on the signed path as it descends to a nice viewpoint of picturesque Tahkenitch Creek.

0.1   Cross the creek over a wooden footbridge.

0.2   Turn left at the trail fork.

0.4   Turn right at the trail junction. At the next trail junction and trail sign, go left and start the loop portion of the hike.

◀   *Tahkenitch Creek*

0.6 Turn right at the signed trail junction.

0.7 Turn right at the trail junction.

0.8 The trail parallels the edge of the creek.

1.1 Turn left at the trail junction (you've now completed the loop portion of the hike).

1.5 Arrive back at the trailhead.

Hike Information

Local Information

Oregon Dunes National Recreation Area, 855 Highway Ave., Reedsport, OR 97467; (541) 271-6000; www.fs.fed.us/r6/siuslaw/

Local Events and Attractions

Umpqua Discovery Center, 409 Riverfront Way, Reedsport; (541) 271-4816; umpquadiscoverycenter.com

21 Sunset Bay, Shore Acres, and Cape Arago State Parks

Get your camera ready to snap great photos of the rocky coastline along this scenic stretch of the Oregon coast. This trail begins at Sunset Bay State Park and takes you on a journey along the cliff edges to Shore Acres State Park and Cape Arago State Park. The rocky coastline is a haven for sea lions. As you near Cape Arago State Park, you can hear their raucous cries from almost a mile away.

Start: The trailhead is located at the Oregon Coast Trail marker adjacent to the restrooms in the day-use picnic area in Sunset Bay State Park. Sunset Bay State Park is located 12 miles southwest of Coos Bay on the Cape Arago Highway.
Distance: 8.8 miles out and back
Hiking time: 3 to 4 hours
Difficulty: Moderate due to trail length
Best season: June through Oct
Other trail users: Hikers only
Canine compatibility: Not dog friendly. Dogs are not allowed in Shore Acres State Park. Dogs are allowed in Sunset Bay State Park and Cape Arago State Park.

Land status: State park
Nearest town: Coos Bay
Fees and permits: No fees or permits required in Sunset Bay State Park or Cape Arago State Park. Shore Acres State Park charges a small day-use fee.
Schedule: Year-round
Maps: Maptech CD: Coos Bay/Eugene/Bend, OR; USGS: Charleston, OR; Cape Arago, OR
Trail contact: Oregon State Parks and Recreation, 725 Summer St. NE, Suite C, Salem, OR 97301; (800) 551-6949; oregonstate parks.org

Finding the trailhead: From Coos Bay follow the signs marked CHARLESTON HARBOR AND OCEAN BEACHES. Drive southwest for about 12 miles on the Cape Arago Highway to Sunset Bay State Park. When you reach the park, turn into the day-use picnic area, located on the west side of the highway. Look for the OREGON COAST TRAIL marker located to the right of the restrooms. *DeLorme: Oregon Atlas & Gazetteer:* Page 33 B5. GPS: N43 19.967 / W124 22.375

The Hike

Some of the most beautiful stretches of rocky coast and forest can be found along the Oregon Coast Trail between Sunset Bay and Cape Arago State Parks. Hemmed in and protected by golden sandstone cliffs, the beautiful Sunset Bay forms the focal point of Sunset Bay State Park. This secluded piece of coast is thought to have served as a safe haven for ships waiting out the furious storms that often hit the Oregon coast. The park was once part of the enormous estate of Louis J. Simpson, lumberman, shipbuilder, and founder of North Bend. Simpson had his home 2 miles south in what is now Shore Acres State Park. In 1913 Simpson oversaw the building of the Sunset Bay Inn, situated on the edge of Sunset Bay.

The Oregon Coast Trail takes off from the day-use picnic area and parallels the cliff's edge through a thick Sitka spruce forest. As the trail winds its way south, you'll

GRAY WHALE FACTS

- A gray whale mother carries her calf for thirteen months before giving birth.
- Calves weigh about a ton when they are born, and their mother's milk contains 53 percent butterfat.
- A calf can grow to be 26 feet long in twelve months.
- It takes a calf eight years to reach sexual maturity.

have sneak peeks at the golden, steep-walled sandstone cliffs. Many of the layers in these cliffs are curved, matching the ocean currents that formed them more than forty-five million years ago when this area was under a shallow sea. After 1.4 miles you'll have a scenic view of the bay and the Cape Arago Lighthouse, one of only nine lighthouses that grace Oregon's coastline. Located on a rocky outcrop just off Gregory Point, the scenic lighthouse rises 100 feet above the ocean and stands 44 feet tall. Built in 1934, it's the third lighthouse to occupy this same site. Its predecessors were built in 1866 and 1908, and both fell prey to the harsh elements along this stretch of the Oregon coast.

At mile 2.1 you reach 743-acre Shore Acres State Park, also formerly part of the Louis J. Simpson estate. Simpson discovered this scenic part of the coast in 1905 and bought 320 acres for $4,000. He then built an elaborate estate on the grounds, with stables, a carriage house, tennis courts, and beautiful cultivated gardens. At mile 2.3 you come to a glass-enclosed observation building that stands on the site of Simpson's former estate.

From this vantage point the wild rocky coast stretches for miles in both directions, and thundering waves create many great photo opportunities. From December through June you may also be lucky and spot some gray whales on their semiannual migration from Baja, Mexico, to Alaska. At mile 2.4 you come to a view of the beautiful botanical gardens, which are meticulously maintained by Oregon State Parks and Recreation. Within the botanical gardens are a Japanese garden, two rose gardens, and other formal flower gardens. From February through March daffodils are in peak bloom; April through mid-May, the azaleas and rhododendrons steal the show; and June through September, roses are in full bloom.

You'll arrive at your turnaround point inside of Cape Arago State Park after 4.4 miles. The 134-acre park sits atop a 200-foot rocky cliff. Offshore is Simpson Reef, home to large colonies of seals and sea lions. You'll be able to hear their raucous calling from several wildlife-viewing points in the park. This scenic cape was named for Dominique F. J. Arago, a French physicist and geographer (1786–1853). This rocky headland was also once part of the large Simpson estate. It was handed over to the

◀ *Spectacular rocky outcroppings at Shore Acres State Park*

Sunset Bay, Shore Acres, and Cape Arago State Parks

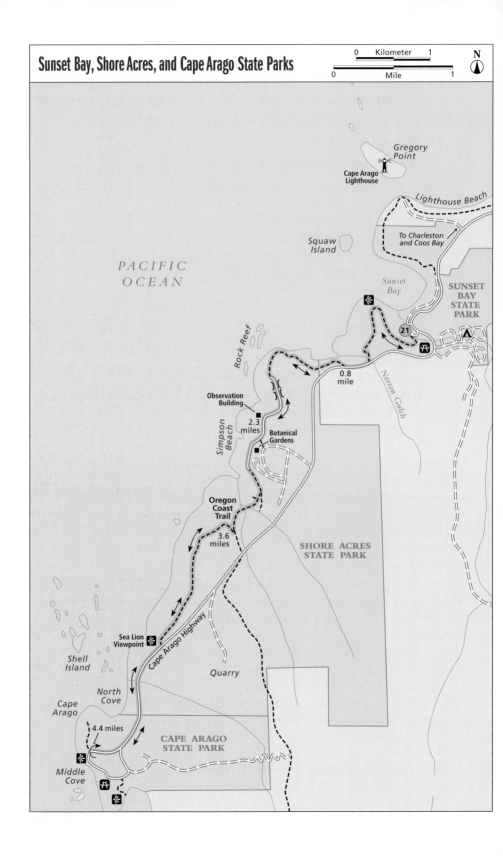

0 Kilometer 1

0 Mile 1

N

Gregory
Point

Cape Arago
Lighthouse

Lighthouse Beach

Squaw
Island

To Charleston
and Coos Bay

PACIFIC
OCEAN

Sunset
Bay

SUNSET
BAY
STATE
PARK

21

Rock Reef

0.8
mile

Norton Gulch

Observation
Building

Simpson
Beach

2.3
miles

Botanical
Gardens

Oregon
Coast
Trail

3.6
miles

SHORE ACRES
STATE PARK

Sea Lion
Viewpoint

Cape Arago Highway

Quarry

Shell
Island

North
Cove

Cape
Arago

4.4 miles

CAPE ARAGO
STATE PARK

Middle
Cove

state of Oregon in 1932. There are three coves you can hike to in this park—North, Middle, and South. If you enjoy exploring tide pools, be sure to take a side trip to South Cove. North Cove is closed from March 1 to July 1 each year to protect sea lions and seal pups.

Miles and Directions

0.0 Start at the day-use picnic area at Sunset Bay State Park. Look for the wooden OREGON COAST TRAIL marker located just to the right of the restrooms, which indicates the start of the trail. As you begin walking on the trail, you'll see a sign that reads SHORE ACRES 2 MILES.

0.1 Turn right at the trail fork. (The left opens into a grassy picnic area.)

0.3 Enjoy good views of Sunset Bay and offshore rock formations.

0.6 Turn left at a trail junction. The trail winds up a fern-covered hillside to a paved road.

0.8 Reach the paved road and turn right. Walk along the road. Approach a set of wooden steps on your right and turn right. Take the steps over the metal road barrier.

1.3 Turn right at the trail fork.

1.4 Pass a good viewpoint of the bay and the Cape Arago Lighthouse to your right.

2.1 Reach Shore Acres State Park. The path turns from dirt to pavement when you enter the park. (**Note:** Dogs are not allowed in the park.)

2.2 Turn right at the trail fork. (If you go left, you'll enter a parking area.) Come to another fork and stay right. The trail parallels a wooden rail fence.

2.3 Arrive at an observation building on your right.

2.4 Turn right where a sign indicates SIMPSON BEACH. **Option:** You can turn left here and view the botanical gardens.

2.7 Arrive at Simpson Beach. The paved path ends; turn left and cross a stream. Continue walking on the trail and cross a second stream.

2.9 Turn right at a T junction.

3.5 Turn right at the trail fork. (**Note:** Listen closely for the calls from the sea lion colony in Cape Arago State Park.)

3.6 Turn right at a T junction.

3.8 Turn right at the junction with a paved road. Walk into the paved parking area of Sea Lion Viewpoint. Continue walking parallel to US 101 for another 0.6 mile.

4.4 Arrive at your turnaround point inside Cape Arago State Park and return on the same route back to your vehicle.

8.8 Arrive back at the trailhead.

Hike Information

Local Information

Bay Area Chamber of Commerce, 145 Central Ave., Coos Bay, OR 97420; (541) 266-0868; oregonsbayarea.org

Local Events and Attractions

Charleston Merchants' Annual Crab Feed, February, Charleston; (800) 824-8486

22 Cape Ferrelo to Whalehead Beach

This hike takes you on the Oregon Coast Trail through the heart of Samuel H. Boardman State Park. You'll walk through thick Sitka spruce forest, past bubbling coastal creeks, on wild and windy headlands with fantastic views of offshore sea stacks and rocky islands, and on a beautiful secluded beach.

Start: The trailhead is located 5 miles north of Brookings on US 101 at the Cape Ferrelo Viewpoint parking area.
Distance: 9.4 miles out and back
Hiking time: 3 to 4 hours
Difficulty: Moderate; steep ascents and descents through forest and open headlands. The beach walking can be difficult due to high winds and soft sand.
Best season: June through Oct
Other trail users: Hikers only

Canine compatibility: Leashed dogs permitted
Land status: State park
Nearest town: Brookings
Fees and permits: None
Schedule: Year-round
Maps: Maptech CD: Coos Bay/Eugene/Bend, OR; USGS: Brookings, OR; Carpenterville, OR
Trail contact: Oregon State Parks and Recreation, 725 Summer St. NE, Suite C, Salem, OR 97301; (800) 551-6949; oregonstateparks .org/ park_77.php

Finding the trailhead: From Brookings travel 4.8 miles north on US 101 and turn left (west) at the Cape Ferrelo Viewpoint. Continue 0.2 mile to the parking area. The hike begins in the northwest corner of the parking area. *DeLorme: Oregon Atlas & Gazetteer:* Page 17 C13. GPS: N42 06.415 / W124 20.784.

The Hike

The charming coastal town of Brookings lies 6 miles north of the California–Oregon border on the bay of the Chetco River and boasts uncrowded beaches, spectacular bluffs and offshore rock formations, a busy fishing harbor, prize fishing on the Chetco River, and some of the warmest weather on the Oregon Coast. Established in 1908, Brookings is the namesake of the Brookings family, who founded the Brookings Lumber and Box Company. In the past, logging was the chief industry here, but now tourism, Easter lily bulb production (Brookings is the nation's leader), and sportfishing are also major industries in this bustling seaport. Large-scale Easter lily bulb production in the Chetco Valley began during World War II when Japanese and Holland lily bulb imports were halted in the United States. Bulbs that sold for about a nickel apiece before the war were going for $1 during the war. This high price soon made bulb production a profitable way to make a living in Curry County. During the war the number of lily bulb growers exploded to about 1,000. Some growers were making $10,000 to $20,000 per acre growing bulbs. Currently, ten large production farms are active in the Brookings area, producing about 95 percent of the Easter lily bulbs worldwide.

Whalehead Beach

Another highlight of the Brookings area is Samuel H. Boardman State Park. This 1,471-acre park stretches more than 12 miles along the rugged coastline north of Brookings and has several access points off US 101. The Oregon Coast Trail runs right through the heart of this scenic area and promises you a pleasant, uncrowded coastal trek.

Begin the hike from the Cape Ferrelo parking area and wind through a Sitka spruce and red cedar forest interspersed with open meadows filled with vibrant purple lupine. Several viewpoints along this section give you a sneak peek at the rugged rocky sea stacks located just off Whalehead Beach. After 1.4 miles you come to House Rock Viewpoint, an excellent vantage point for spotting migrating gray whales. There is also a memorial for Samuel H. Boardman—the founder of the park. As you continue north the trail reenters the forest and begins to descend steeply down a series of switchbacks. After 2.8 miles you emerge from the forest onto a scenic open headland. The trail descends steeply to sandy Whalehead Beach. Continue walking north on the beach past large rocky outcrops; offshore you'll see Whalehead Island—which clearly resembles the shape of a whale. At last you arrive at your turn-around point, where you'll find a scenic picnic spot and restrooms.

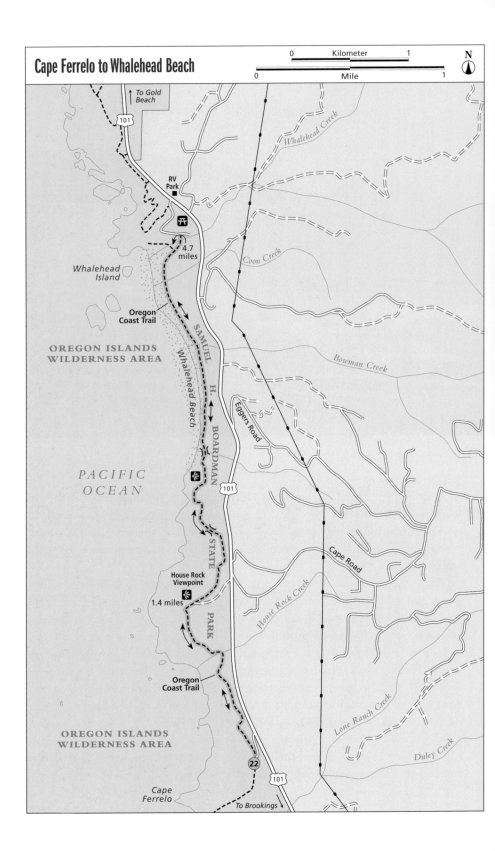

0   Kilometer   1

0   Mile   1

N

To Gold
Beach

101

RV
Park

4.7
miles

Whalehead
Island

Oregon
Coast Trail

OREGON ISLANDS
WILDERNESS AREA

SAMUEL H. BOARDMAN STATE PARK

Whalehead Beach

Coon Creek

Bowman Creek

Eggers Road

101

PACIFIC
OCEAN

Cape Road

House Rock
Viewpoint

1.4 miles

House Rock Creek

Oregon
Coast Trail

OREGON ISLANDS
WILDERNESS AREA

Lone Ranch Creek

Duley Creek

22

101

Cape
Ferrelo

To Brookings

Whalehead Creek

Miles and Directions

0.0 Start at the north end of the viewpoint parking area at the wooden OREGON COAST TRAIL marker.

1.4 Reach House Rock Viewpoint. Continue walking straight on the paved sidewalk. **Side trip:** You can take a detour here by turning left to view the Samuel H. Boardman monument.

2.0 Cross a wooden bridge over a creek. Notice the small, cascading waterfall to your right.

2.3 Enjoy a good viewpoint to your left.

2.5 Turn left at the trail fork. Cross a wooden bridge over a creek.

2.8 The trail takes you into an open area on a scenic headland above Whalehead Beach. Descend steeply down a series of switchbacks to the beach.

3.1 Reach Whalehead Beach. Cross a small stream and continue walking north on the sandy beach.

4.2 Cross a stream.

4.3 Near the end of the beach. Veer to the right and look for the wooden OREGON COAST TRAIL marker.

4.4 Reach the marker indicating the continuation of the trail north.

4.6 Pass the wooden stairs to your left. (**Note:** If you take these stairs, you'll walk through a 0.25-mile tunnel to an RV park.)

4.7 Arrive at a paved parking and picnic area with restrooms. Turn around here and retrace the same route back to the trailhead.

9.4 Arrive back at the trailhead.

Hike Information

Local Information

The Brookings-Harbor Chamber of Commerce, 16330 Lower Harbor Rd., Brookings, OR 97415; (800) 535-9469; brookingsharborchamber.com

Local Events and Attractions

Azalea Festival, Memorial Day weekend, Brookings; (800) 535-9469
Oregon Caves National Monument, 19000 Caves Hwy., Cave Junction; (541) 592-2100; www.nps.gov/orca

23 Alfred A. Loeb State Park Nature Trails

This hike through Alfred A. Loeb State Park offers a rare glimpse of two hard-to-find tree species: the Oregon myrtle and the redwood. The Riverview Trail follows the banks of the salmon- and steelhead-rich Chetco River through an old grove of Oregon myrtle trees. The Redwood Nature Trail loops through a grove of immense coast redwood trees. Both trails include numbered markers that correspond to a detailed brochure pointing out all the highlights. The state park also has a campground and all kinds of fun things to see and do. You can swim in the Chetco River, fish, or rent a charter boat in nearby Brookings Harbor. In addition, the park is the gateway to the 179,655-acre Kalmiopsis Wilderness and its hundreds of miles of trails, numerous lakes, and rugged river gorges.

Start: The trailhead is located 7.5 miles east of Brookings in Alfred A. Loeb State Park.
Distance: 4.2-mile lollipop
Hiking time: 1.5 to 2 hours
Difficulty: Easy
Best season: June through Oct
Other trail users: Hikers only
Canine compatibility: Leashed dogs permitted
Land status: State park
Nearest town: Brookings

Fees and permits: None
Schedule: Year-round
Maps: Maptech CD: Siskiyou National Forest/ Crater Lake/Medford, OR; USGS: Mount Emily, OR
Trail contact: Oregon State Parks and Recreation, 725 Summer St. NE, Suite C, Salem, OR 97301; (800) 551-6949; oregonstateparks. org/park_72.php

Finding the trailhead: From Brookings at the junction of US 101 and North Bank Chetco River Road, travel 7.5 miles east on North Bank Chetco River Road. Turn right into Alfred A. Loeb State Park. Come to a fork in the road and turn left. Proceed to the picnic area and park in a parking area on your right. *DeLorme: Oregon Atlas & Gazetteer:* Page 17 D3. GPS: N42 06.778 / W124 11.313.

The Hike

The Riverview and Redwood Nature Trails take you on a journey through groves of two hard-to-find tree species: the Oregon myrtle (also known as Coos Bay laurel) and the giant coast redwood. Be sure to pick up the descriptive brochure at the trailhead so you can identify these and other plant species found along the trails.

The trail begins as an easy ramble through a lush grove of Oregon myrtle, Douglas fir, western hemlock, and red alder. As you walk the path, look for the distinctive gumdrop shape of the Oregon myrtle tree. This broad-leafed evergreen grows in small groves in the wet coastal regions of Oregon and California and is a member of the laurel family—the same family as avocado, camphor, cinnamon, and sassafras. The oil from the myrtle's fragrant and spicy leaves is often used to scent candles and perfumes. The leaves are also an excellent seasoning for soups and sauces, and Native Americans made a soothing tea from the leaves. The beautiful wood is used to make furniture and souvenirs.

The trees provide a shady canopy that creates a perfect growing environment for feathery maidenhair fern, spiked sword fern, deer fern, and the edible salmonberry. You'll also notice an abundance of English ivy, a non-native plant that competes with the indigenous species for precious forest real estate. Poison oak also can be found lurking along this trail, so watch out. As you walk you'll catch glimpses of the wide-running Chetco River. This calm, deep river meets the Pacific Ocean at Brookings Harbor—home to one of Oregon's largest fishing fleets. The river has some of the largest steelhead and salmon runs on the Oregon coast and is popular with sportfishermen. It's also home to several good swimming holes—keep your eyes peeled. At mile 1.1 the Riverview Trail comes to a paved road. Across the road is the beginning of the Redwood Nature Trail. From here it's a series of steep switchbacks through a tall, silent grove of 300- to 800-year-old coast

A giant redwood tree in Alfred A. Loeb State Park

redwood trees (*Sequoia sempervirens*). Redwood trees (there are three varieties) are found in only three regions of the world: The coast redwood is found along the northern California coast and at the tip of the southern Oregon coast; the Sierra redwood (*Sequoiadendron gigantea*) is found in a small section of the Sierra Nevada; and the dawn redwood (*Metasequoia*) is found in a remote area of China.

Coast redwoods can live for more than 2,000 years, growing as high as 300 feet with a diameter of 20 feet. These hardy trees have several survival strategies that account for their longevity. Their thick bark is fire and rot resistant, and they have the ability to grow a lateral root system, which allows them to reestablish themselves after floods. If a redwood tree falls over, new trees spring up from the limbs of the parent tree to create a grove of small trees in fairly straight rows.

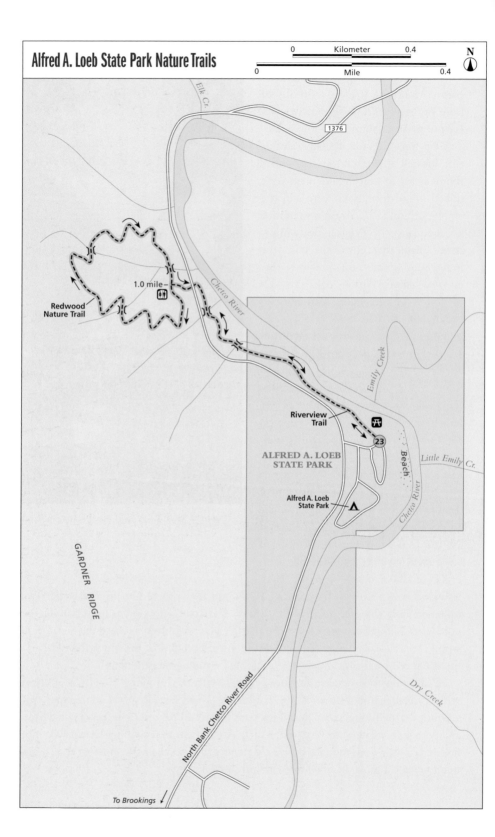

0   Kilometer   0.4

0   Mile   0.4

N

Elk Cr.

1376

1.0 mile

Chetco River

Redwood
Nature Trail

Emily Creek

Riverview
Trail

23

Beach

Little Emily Cr.

ALFRED A. LOEB
STATE PARK

Chetco River

Alfred A. Loeb
State Park

GARDNER RIDGE

North Bank Chetco River Road

Dry Creek

To Brookings

As you continue walking up the path, you'll see native rhododendrons and tan oak trees, which commonly grow in the company of redwoods. The bright-red and pink flowers of the rhododendron bloom in early spring. The tan oak tree can be identified by its fuzzy acorns. Finally, you'll see the delicate pink flowers and clover-like leaves of redwood sorrel. The Redwood loop ends after 1.9 miles. Continue back to your starting point on the Riverview Trail. If you want to stay and explore more of the state park, check out the campground. If you don't want to rough it, stay in one of the park's cabins.

Miles and Directions

0.0 Start in the parking area signed for the Riverview trailhead. Walk across the paved road to the trailhead sign that indicates the start of the Riverview Trail. (**Note:** Be sure to pick up a trail brochure. There are trail markers that correspond to descriptions in the brochure. Take the time to read about the plants and wildlife described in the brochure.)

0.5 Walk through an area that has edible salmonberries.

1.0 Cross North Bank Chetco River Road and arrive at the Redwood Nature Trailhead. There are restrooms and a picnic table here.

1.1 Turn left on the Redwood Nature Trail. (This trail also has trail markers that are described in the brochure.)

3.1 The loop trail ends. Turn left and walk 1.1 miles on the Riverview Trail back to your car.

4.2 Arrive back at the Riverview Trailhead.

Hike Information

Local Information

The Brookings-Harbor Chamber of Commerce, 16330 Lower Harbor Rd., Brookings, OR 97415; (800) 535-9469, brookingsharborchamber.com

Local Events and Attractions

Azalea Festival, Memorial Day weekend, Brookings; (800) 535-9469
Oregon Caves National Monument, 19000 Caves Hwy., Cave Junction; (541) 592-2100; nps.gov/orca

24 Vulcan Lake

Experience the raw beauty of the rugged and remote Kalmiopsis Wilderness. This scenic hike takes you over an open, windswept ridge to a viewpoint of the spectacular glacier-carved basin that cradles Vulcan Lake. Once you reach this scenic lake and descend the ridge, you'll want to spend hours sitting on the boulder-strewn lakeshore gazing at the crystal-clear water of the high alpine lake.

Start: The trailhead is located about 30 miles east of Brookings on FR 260.
Distance: 2.2 miles out and back
Hiking time: 1 to 2 hours
Difficulty: Moderate; a fairly steep ascent up a ridge
Best season: July through Oct
Other trail users: Hikers only
Canine compatibility: Leashed dogs permitted
Land status: Wilderness

Nearest town: Brookings
Fees and permits: None
Schedule: Open mid-June through Oct
Maps: Maptech CD: Siskiyou National Forest/ Crater Lake/Medford, OR; USGS: Chetco Peak, OR
Trail contact: Siskiyou National Forest, Chetco Ranger District, 555 Fifth St., Brookings, OR 97415; (541) 469-2196; www.fs.fed.us/r6/siskiyou/

Finding the trailhead: From Brookings turn onto North Bank Chetco River Road from US 101 and drive 15.8 miles to FR 1909. Turn right. At mile 18.4 come to a fork and go right. Follow the signs indicating Vulcan Peak and the Kalmiopsis Wilderness. At mile 23.6 the road comes to a T intersection. Turn right where a sign indicates Vulcan Lake. The road becomes very rough and rocky. At mile 25.6 come to a fork and turn left. At mile 28.4 pass Red Mountain Prairie Campground on your left. At mile 29.1 come to a fork and turn left onto FR 260, where the sign indicates Vulcan Lake. The road becomes rougher, rockier, and narrow, making it difficult to turn around. At mile 30.8 reach the trailhead at the road's end. *DeLorme: Oregon Atlas & Gazetteer:* Page 18 C1. GPS: N42 11.755 / W123 59.560

The Hike

Established in 1907, the 1,163,484-acre Siskiyou National Forest contains within its boundaries the Klamath, Coast, and Siskiyou mountain ranges. The wild and rugged Siskiyou National Forest boasts five wilderness areas: Grassy Knob, Red Buttes, Siskiyou, Wild Rogue, and the Kalmiopsis. Of these five, the 179,655-acre Kalmiopsis Wilderness is the largest.

The Kalmiopsis Wilderness is the namesake of a pre–Ice Age shrub named *Kalmiopsis leachiana*—one of the oldest members of the heath family. More than 153 miles of trails wander through this rugged area of steep ridges and rugged river gorges. This diverse wilderness area is also known for its rare and unique plants, many of which have adapted to the harsh soils derived from peridotite and serpentinite rocks. Weather, climate, and geological forces have also played a role in the type of plants

Vulcan Lake

that live in this remote corner of southern Oregon. Some of the hardwood tree species you'll find here include golden chinquapin, Pacific madrone, Oregon myrtle, California black oak, tan oak, canyon live oak, and Oregon white oak. Rare and sensitive woody shrubs found here include Howell's manzanita, kalmiopsis plant, Sierra laurel, Del Norte willow, and Tracy's willow. Rare and sensitive herbaceous plants found here include Bolander's onion, Waldo rockcress, Siskiyou sedge, purple toothwort, short-lobed paintbrush, clustered lady's slipper, rigid willow herb, deer fleabane, Siskiyou fritillaria, and Siskiyou monardella, plus many more.

For millions of years erosional forces have been shaping the Kalmiopsis Wilderness. Now-extinct glaciers carved many of the lake basins, such as Babyfoot Lake, the Vulcan Lakes, Rough and Ready Lakes, and Chetco Lake. The hike to Vulcan Lake gives you an inside look at the geological forces that have shaped this area. The trail begins by switchbacking steeply up an open ridge to a spectacular overlook. The trail then crosses a saddle on the ridge and descends across an open slope filled with different species of manzanita plants. There are numerous viewpoints of the lake along the way. After a mile you reach Vulcan Lake. This 7-acre lake rests at an elevation of approximately 4,000 feet in a spectacular red-rock basin at the foot of 4,655-foot

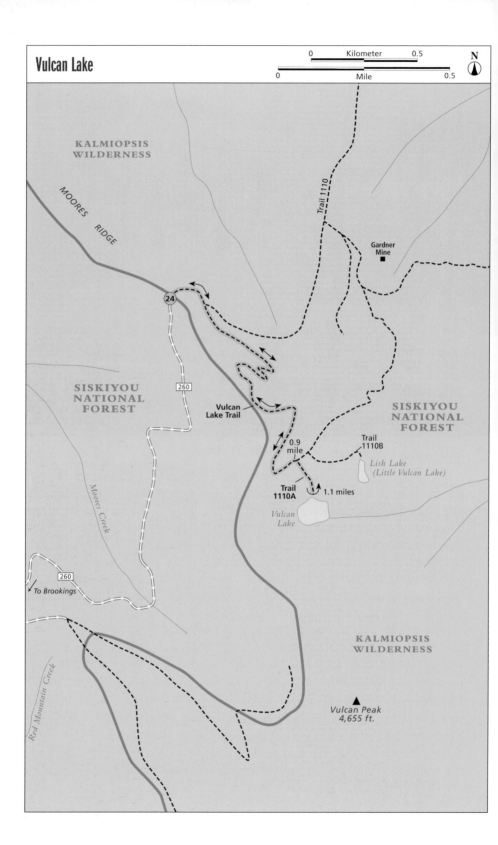

Vulcan Lake

KALMIOPSIS
WILDERNESS

MOORES RIDGE

Trail 1110

Gardner
Mine

24

260

SISKIYOU
NATIONAL
FOREST

Vulcan
Lake Trail

Moores Creek

260

To Brookings

SISKIYOU
NATIONAL
FOREST

Trail
1110B

Lish Lake
(Little Vulcan Lake)

0.9
mile

Trail
1110A

1.1 miles

Vulcan
Lake

KALMIOPSIS
WILDERNESS

Red Mountain Creek

Vulcan Peak
4,655 ft.

Nice mountain views from the Vulcan Lake Trail

Vulcan Peak. The blue-green lake is stocked with rainbow trout and is the home to the California newt (salamander). The lake's shoreline is strewn with large, oddly shaped boulders that make wonderful places to hang out, eat your lunch, and gaze at the lake before heading back to the trailhead.

Miles and Directions

0.0 Start from the trailhead sign located at the end of FR 260. Be sure to fill out a self-issue wilderness permit.

0.1 Turn right at the trail fork.

0.9 Turn right where a sign indicates trail 1110a. (Trail 1110B goes left toward Little Vulcan Lake.)

1.1 Reach Vulcan Lake and your turnaround point. Retrace the same route back to the trailhead.

2.2 Arrive back at the trailhead.

Hike Information

Local Information

The Brookings-Harbor Chamber of Commerce, 16330 Lower Harbor Rd., Brookings, OR 97415; (800) 535-9469, brookingsharborchamber.com

Local Events and Attractions

Azalea Festival, held Memorial Day weekend, Brookings; (800) 535-9469; brookingsharborchamber.com

Oregon Caves National Monument, 19000 Caves Hwy., Cave Junction; (541) 592-2100; nps.gov/orca

25 Babyfoot Lake

This easy 2.0-mile out-and-back trail takes you through part of the Babyfoot Lake Botanical Area, home to many rare plant species that are found only in the unspoiled Kalmiopsis Wilderness. After 1 mile of hiking, you reach Babyfoot Lake, which sits in a dramatic glacial cirque surrounded by timbered hillsides that contain a large population of rare Port Orford cedar and Brewer's spruce trees.

Start: The trailhead is located 15.6 miles north of Cave Junction and about 60 miles northeast of Brookings off US 199 (the Redwood Highway).
Distance: 2.0 miles out and back
Hiking time: 1 hour
Difficulty: Easy; smooth trail surface and minimal elevation gain
Best season: July through Oct
Other trail users: Hikers only
Canine compatibility: Dogs permitted
Land status: Wilderness
Nearest town: Cave Junction

Fees and permits: Northwest Forest Pass (small fee) required. Purchase a pass online at www.fs.usda.gov/main/r6/passes-permits/recreation or by calling (800) 270-7504. Self-issue wilderness permit (free and available at the trailhead) also required.
Schedule: Open mid-June through Oct
Maps: Maptech CD: Siskiyou National Forest/Crater Lake/Medford, OR; USGS: Josephine Mountain, OR
Trail contact: Wild Rivers Ranger District, 2164 NE Spaulding Ave., Grants Pass, OR 97526; (541) 471-6500; www.fs.fed.us/r6/siskiyou/

Finding the trailhead: From Brookings: Travel 20 miles south on US 101 to Crescent City and turn east onto US 199. Travel about 45 miles northeast on US 199 to Cave Junction. From Cave Junction travel north for 4 miles on US 199 (the Redwood Highway) and turn left (west) onto Eight Dollar Road (which becomes FR 4201 after you enter the Siskiyou National Forest). Drive on FR 4201 for 11.3 miles to the intersection with FR 140. Turn left onto FR 140 and drive 0.3 mile to the trailhead on the right side of the road. *DeLorme: Oregon Atlas & Gazetteer:* Page 18 C2 GPS: N42 13.490 / W123 47.567

The Hike

Babyfoot Lake is located in a glacial cirque surrounded by forested hills and rocky bluffs. This high mountain lake is situated in the wild and rugged 179,655-acre Kalmiopsis Wilderness—one of five wilderness areas located in the Siskiyou National Forest. A short, easy 1.0-mile trail leads you to this quiet lake through an old-growth forest—part of the 352-acre Babyfoot Lake Botanical Area, which was established in 1963 to protect the Brewer's spruce and other rare plant species.

Because of its gentle terrain and easy access off FR 140, the Babyfoot Lake Trail can be crowded during the summer months. The trail begins by winding through an old-growth forest of Brewer's spruce, Douglas fir, Shasta red fir, sugar pine, Port Orford cedar, and incense cedar. Interspersed on the forest floor are vine maple,

Snow can still be present on this hike in June.

western sword fern, parsley fern, and fragile fern. In open areas you may see the bright colors of such wildflowers as bleeding hearts, rattlesnake orchid, Siskiyou iris, Newberry's penstemon, pussy paws, spreading phlox, and twinflower.

When you reach the lake, you'll want to plan on staying for a while. You may want to take a refreshing swim, search for rare endemic plants (be sure to bring your plant field guide), or have a picnic. If you love to fish, try your luck at catching some brook trout, which are present in small quantities in the lake.

While you are in the Cave Junction area, be sure to check out Oregon Caves National Monument, located 20 miles southeast of Cave Junction on OR 46. This national monument was established in 1909 to showcase its main attraction, a large cave carved by the Styx River. You can see this magnificent cave by taking the 90-minute guided tour. You'll see almost a half mile of fascinating rock chambers filled with stalactites and intricately carved rock columns. This national monument also contains nature trails that will help you learn about the eighty species of birds, thirty-five species of mammals, and more than 110 species of plants present in the park. The 3.3-mile Big Tree Trail loop takes you on a tour of an old-growth Douglas fir forest.

Babyfoot Lake

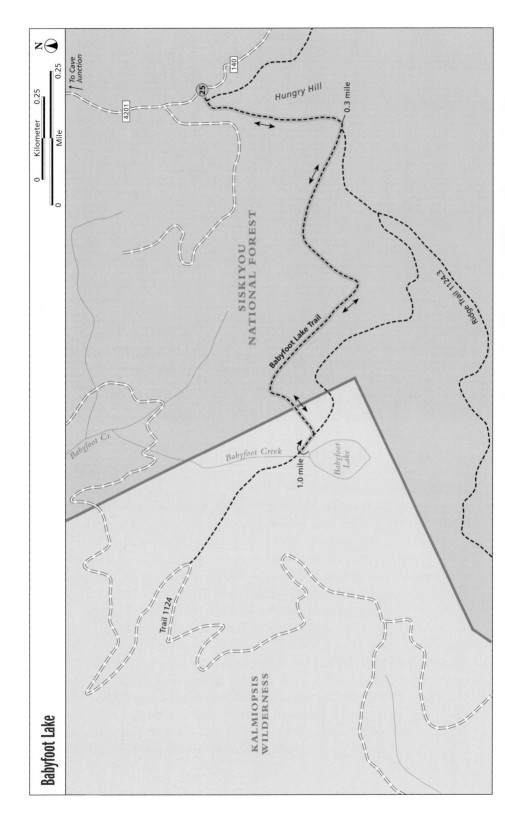

N

0 Kilometer 0.25
0 Mile 0.25

To Cave
Junction

4201

25

140

Hungry Hill

0.3 mile

SISKIYOU
NATIONAL FOREST

Babyfoot Lake Trail

Ridge Trail 1124.3

Babyfoot Cr.

Babyfoot Creek

1.0 mile

Babyfoot
Lake

Trail 1124

KALMIOPSIS
WILDERNESS

The 1.0-mile Cliff Nature Trail has interpretive signs that help you learn about the geology, plants, and animals present in the wild and rugged Siskiyou Mountains.

Miles and Directions

0.0 Start from the wooden trailhead sign. A sign indicates Babyfoot Lake .75/Canyon Peak Trail 4. (**Note:** The trail is actually a mile in length.) Be sure to fill out a self-issue wilderness permit at the trailhead.

0.3 Turn right at the trail fork. (**Note:** If you go left here, a sign indicates Ridge Trail 1124.3.

1.0 Reach Babyfoot Lake and your turnaround point. Retrace the same route back to your starting point.

2.0 Arrive back at the trailhead.

Hike Information

Local Information

The Brookings-Harbor Chamber of Commerce, 16330 Lower Harbor Rd., Brookings, OR 97415; (800) 535-9469; brookingsharborchamber.com

Local Events and Attractions

Azalea Festival, held Memorial Day weekend, Brookings; (800) 535-9469; brookingsharbor chamber.com

Oregon Caves National Monument, 19000 Caves Hwy., Cave Junction; (541) 592-2100; nps.gov/orca

26 Illinois River Trail

Take a tour in a rugged gorge carved by the wild and scenic Illinois River. This remote, well-maintained trail follows the Illinois River for 27 miles and gives you a unique glimpse into the wonders of the Kalmiopsis Wilderness, a 179,655-acre wilderness filled with deep gorges and rocky ridges and home to many rare plant species. Be prepared for a long, twisty drive to the trailhead. Because of this trail's remoteness, I recommend that you plan on backpacking the trail. If you don't want to backpack, the 8.0-mile out-and-back section of the trail described here gives you a good introduction to this beautiful, uncrowded wilderness area. If you care to stay the night, there's a campground at the trailhead.

Start: The Briggs Creek trailhead is located about 40 miles south of Grants Pass off US 199 (the Redwood Highway).
Distance: 8.0 miles out and back
Hiking time: 3 to 4 hours
Difficulty: Moderate
Best season: June through Oct
Other trail users: Hikers only
Canine compatibility: Dogs permitted
Land status: Wilderness

Nearest town: Selma
Schedule: Open May through Oct
Fees and permits: None
Maps: Maptech CD: Siskiyou National Forest/ Crater Lake/Medford, OR; USGS: York Butte, OR
Trail contact: Gold Beach Ranger District, 29279 Ellensburg Ave., Gold Beach, OR 97444; (541) 247 3600; www.fs.fed.us/r6/ siskiyou/

Finding the trailhead: From Grants Pass take I-5 exit 55, indicated by the OREGON CAVES AND CRESCENT CITY sign. Turn south onto US 199 (the Redwood Highway) and drive 21.6 miles to Selma. From US 199 in Selma, turn right (west) onto FR 4103 (Illinois River Road) at the flashing yellow light. The pavement ends and becomes a rough, rocky dirt road after 11 miles. At mile 17.8 the road forks; go left. At mile 18 the road forks again; go right. There is a sign that warns you that this road is not recommended for low-clearance vehicles. If you are driving a passenger car, it is recommended that you park here and walk the remaining mile to the trailhead.

From Brookings travel 20 miles south on US 101 to Crescent City and turn east onto US 199. Travel about 55 miles northeast on US 199 to Selma. From US 199 in Selma, turn left (west) onto FR 4103 (Illinois River Road) at the flashing yellow light. The pavement ends and becomes a rough, rocky dirt road after 11 miles. At mile 17.8 the road forks; go left. At mile 18 the road forks again; go right. There is a sign that warns you that this road is not recommended for low-clearance vehicles. If you are driving a passenger car, it is recommended that you park here and walk the remaining mile to the trailhead. *DeLorme: Oregon Atlas & Gazetteer:* Page 18 A2. GPS: N42 22.657 / W123 48.188

The Illinois River gets its dark-green color from the serpentinite rock that's present along the river's course. ▶

The Hike

The Illinois River Trail is located in the 179,655-acre Kalmiopsis Wilderness—one of Oregon's biggest and least-crowded wilderness areas. Two words describe this wilderness best: rugged and remote. Characterized by deep river and creek gorges and high ridges, this part of Oregon is home to many rare plant species. The namesake of the Kalmiopsis Wilderness, the pink-flowering *Kalmiopsis leachiana,* can be found clinging to rocky ridges and hillsides. This plant begins blooming in late April and blooms through the end of June. Plants that live in this region are tolerant of the high rainfall in winter—the average winter rainfall can range from 100 to 150 inches—and the dry, scorching summers, when temperatures can reach the mid- to upper nineties.

The Kalmiopsis Wilderness is part of the ancient Klamath Mountains. The mountains were formed when the North American plate pushed up against the Pacific Ocean bottom approximately 200 million years ago. This push-and-shove affair produced high mountain ridges, where ocean fossils have been found. The rocks found in this wilderness area are of varied origins, from oceanic crust to ocean-floor lavas. This mountainous region is also rich in such metals as copper, cobalt, platinum, chromite, nickle, iron, manganese, and gold. Old mining operations are dotted throughout the region; the largest producing mine, Gold Peck (located north of Baby Creek), was shut down in 1952.

The Illinois River Trail takes you right through the heart of this wilderness. The trail follows the river along a high ridge, taking you over Bald Mountain on a well-graded path for 27 miles to its terminus at Oak Flat, near Agness. Before you begin hiking on the trail, be sure to fill out a wilderness permit. You begin by walking on a path that crosses Briggs Creek and then slowly ascends through a forest of Douglas fir, canyon live oak, and orange madrone trees (identifiable by their rusty orange–colored, papery bark). Along the way you'll see the low-growing, bushy manzanita and chinquapin. Another plant to look out for, though you may not appreciate it as much, is poison oak. When you catch your first glimpse of the Illinois River, you'll notice its dark-green color, caused by the serpentinite rock that's present along the river's course.

As the trail climbs you'll pass rough, rocky outcrops of lava rock that offer scenic viewpoints of the river and the river gorge. The river flows over large boulders and through narrow shoots, filling the current with huge, challenging rapids. Not

THE COBRA LILY

The odd-looking cobra lily (pitcher plant) grows in boggy areas along the Illinois River and other places in the Kalmiopsis Wilderness. This ingenious plant lures unwary insects into its bulblike opening and then traps them. The insect is then digested with enzymes, making a meal that provides many needed nutrients.

Illinois River Trail

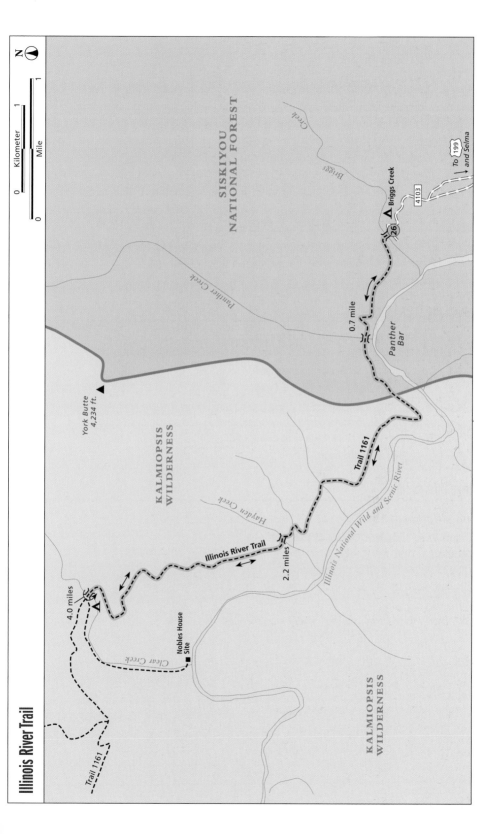

surprisingly, this river is the most difficult whitewater-rafting river in Oregon and attracts a few brave rafters and kayakers to run its rapids. The greatest obstacle on the river is the Green Wall—a rip-roaring, Class V boulder-strewn rapid that tests even the most experienced rafters and kayakers. (This rapid is located several miles away from the section of trail on which you're hiking, but you'll also see many rapids along this section.)

If you plan on backpacking this trail, you'll reach a good camping spot at Clear Creek (the hike's turnaround point). Cross a bridge over the creek, and there are some level campsites to your left. There is also an unmaintained trail that leads down to bubbling Clear Creek, where you can wade or filter water if you're running low. Keep in mind that black bears live in this wilderness area, so you should hang your food if you are camping. Other critters you may see on your journey include blue-tailed skinks, chattering Douglas squirrels, western fence lizards, and (last but certainly not least) rattlesnakes.

Miles and Directions

0.0 Start at the wooden trailhead marker at the end of FR 4103. Start walking on the Illinois River Trail (Trail 1161) and cross a wooden bridge spanning Briggs Creek.

0.7 Cross a wooden bridge over Panther Creek.

2.2 Cross a wooden bridge over Hayden Creek.

4.0 Cross a bridge over Clear Creek. This is your turnaround point. (**Note:** After you cross the bridge, there are some campsites to your left. There is also an unmaintained trail that leads down to the creek if you want to cool off.)

8.0 Arrive back at the trailhead.

Hike Information

Local Information

Grants Pass/Josephine County Chamber of Commerce, 1995 NW Vine St., Grants Pass, OR 97528; (541) 476-7717; grantspass chamber.org

27 Mount McLoughlin

Located in the heart of volcano country, 9,495-foot Mount McLoughlin rises above the pristine Sky Lakes Wilderness. It's a difficult trek to the top of this Cascade volcano. Along the way you pass through a scenic forest of Douglas fir and western red cedar and have many opportunities to view the lakes of the surrounding wilderness area. While you're in the area, be sure to visit Crater Lake National Park, located about 75 miles to the north via OR 62.

Start: The trailhead is located approximately 41 miles west of Klamath Falls off OR 140.
Distance: 11.0 miles out and back
Hiking time: 6 to 8 hours
Difficulty: Difficult; significant elevation gain, rocky terrain, and trail length
Best season: July through Oct
Other trail users: Equestrians
Canine compatibility: Leashed dogs permitted
Land status: National forest
Nearest town: Klamath Falls
Fees and permits: Northwest Forest Pass (small fee) required. You can purchase a

pass online at www.fs.usda.gov/main/r6/passes-permits/recreation or by calling (800) 270-7504. Self-issue wilderness permit (free) is also required and can be obtained at the trailhead.
Schedule: July through Sept
Maps: Maptech CD: Siskiyou National Forest/Crater Lake/Medford, OR; USGS: Mount McLoughlin
Trail contact: Fremont-Winema National Forest, Klamath Ranger District, 2819 Dahlia St., Suite A, Klamath Falls, OR 97601; (541) 885-3400; www.fs.usda.gov/fremont-winema

Finding the trailhead: From Klamath Falls head approximately 38 miles west on OR 140 and turn right (north) onto FR 3661 at the FOURMILE LAKE sign. Drive 2.9 miles on this gravel road to the junction with FR 3650. Turn left onto FR 3650 and drive 0.2 mile to the Trail 3716 trailhead. *DeLorme: Oregon Atlas & Gazetteer:* Page 21 A6. GPS: N42 25.230 / W122 15.265

The Hike

At 9,495 feet, Mount McLoughlin stands prominently above the pristine Sky Lakes Wilderness. The 113,590-acre wilderness area, established in 1984, stretches 27 miles by 6 miles and is bordered to the east by the 1.1 million–acre Winema National Forest and to the west by the 630,000-acre Rogue River National Forest. To the north is Crater Lake National Park, home to the deep blue waters of Crater Lake—at 1,932 feet, the deepest lake in the United States.

Mount McLoughlin has gone by a variety of names. Native Americans called the volcano **M'laiksini Yaina** because of its steep slopes. Early on, settlers dubbed it Mount Pit (also spelled

PACIFIC CREST TRAIL

The famous Pacific Crest Trail, which stretches more than 2,650 miles from Canada to Mexico, skirts the east flank of Mount McLoughlin.

Mount McLoughlin is 9,495 feet tall and is located in the Sky Lakes Wilderness. © CHRIS
BOSWELL/DREAMSTIME.COM

"Pitt"), borrowing on the nearby Pit River moniker, a name derived from the game-
trapping pits that Native Americans dug out along its banks. Snowy Butte and Big
Butte were also tossed around from time to time, but in 1905 Congress officially
named the mountain after Dr. John McLoughlin, a valued administrator in the Hud-
son's Bay Company from 1824 to 1849. McLoughlin established the company's Fort
Vancouver outpost in 1824. He retired to Oregon City (southeast of Portland), where
he ran a milling business until his death in 1857.

Geologically speaking, Mount McLoughlin is quite young—only about 700,000
years old. When viewed from the south or southeast, the mountain has a very symmetrical shape, characteristic of a young volcano. Glaciers have carved large cirques
on the mountain's northeast side, exposing rock within the volcano's cone that geologists have dated to as recently as 200,000 years ago.

To see this mountain for yourself, take the strenuous 11.0-mile out-and-back
trek to the mountain's summit. The hike begins winding through a forest of mixed
Douglas fir and western hemlock, ascending at a moderate-level pace. As you

CRATER LAKE

Crater Lake is nestled in the mountains of southern Oregon—some would say "mountains" and "southern Oregon" is a contradiction of terms. Sure, the region is virtually peakless when compared to the monstrous summits rising to the north and south, but this view has earned southern Oregon the undeserved reputation as less wild. Certainly, the more mountainous regions to the north and south are, at a glance, more spectacular, but southern Oregon's drama is meant to be less vertical. It doesn't boast skyscraping volcanic peaks like Mount Hood, Mount Jefferson, and Mount Shasta (though it has its share: Mount Thielsen at 9,182 feet, Mount McLoughlin at 9,495 feet, and Mount Bailey at 8,363 feet to name a few). It instead bears the more salient scars of a violent volcanic past.

Mount Mazama, a 12,000-foot volcano, once rose from the southern Oregon mountains to rival its northern and southern neighbors. But in 4,860 BC, it decided to blow. The explosion was of unfathomable proportion, with debris being flung as far off as British Columbia. Once the terrific violence had ceased, the mountain collapsed on itself, creating a 6-mile-wide, 4,000-foot-deep caldera. Over time, underground springs, rain, and snowmelt filled the crater, giving us what is today Crater Lake—which at 1,932 feet deep is the deepest lake in North America and the seventh-deepest lake in the world. Perhaps the greatest thing about this sapphire jewel of the southern Cascades is that it's unassuming. Unlike the flaunting peaks of Mount Hood, Mount Jefferson, and Mount Shasta, you must crest its 1,000-foot rim before ever having the slightest hint of the stunning beauty you're about to behold. And there's no describing it to you. You'll see for yourself, without a degree of diminishment, just how John Wesley Hillman felt when he stumbled upon this treasure in 1853.

approach the southeast side of the mountain, you'll encounter a number of ups and downs, and the trail becomes scattered with numerous rocks and boulders. After approximately 3.5 miles you're afforded great views of Fourmile Lake and Pelican Butte to the northeast and Lake of the Woods to the south. At mile 5.5 you reach the summit to grand views of the surrounding Sky Lakes Wilderness. Pay close attention to the route on the way up—many people lose the trail on the way down because of the numerous spur trails.

Miles and Directions

0.0 Start hiking on Trail 3716 and cross a bridge over Cascade Canal. (**Note:** Be sure to sign in at the climber's register.)

0.2 Enter the Sky Lakes Wilderness.

1.0 Turn right onto the Pacific Crest Trail where a sign indicates Mount McLoughlin Trail.

Mount McLoughlin

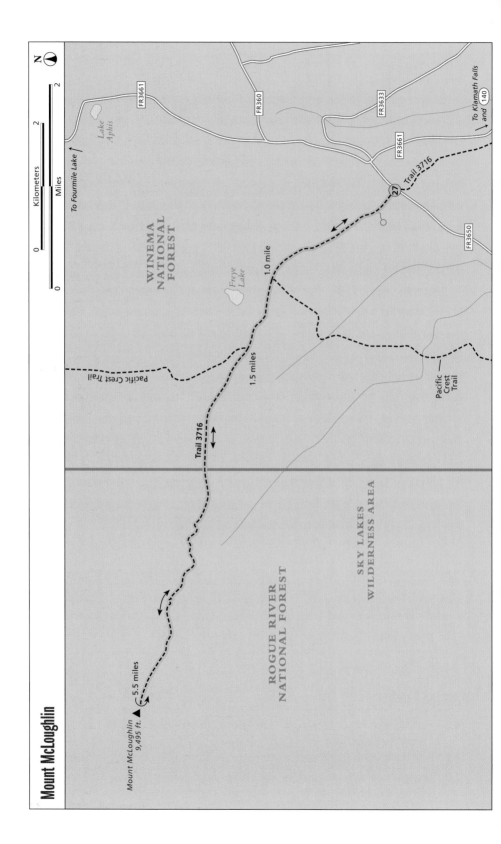

To Fourmile Lake

Lake Aphis

FR3661

WINEMA NATIONAL FOREST

Freye Lake

Pacific Crest Trail

1.0 mile

1.5 miles

Trail 3716

Pacific Crest Trail

27

Trail 3716

FR360

FR3661

FR3633

FR3650

To Klamath Falls and 140

5.5 miles

Mount McLoughlin ▲ 9,495 ft.

ROGUE RIVER NATIONAL FOREST

SKY LAKES WILDERNESS AREA

Kilometers

0   2

Miles

0   2

N

1.5   Turn left at the Mount McLoughlin Trail sign. (The Pacific Crest Trail goes right at this junction.) After this point the trail becomes rocky. Look for carvings in the trees for trail directions; in some places the trail is lined with rocks.

2.3   The trail becomes very steep and is scattered with boulders and other large rocks.

3.5   Enjoy great views of Fourmile Lake and Pelican Butte to the northeast and Lake of the Woods to the south.

4.2   Look for rocks with spray-painted red arrows to guide you on the trail.

4.5   Reach the top of a ridge. If you look at the north slope of the mountain, you can see the summit. Make a note of your position here, because at this point many hikers become lost during their descent.

4.7   The trail is very hard to distinguish in this section. Head to the right (uphill) and follow the ridge. Eventually a faint trail leaves the ridge, paralleling it to the south, and then after 200 yards comes back to the ridge.

5.5   Reach the summit and a foundation of the old lookout. Here are grand views of the surrounding Sky Lakes Wilderness. Retrace the same route back to the trailhead.

11.0   Arrive back at the trailhead.

Hike Information

Local Information

Crater Lake National Park, P.O. Box 7, Crater Lake, OR 97604; (541) 594-3100; nps.gov/ crla/index.htm

Discover Klamath, 205 Riverside Dr., Suite B, Klamath Falls, OR 97601; (800) 445-6728; discoverklamath.com

28 Mount Thielsen

This hike takes you through the pristine Mount Thielsen Wilderness and challenges you with a thrilling rock scramble and technical Class 4 rock climb to the pinnacle of 9,182-foot Mount Thielsen. From this high vantage point you'll have outstanding views of the surrounding Cascade peaks and Diamond Lake to the west.

Start: The trailhead is located 30 miles southwest of Chemult off OR 138. Chemult is located about 65 miles south of Bend on US 97.
Distance: 8.4 miles out and back
Hiking time: 5 to 7 hours
Difficulty: Moderate up to the junction with the Pacific Crest Trail. The trail then becomes difficult due to a rock scramble and a technical Class 4 rock climb to the summit.
Best season: Aug through Oct
Other trail users: Hikers only
Canine compatibility: Dogs permitted. If you have your canine hiking partner with you, it is recommended you hike only to the junction with the Pacific Crest Trail at mile 3.8. Due to the trail's technical nature, do not attempt to take your dog to the summit.

Land status: National forest and wilderness area
Nearest town: Chemult
Fees and permits: Northwest Forest Pass (small fee) required. You can purchase a pass online at www.fs.usda.gov/main/r6/passes-permits/recreation or by calling (800) 270-7504.
Schedule: Open July through Oct
Maps: Maptech CD: Siskiyou National Forest/Crater Lake/Medford, OR; USGS: Mount Thielsen, OR; Diamond Lake, OR
Trail contact: Chemult Ranger District, Winema National Forest, P.O. Box 150, Chemult, OR 97731; (541) 365-7001; www.fs.fed.us/r6/winema

Finding the trailhead: From Chemult drive 10 miles south on US 97. Turn west onto OR 138 and drive about 20 miles to the Mount Thielsen trailhead, located on the right (east) side of the road. *DeLorme: Oregon Atlas & Gazetteer:* Page 37 C8. GPS: N43 08.388 / W122 07.593

The Hike

Mount Thielsen is located in the Mount Thielsen Wilderness, north of Crater Lake National Park and just east of Diamond Lake. The 55,100-acre Mount Thielsen Wilderness, established in 1984, contains more than 78 miles of hiking trails, including a 26-mile section of the famed Pacific Crest Trail. The wilderness area falls under the management of the Deschutes, Umpqua, and Winema National Forests.

Portlander John A. Hurlburt named the peak in 1872 for prominent railroad engineer and builder Hans Thielsen, but prior to its official naming, locals referred to the peak as Big Cowhorn. Native Americans called it *His-chok-wol-as.* Mount Thielsen is often referred to as the "lightning rod of the Cascades" because of its pointed summit, which tends to attract numerous lightning strikes each year.

Mike Paholsky on the summit of Mount Thielsen PHOTO SHANNON VANDER GIESSEN

Technically speaking, Mount Thielsen is a shield volcano (a broad, domed-shaped cone made up of solidified layers of lava) thought to be 290,000 years old—relatively young on a geologic time scale. The volcano is composed of a central pyroclastic (rock formed by a volcanic explosion) cone that consists of tuff (rock formed from fine-grained ash and dust particles) and breccia (fragmented pieces of volcanic rock). Some of the breccia present on this ancient mountain forms layers up to 33 feet thick. The north and east sides of this peak have spectacular cirque walls that were carved by now-extinct glaciers.

The hike described here takes you through the Mount Thielsen Wilderness to the summit of 9,182-foot Mount Thielsen. You begin by hiking through a Douglas fir forest and after about 3 miles enjoy your first views of the sharp, pointed summit of the volcano's central basalt plug. At mile 3.8 you cross the Pacific Crest Trail. If you're not planning to attempt the rock climb to the summit, this is a good place to turn

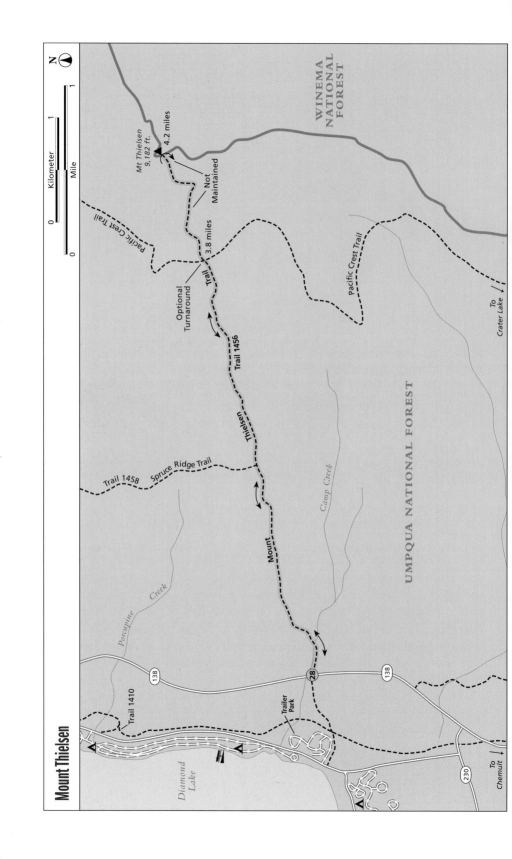

Mount Thielsen

around. After 4 miles the trail becomes hard to distinguish, so you'll have to navigate your way to the summit on one of several unmaintained trails. A helmet is advised beyond this point, and you'll need to use your hands to scramble over large rocks. If you don't have rock-climbing experience, do not attempt to climb to the summit of this peak—exposure, falling rock, and the chance of falling make it too dangerous.

Miles and Directions

0.0 Start hiking from the Mount Thielsen trailhead (Trail 1456/1458) and hike through an open Douglas fir forest.

1.8 Arrive at a junction with the Spruce Ridge Trail (Trail 1458). Continue straight (right) on the Mount Thielsen Trail (Trail 1456).

2.0 Enter the Mount Thielsen Wilderness.

3.0 Enjoy views of Mount Thielsen. Pass through a popcorn pumice–like area.

3.8 Come to a junction with the Pacific Crest Trail. Continue straight. **Option:** Those not wanting to continue to the summit should turn around at this point.

4.0 The trail becomes indistinct. There are several "goat" trails to the summit. You can either switchback to the right on looser scree or scramble directly up the ridge along a steep route. Stay on the right side of the ridge and ascend to a notch at the southwest edge of the summit plug. **Warning:** The final 30 feet to the summit is a Class 4 technical rock climb, and a belayed ascent (rope and harness with protection) is recommended. Also, because of the eroding rock conditions near the summit, a helmet is recommended.

4.2 Reach the 9,182-foot summit. There are stunning views of Diamond Lake to the west and of the surrounding Mount Thielsen Wilderness. Retrace the same route back to the trailhead.

8.4 Arrive back at the trailhead.

Hike Information

Local Information

Visit Bend, 750 NW Lava Rd., Suite 160, Bend, OR 97701 (877) 245-8484; visitbend.com

Restaurants

Deschutes Brewery Bend Public House, 1044 NW Bond St., Bend; (541) 382-9242; deschutesbrewery.com

Honorable Mentions

Southwest Oregon

Z Sweet Creek Falls

This easy 2.2-mile out-and-back route takes you on a tour along the banks of bouldery Sweet Creek to a viewpoint of Sweet Creek Falls. To get there from Florence, head 15 miles east (or 46 miles west of Eugene) on OR 126 to Mapleton and the junction with Sweet Creek Road. Turn south onto Sweet Creek Road and travel 10.2 miles to the Homestead Trailhead on the right. From the Homestead trailhead, start walking upstream. You'll pass small waterfalls and after 1.1 miles reach 20-foot Sweet Creek Falls (your turnaround point). Head up a short side trail to a fantastic viewpoint of the upper falls.

For more information, contact Siuslaw National Forest, Mapleton Ranger District, 4480 Highway 101, Building G, Florence, OR 97439; (541) 902-8526; www.fs.fed.us/r6/siuslaw. *DeLorme: Oregon Atlas & Gazetteer:* Page 40 A1.

AA Kentucky Falls

This moderate 4.0-mile out-and-back route descends 760 feet through a mossy forest of western hemlock and Douglas fir dotted with trillium, sword fern, and oxalis. After about 0.5 mile you'll arrive at the shimmering double cascade of Upper Kentucky Falls. Continue about another 1.5 miles to a viewpoint of Lower Kentucky Falls and North Fork Falls (your turnaround point).

To get there from Reedsport, head north on US 101, cross a bridge over the Umpqua River, and turn right (northeast) onto Smith River Road (FR 48). Go approximately 14.5 miles and turn left (north) onto North Fork Road. Go about 10 miles to the intersection with FR 23. Turn right onto FR 23 and follow signs to Kentucky Falls. After another 9.8 miles you'll arrive at a T intersection. Turn left onto FR 919 and continue 2.6 miles to the trailhead.

For more information, contact Oregon Dunes NRA Visitor Center, 855 Highway Ave., Reedsport, OR 97467; (541) 271-6000; www.fs.fed.us/r6/siuslaw. *DeLorme: Oregon Atlas & Gazetteer:* Page 40 A2.

BB North Fork Smith River

This difficult 17.4-mile out-and-back route travels along the banks of the North Fork Smith River, which is filled with many great swimming spots. You'll hike through a jungly coastal forest where you can admire huge old-growth Douglas firs. You are treated at the trail's turnaround point with a great view of Kentucky Falls. To get there from Reedsport, head north on US 101, cross a bridge over the Umpqua River, and then turn right (northeast) onto Smith River Road (FR 48). After about 15 miles turn left (north) onto North Fork Road 48A. Continue about 9.5 miles to a road junction and go right toward Mapleton. Go 0.5 mile to another road junction and turn right onto FR 23. Continue 4 miles to the trailhead parking area on the left side of the road.

For more information, contact the Oregon Dunes NRA Visitor Center, 855 Highway Ave., Reedsport, OR 97467; (541) 271-6000; www.fs.fed.us/r6/siuslaw. *DeLorme: Oregon Atlas & Gazetteer:* Page 40 A2.

CC Umpqua Dunes

This 1.0-mile interpretive loop takes you through a madrone and manzanita forest, wetlands, and magnificent coastal dunes. If you feel like a longer hiking adventure, continue through the dunes 2.5 miles to the beach. Look for posts with blue bands to guide your way. To get to this hike, travel 10.5 miles south of Reedsport on US 101 (or 12 miles north of North Bend) to the signed Umpqua Dunes trailhead located on the west side of US 101.

This hike requires a Northwest Forest Pass, which you can purchase online at www.fs.usda.gov/main/r6/passes-permits/recreation or by calling (800) 270-7504. For more information, contact Oregon Dunes NRA Visitor Center, 855 Highway Ave., Reedsport, OR 97467; (541) 271-6000; www.fs.fed.us/r6/siuslaw/. *DeLorme: Oregon Atlas & Gazetteer:* Page 32, Inset 3, C3.

DD South Slough Estuarine Preserve

You can explore a series of trails through a wetland ecosystem at this 4,800-acre Coos Bay estuary. Paths lead through fresh- and saltwater marshes, mudflats, and floodplains. The visitor center is open from 10 a.m. to 4:30 p.m. Tuesday through Saturday and is closed major holidays.

To get there from Coos Bay or North Bend, follow signs to Charleston, Shore Acres State Park, and Ocean Beaches. From Charleston head west on Cape Arago Highway and in 0.1 mile turn left (south) onto Seven Devils Road. Follow signs to South Slough Sanctuary and Bandon. Drive 4.5 miles, turn left at the interpretive center, and continue to a parking area. The trailhead is past the interpretive center to the left of a panel titled Journey to the Sea.

For more information, contact South Slough National Estuarine Research Reserve, 61907 Seven Devils Rd., Charleston, OR 97420; (541) 888-5558; oregon.gov/dsl/SSNERR/Pages/index.aspx. *DeLorme: Oregon Atlas & Gazetteer:* Page 33 B6.

EE Golden and Silver Falls State Natural Area

This spectacular trail takes you on a tour of the shimmering cascades of Golden Falls and Silver Falls. To get there from US 101 in Coos Bay, head east on the Coos River Highway, following signs to Allegany. Travel 13.5 miles east on the north side of the

Coos River to the town of Allegany. From here follow state park signs another 9.5 miles to the Golden and Silver Falls State Natural Area.

Start by crossing a bridge over Silver Creek. At the trail junction head left and enjoy the shady canopy of old-growth Douglas fir trees. At 0.4 mile turn left to view the billowing 160-foot cascade of Silver Falls. After viewing the falls head back to the main trail and turn left. Continue uphill as the trail follows the edge of a steep cliff to the viewpoint of Golden Falls at 0.9 mile (your turnaround point). For a less precipitous view of Golden Falls, take the right fork at the beginning of the hike and walk 0.3 mile to the viewpoint.

For more information, contact Oregon State Parks and Recreation, 725 Summer St. NE, Suite C, Salem, OR 97301; (800) 551-6949; oregonstateparks.org/park_96.php. *DeLorme: Oregon Atlas & Gazetteer:* Page 34 A1. GPS: N43 28.946 / W123 55.984.

FF Cape Blanco State Park

This uncrowded state park is a great place to enjoy the sights and sounds of the southern Oregon coast. Set up a base camp at the scenic campground and spend a few days exploring 8 miles of hiking trails through a diverse coastal ecosystem. The Oregon Coast Trail can be accessed from the south end of the campground. Additional hiking trails lead to several viewpoints and to the beach.

To get to Cape Blanco State Park, drive 46 miles south of Coos Bay or 4 miles north of Port Orford on US 101 to the junction with Cape Blanco Road. Turn west and drive 5 miles on Cape Blanco Road to Cape Blanco State Park. Photographers and wildlife lovers will enjoy the natural beauty of this park, with its high chalky bluffs, black-sand beach, and offshore sea stacks, which are home to herds of sea lions and prime nesting sites for seabirds. If you're a history buff, don't miss exploring the 59-foot Cape Blanco Lighthouse, the oldest lighthouse in Oregon. Another historical structure at this state park is the Hughes House Museum, built in 1898 by Patrick Hughes. This eleven-room, two-story Victorian-style mansion was built out of old-growth Port Orford cedar at a cost of $3,800. It's open for tours April through October and is filled with delightful antique furniture and old photos depicting the life of the former 1,000-acre dairy ranch that the house sits on.

For more information, contact Oregon State Parks and Recreation, 725 Summer St. NE, Suite C, Salem, OR 97301; (800) 551-6949; www.oregonstateparks.org/park_62.php. *DeLorme: Oregon Atlas & Gazetteer:* Page 24 B4. GPS: N42 50.146 / W124 33.647.

GG Susan Creek Falls

This easy 1.4-mile out-and-back hike takes you to a viewpoint of Susan Creek Falls. Start the hike from the picnic area by crossing OR 138 and picking up the trail on the other side. Continue 0.7 mile through an old-growth Douglas fir, cedar, and hemlock forest to 70-foot Susan Creek Falls. After enjoying the view retrace the route back to the trailhead. To get there from I-5 in Roseburg, take exit 124 and head 28.3 miles east on OR 138 to the Susan Creek picnic area on the right side of the road.

For more information, contact the Umpqua National Forest, North Umpqua Ranger District, 18782 N. Umpqua Hwy., Glide, OR 97443; (541) 496-3532; fs.usda.gov/main/umpqua/home. *DeLorme: Oregon Atlas & Gazetteer:* Page 36 B1.

⊢⊣ Tipsoo Peak

You'll enjoy this difficult 6.2-mile out-and-back trek that climbs 1,780 feet to the 8,034-foot summit of Tipsoo Peak in the Mount Thielsen Wilderness. To get there from I-5 in Roseburg, take exit 124 and travel 75 miles east on OR 138 to the junction with Cinnamon Butte Road (FR 4793). Turn east and travel 1.7 miles to the junction with Wits End Road (FR 100). Go straight and continue 3.2 miles on a rough road to a small, signed trailhead on the right.

The trail ascends through a fragrant mountain hemlock forest and skirts the edge of Tipsoo Meadow after 2.8 miles. As you continue you'll see twisted and bent whitebark pine along the trail. These trees are found only at high elevations and are a reminder of the area's harsh winter storms. As you near the top, the trail follows a lava-strewn ridgeline until you reach the summit at 3.1 miles. From the top you'll have a commanding view of North, Middle, and South Sister, Mount Thielsen, Mount Bailey, Diamond Lake, and Diamond Peak. Retrace the route back to the trailhead.

This trail requires a Northwest Forest Pass, which you can purchase online at www.fs.usda.gov/main/r6/passes-permits/recreation or by calling (800) 270-7504. For more information, contact the Umpqua National Forest, Diamond Lake Ranger District, 2020 Toketee Ranger Station Rd., Idleyld Park, OR 97447; (541) 498-2531; fs.usda.gov/main/umpqua/home. *DeLorme: Oregon Atlas & Gazetteer:* Page 37 C8.

‖ Mount Bailey Hike

This difficult 9.8-mile out-and-back trail takes you to the 8,368-foot summit of Mount Bailey. To get there from Medford, travel about 60 miles north on OR 62 to the junction with OR 230. Turn left (north) onto OR 230 and continue about 24 miles to the Diamond Lake Recreation Area turnoff. Continue on FR 6592 to a SOUTH SHORE PICNIC AREA sign. Turn left onto FR 4795, travel 1.7 miles, and turn left onto FR 300. Continue 0.4 mile to the trailhead parking area.

The challenging route climbs more than 3,100 feet through a lodgepole pine forest lined with manzanita. After 2.2 miles the trail intersects a dirt road. Cross the road and continue your steep ascent through a mountain hemlock forest that eventually thins to whitebark pine. You'll reach the spectacular summit after another 2.7 miles. Enjoy the views of Diamond Lake, Mount Thielsen, and Mount Scott, and then return on the same route.

Mount Scott

For more information, contact the Umpqua National Forest, Diamond Lake Ranger District, 2020 Toketee Ranger Station Rd., Idleyld Park, OR 97447; (541) 498-2531; fs.usda.gov/main/umpqua/home. *DeLorme: Oregon Atlas & Gazetteer:* Page 37 C7.

JJ Mount Scott

This trail takes you on a 5.0-mile out-and-back trek to the top of 8,929-foot Mount Scott. From the top you have a fantastic view of the deep blue waters of Crater Lake and Crater Lake National Park. To get there from Fort Klamath, drive north on OR 62 for approximately 16 miles to Mazama Village. Turn right onto Munson Valley Road and drive about 6 miles to the junction with Rim Drive. Turn right onto Rim Drive and continue east for 14 miles to the trailhead on the right.

For more information, contact Crater Lake National Park, P.O. Box 7, Crater Lake, OR 97604; (541) 594-3000; nps.gov/crla/. *DeLorme: Oregon Atlas & Gazetteer:* Page 29 A8.

Central Oreɡon

A high-desert ecosystem of sagebrush, juniper, and ponderosa pine charac-terizes the dry, central part of Oregon, where volcanic activity and ero-sion have formed amazing gorges and unique rock formations. Coursing through all of this is the mighty Deschutes River, beginning high in the Cascade Mountains and traveling north to south through the heart of Bend, central Oregon's largest city.

Many consider Bend the gateway to the High Cascade Lakes Region and Deschutes National Forest. It serves as the geographic and popular center of this area of the state. Just northwest of here is the small western town of Sisters, a major access point to both the Mount Washington and Mount Jefferson Wilderness Areas—serious volcano country.

Here, two trails not to be missed are the Black Crater Trail and the Little Belknap Crater Trail. The Black Crater Trail winds its way through a mountain hemlock for-est to the craggy, red-cinder summit of Black Crater, providing a panoramic view of the Three Sisters, Belknap Crater, Mount Washington, Mount Jefferson, and Mount Hood. The Little Belknap Crater Trail takes you across the moonlike landscape of an ancient lava flow to the summit of Little Belknap Crater. From the summit of the crater, you can enjoy sweeping views of the snow-topped Three Sisters Mountains, Mount Washington, and the surrounding lava flows and craters that make up the Mount Washington Wilderness. For a pristine river hike, be sure to take a tour on the Metolius River Trail and admire the lush, spring-fed river ecosystem.

Afterward consider the Three Sisters Wilderness and the Newberry National Vol-canic Monument; both of these areas can be easily accessed from the city of Bend. To experience one of the best views in the Central Cascade Range, hike to the top of 10,358-foot South Sister (located in the Three Sisters Wilderness). This strenuous 11.0-mile out-and-back trail is located approximately 27 miles west of Bend off the Cascade Lakes Highway. From the summit you'll have a panoramic view to the north of Middle Sister, North Sister, and Chambers Lakes; to the southeast you'll be able to see Broken Top, Mount Bachelor, and Green Lakes.

The Newberry National Volcanic Monument (southeast of Bend off US 97) is home to Newberry Caldera—a 500-square-mile crater that houses Paulina and East

Scenic Square Lake with South Sister in the background

Lakes. This national monument has a rich geologic history, evident in its hot springs, lava flows, and cinder cones. The 1.0-mile Big Obsidian Flow Trail takes you on a fascinating tour of Oregon's youngest lava flow. To see the national monument from a different perspective, tackle the strenuous Paulina Peak Trail. This trail climbs to the summit of 7,984-foot Paulina Peak, where from the top you'll have quite a view of the magnificent caldera, as well as vistas of Paulina and East Lakes and the surrounding high alpine country.

Smith Rock State Park is also located right in the center of this open, high-desert country and features spectacular pinnacles, columns, and cathedral-like cliffs that rise more than 400 feet above a mammoth gorge carved by the Crooked River. Tour this unusual landscape on a 4.0-mile loop trail, located about 8 miles northeast of Redmond off US 97.

A less frequently visited but no less stunning area is Mill Creek Wilderness, located about 20 miles northeast of Prineville off US 26. The Twin Pillars Trail takes you through this wilderness, which is characterized by open, parklike stands of ponderosa pine, grand fir, and Douglas fir.

Unlike the Willamette Valley to the west, the central part of the state is much sunnier and dryer. The average rainfall in this part of the state is about 12 inches, and blue skies are the norm. Summers are hot and winters are cold. Be prepared for a substantial amount of snow in the high-mountain areas and periodic snow showers at lower elevations.

29 Triangulation Peak

This trail begins in a lush forest filled in summer with colorful wildflowers and juicy raspberries. Near the summit of Triangulation Peak, a side trail leads steeply downhill to Boca Cave, which is well worth exploring. From the cave's entrance there's a great view of the immense glaciated summit of Mount Jefferson. As you continue to the pointed summit of Triangulation Peak, you'll enjoy another sweeping view of Mount Jefferson and the surrounding Mount Jefferson Wilderness.

Start: The trailhead is located approximately 15 miles southeast of Detroit off OR 22.
Distance: 5.4 miles out and back with an optional 0.6-mile side trail to Boca Cave
Hiking time: 2 to 3 hours
Difficulty: Moderate; steep push to the summit. The trail to Boca Cave is challenging—steep, loose, and unmaintained.
Best season: July through Oct
Other trail users: Hikers only
Canine compatibility: Dogs permitted

Land status: National forest and wilderness area
Nearest town: Detroit
Fees and permits: Wilderness permit (free) required and available at trailhead
Schedule: Open June through Oct
Maps: Maptech CD: Coos Bay/Eugene/Bend, OR; USGS: Mount Bruno, OR
Trail contact: Willamette National Forest, Detroit Ranger District, 44125 N. Santiam Hwy. SE, Detroit, OR 97342; (503) 854-3366; fs.usda.gov/main/willamette/home

Finding the trailhead: From Detroit travel 6 miles southeast on OR 22 and turn left onto FR 2233 (McCoy Creek Road). Drive 7.8 miles (the road becomes gravel after 4 miles) to a road junction. Stay to the right and drive another 1.3 miles to the junction with FR 635. Turn right onto FR 635 and park in the trailhead parking area on the right side of the road. *Delorme: Oregon Atlas & Gazetteer:* Page 56 C1. GPS: N44 43.296 / W121 56.964

The Hike

The rocky summit of 5,434-foot Triangulation Peak rises prominently above the 1.6 million–acre Willamette National Forest, offering up a grand view of 10,497-foot Mount Jefferson. Jefferson is the second-highest peak in Oregon and one of thirteen major volcanoes in the Cascade Mountain Range. It forms the centerpiece of the 111,177-acre Mount Jefferson Wilderness. Sporting five glaciers (Jefferson Park, Milk Creek, Russell, Waldo, and Whitewater), Mount Jefferson is an active composite volcano that has erupted periodically over the past 300,000 years. One of its largest eruptions occurred between 35,000 and 100,000 years ago, depositing ash as far as southeast Idaho. Jefferson's last major eruption occurred almost 15,000 years ago. A more recent eruption, about 6,500 years ago, occurred about 5 miles south of Mount Jefferson at a Forked Butte cinder cone.

The author climbs to the summit of Triangulation Peak. PHOTO KEN SKEEN

The base of this highly glaciated peak consists of picturesque alpine meadows and more than 150 small trout-stocked lakes. The high, parklike setting is popular with hikers and backpackers, as evidenced by the more heavily trafficked areas: Jefferson Park, Eight Lakes Basin, Marion Lake, Pamelia Lake, Jack Lake, Duffy Lake, and Santiam Lake. In an effort to control what could become a threat to the local ecosystem, the USDA Forest Service now restricts camping to designated areas. Campfires are not permitted within 100 feet of lakes, and in many areas they're outright prohibited.

Begin this hike with a downhill walk along a gentle ridge surrounded by Douglas fir, subalpine fir, and mountain hemlock. Notice the showy pink blooms of wild rhododendron, purple lupine, fiery Indian paintbrush, and other colorful wildflowers. The trail wanders at a pleasant pace for about the first 2 miles. It then turns right at a junction with the Triangulation Trail and winds steeply up the north side of Triangulation Peak. At mile 1.9 you pass the rocky tower of Spire Rock. A little more than half a mile later, you arrive at a second trail junction, where you have the option of turning left and scrambling down a steep, eroded trail to Boca Cave. Inside the cave, ferns cling precariously to jumbled rocks as water trickles from the sides and floor.

Triangulation Peak

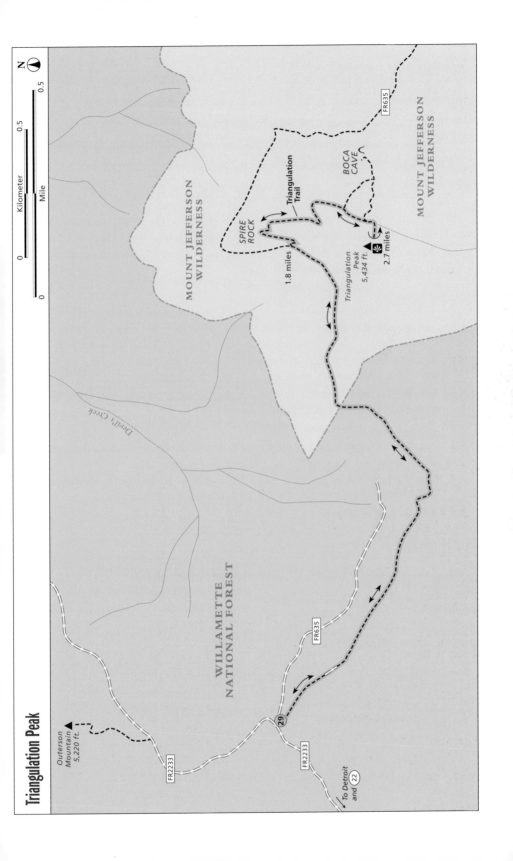

RASPBERRY BASICS

Wild raspberries are common along this trail. The plants begin blooming in June, and the berries start to ripen in mid-July. You can recognize the plant by its white petals and clusters of three or five green leaves. The berries are half-sphere shaped and range in color from light pink to dark red. The wild berries aren't quite as sweet as their domesticated cousins, but they are a delight to eat.

When you're through exploring the cave, climb back up to the main trail and turn left for a short hike and scramble over several large boulders to the summit of Triangulation Peak. Take in the sweeping views (especially of Mount Jefferson) before returning to the trailhead the way you came.

Miles and Directions

0.0 Start at the wooden trailhead sign off FR 635. (**Note:** Be sure to fill out a wilderness permit at the trailhead.)

0.2 Stay to the right. The trail becomes a doubletrack dirt road and changes back to a dirt path after approximately 50 yards.

1.8 Turn right onto Triangulation Trail. You'll begin a steep ascent up the north slope of Triangulation Peak on a series of switchbacks.

1.9 Reach the base of Spire Rock.

2.6 Stay to the right. **Option:** If you go left, you can scramble 0.3 mile down a steep, rocky trail to Boca Cave.

2.7 Reach the pointed, rocky summit of Triangulation Peak. There are first-class views of Mount Jefferson (your turnaround point). Retrace the same route back to the trailhead.

5.4 Arrive back at the trailhead.

Hike Information

Local Information

Detroit Lake State Park, Oregon State Parks and Recreation, 725 Summer Street NE, Suite C, Salem, OR 97301; (800) 551-6949; oregonstateparks.org/park_93.php

Willamette National Forest, Detroit Ranger District, 44125 N. Santiam Hwy. SE, Detroit, OR 97342; (503) 854-3366; fs.usda.gov/main/willamette/home

30 West Metolius River Trail

This unique trail traces the banks of the clear, fast-moving Metolius River and meanders through a lush riparian ecosystem of bright wildflowers and riverside vegetation. The spring-fed river rushes over lava to create swirling rapids and big eddies that are home to various species of salmon and trout. At the turnaround point is the Wizard Falls Fish Hatchery, a great place to take a break and explore. Water and restrooms are available at the fish hatchery.

Start: The trailhead is located 19.3 miles northwest of Sisters off US 20.
Distance: 5.0 miles out and back (with longer options)
Hiking time: 2 to 3 hours
Difficulty: Easy; smooth trail surface and minimal elevation gain
Best season: May through Oct
Other trail users: Hikers only
Canine compatibility: Dogs permitted
Land status: National forest

Nearest town: Sisters
Fees and permits: None
Schedule: Year-round
Maps: Maptech CD: Coos Bay/Eugene/Bend, OR; USGS: Black Butte, OR; Candle Creek, OR; Prairie Farm Spring, OR
Trail contact: Deschutes National Forest, Sisters Ranger District, Pine Street and Highway 20, Sisters, OR 97759; (541) 549-7700; fs.usda.gov/main/centraloregon/home

Finding the trailhead: From Sisters head 10 miles west on US 20 to Camp Sherman Road (FR 14). Turn right (north) and travel 2.7 miles to the junction with Forest Service Road 1419. Turn left and go 2.3 miles to another road junction and stop sign. Continue straight (you're now on FR 1420) for another 3.4 miles to the junction with FR 400. Turn right onto FR 400 toward Canyon Creek Campground; go 0.9 mile through the campground to the road's end and the trailhead. *DeLorme: Oregon Atlas & Gazetteer:* Page 50 A3. GPS: N44 30.057 / W121 38.471

The Hike

The Metolius River, known for its world-class fly fishing, originates as a natural spring at the base of Black Butte before winding its way north through the Metolius Basin and into Lake Billy Chinook. Numerous springs, fed via porous volcanic rock high in the Central Cascade Mountains, continue to feed the river along its length, keeping the flow rate fairly steady at 1,200 to 1,800 cubic feet per second.

The Northern Paiute and Tenino Indians were the first known people to inhabit the Metolius Basin. They fished for salmon, hunted deer and small game, and gathered nuts and berries on the slopes of Black Butte. In the mid–nineteenth century, several well-known explorers traveled through the area. Among them were Captain John Charles Frémont, who passed through in 1843, and Lieutenant Henry Larcom Abbott, who arrived in 1855 as a surveyor for the Pacific Railroad.

Josh Hubbell fly fishing on the Metolius River PHOTO KEN SKEEN

Homesteading in the Metolius Valley didn't occur until 1881. Settlers were attracted to the area by the thick timber and abundant grass that provided good grazing for livestock. The numerous springs and creeks in the valley also provided a plentiful supply of water. In 1893, with the passage of the Forest Reserve Act by President Grover Cleveland, the Metolius Valley became part of the Cascade Range Forest Reserve. In 1908 the area was incorporated into Deschutes National Forest.

If you want to explore this beautiful river, the West Metolius River Trail is the easiest way to do it. The trail starts at Canyon Creek Campground, located approximately 20 miles northwest of Sisters, and continues on a scenic journey to Wizard Falls Fish Hatchery. Along the way there is lush streamside greenery (including pinkish-lavender streambank globe mallow and bright-orange fragrant honeysuckle) as well as open forest dotted with purple lupine, crimson columbine, lavender-tufted thistle, and white-headed yarrow. Large ponderosa pines shade the path, and the

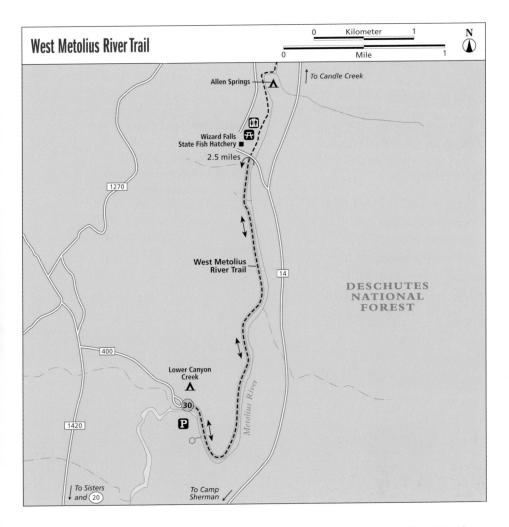

river's deep rock pools and logs provide a haven for trout and salmon. After 2.5 miles the trail arrives at Wizard Falls Fish Hatchery, which raises almost 3.5 million salmon and trout every year. This is a great place to rest before the return trip to the trailhead. Restrooms and water are available here.

Miles and Directions

0.0 Start this stunning river hike at the wooden West Metolius River trail sign, located in the Canyon Creek Campground. A sign indicates that you'll reach Wizard Falls Fish Hatchery in 2.5 miles.

0.3 Look off to the right to view an amazing natural spring that splashes into the river from underground.

2.5 Arrive at Wizard Falls Fish Hatchery. If you are feeling curious, take the time to explore the fish hatchery before you head back to the trailhead. Water and restrooms are available here. **Option:** If you want to enjoy a longer river route, continue on the trail on the west or east side of the river for about 5 more miles.

5.0   Arrive back at the trailhead.

Hike Information

Local Information

Sisters Area Chamber of Commerce,
291 E. Main Ave., Sisters, OR 97759;
(866) 549-0252

Local Events and Attractions

Sisters Folk Festival, second weekend in
September, Sisters; (541) 549-4979;
sistersfolkfestival.org

Sisters Rodeo and Parade, second weekend
in June, Sisters; (541) 549-0121;
sistersrodeo.com

Wizard Falls Hatchery, 7500 Forest Service
Rd. 14, Camp Sherman, OR 97730; (541)
595-6611; sisterscountry.com

31 Three Fingered Jack

This hike follows the Pacific Crest Trail 2000 through a pristine forest of fragrant Douglas and alpine fir, blue spruce, and mountain hemlock to the base of 7,841-foot Three Fingered Jack, an eroded remnant of an ancient volcanic plug. The plug itself is impressive; if you have climbing experience and the appropriate gear, you may be tempted to continue up its south ridge to the summit.

Start: The trailhead is located 20.4 miles west of Sisters on US 20.
Distance: 11.6 miles out and back
Hiking time: 4 to 6 hours
Difficulty: Difficult; steep ascent to the base of Three Fingered Jack
Best season: July through Oct
Other trail users: Equestrians
Canine compatibility: Dogs permitted
Land status: National forest and wilderness area
Nearest town: Sisters

Fees and permits: Wilderness permit (free) required. Northwest Forest Pass (small fee) also required. Purchase a pass online at www.fs.usda.gov/main/r6/passes-permits/recreation or by calling (800) 270-7504.
Schedule: Open June through Oct
Maps: Maptech CD: Coos Bay/Eugene/Bend, OR; USGS: Three Fingered Jack, OR
Trail contact: Deschutes National Forest, Sisters Ranger District, Pine Street and Highway 20, Sisters, OR 97759; (541) 549-7700; fs.usda.gov/main/centraloregon/home.

Finding the trailhead: From Sisters travel 20.4 miles west on US 20 to a gravel parking area on the north side of the road and a trailhead for the Pacific Crest Trail. *DeLorme: Oregon Atlas & Gazetteer:* Page 50 A1. GPS: N44 25.527 / W121 50.959

The Hike

The ragged spires of Three Fingered Jack—named in honor of Joaquin Murietta, an aspiring gold rusher with a mutilated, three-fingered hand—rise abruptly out of central Oregon's Mount Jefferson Wilderness to form a geologic slice of time. Hundreds of thousands of years ago, the mountain—formed by hot basaltic lava flows—resembled a broad, dome-shaped cone. Since that time, volcanic activity and glaciation have left the southern side of the peak a skeleton of its previous majesty. Today the formation is what geologists call a shield volcano.

To view this decaying volcano for yourself, walk to its base on the Pacific Crest Trail 2000. The trail, which tends to be very dusty because of the area's soft volcanic soil, starts out fairly gently as it passes through a forest of Douglas and alpine fir, blue spruce, and mountain hemlock. Scattered along the path, resembling green, grassy wigs, are large clumps of bear grass. This interesting plant is a member of the lily family. When it blooms it produces tiny white flowers in dense clusters on top of a stout, leafy stem. Bears love to dig it up and munch on its succulent roots. Native Americans wove the plant's strong leaves into sturdy baskets. Interspersed among

The jagged spires of Three Fingered Jack

these green grass islands are showy clusters of bright-purple lupine and red Indian paintbrush.

After 5.8 miles the trail arrives at the base of 7,841-foot Three Fingered Jack. From there a climbers' trail ascends steeply up the south ridge of the mountain. If you want to climb to the summit, you should have rock-climbing experience and carry the appropriate gear. There are several places where the route is narrow and rocky and, if you're not accustomed to the breathtaking exposure, likely to be difficult.

While day hikers should turn around here, backpackers can continue along the trail as it dives deeper into the wilderness. For the next 15 miles, the path parallels the Cascade Crest, switching back and forth between Deschutes and Willamette National Forests before eventually traversing the west side of 10,497-foot Mount Jefferson. The mountain forms the centerpiece of the magnificent Jefferson Wilderness, the second-most-visited wilderness area in Oregon next to the Three Sisters Wilderness. In 1806 Lewis and Clark named Mount Jefferson in honor of President Thomas Jefferson, who commissioned their famous expedition.

If you chose to continue past the turnaround point at mile 5.8, here's a list of all the trail junctions you'll find as you hike north for the next 15 miles. From the saddle on Cascade Crest, between Three Fingered Jack and Porcupine Rock at mile 7, the

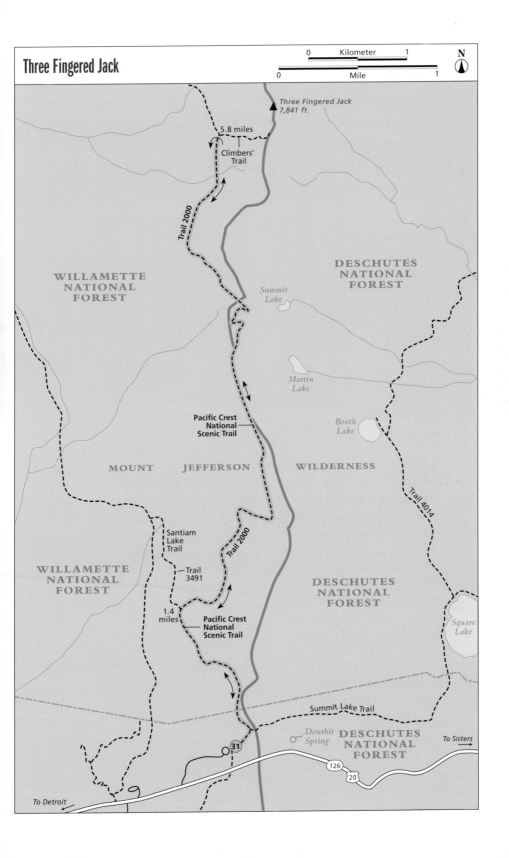

0 Kilometer 1

0 Mile 1

N

Three Fingered Jack
7,841 ft.

5.8 miles

Climbers'
Trail

Trail 2000

WILLAMETTE
NATIONAL
FOREST

DESCHUTES
NATIONAL
FOREST

Summit
Lake

Martin
Lake

Pacific Crest
National
Scenic Trail

Booth
Lake

MOUNT   JEFFERSON   WILDERNESS

Trail 4014

Santiam
Lake
Trail

Trail 2000

Trail
3491

WILLAMETTE
NATIONAL
FOREST

1.4
miles

Pacific Crest
National
Scenic Trail

DESCHUTES
NATIONAL
FOREST

Square
Lake

Summit Lake Trail

Douthit
Spring

31

DESCHUTES
NATIONAL
FOREST

To Sisters

126

20

To Detroit

trail passes around the west side of Three Fingered Jack. At mile 10.2 you'll reach the junction with the Minto Pass Trail 3437 (on your left) and the Minto Pass Tie Trail 4015 (on your right). At mile 10.7 you'll arrive at a junction on your right with Summit Lake Trail 4014. At mile 13.9 you'll reach a junction on the right with Rockpile Lake Trail 4005. At mile 14.4 you'll come to Brush Creek Trail 4004, on your right. At mile 15.4 you'll reach Swallow Lake Trail 3488 on your left. At mile 17.5 you'll intersect the Shirley Lake Trail 4003.1 on your right. Finally, at mile 20.8 you'll arrive at a junction on your left that provides an alternative route to Pamelia Lake.

Miles and Directions

0.0 Start hiking at the wooden trailhead sign adjacent to the gravel parking area. (Fill out a free self-issue wilderness permit before you go.) Walk a short distance and the trail comes to a T. Turn left and head north on Pacific Crest Trail 2000. The trail surface is very soft and dusty.

0.1 Continue straight on Pacific Crest Trail 2000.

1.4 Turn right at the trail junction and continue on Pacific Crest Trail 2000. (**Note:** The Santiam Lake Trail 3491 goes left.)

3.7 Enjoy views of Three Fingered Jack straight ahead. There's also a good view of Summit Lake.

4.0 Enjoy a good view of Black Butte to the east. The trail begins to climb steeply here on a series of switchbacks. There are several rocky sections along this stretch.

5.8 Arrive at a good spot to view the eroding spires of Three-Fingered Jack and the Climbers' Trail that travels up the south side of the mountain. This is your turnaround point. Retrace the same route back to the trailhead.

11.6 Arrive back at the trailhead.

Hike Information

Local Information

Sisters Area Chamber of Commerce, 291 E. Main Ave., Sisters, OR 97759; (866) 549-0252

Local Events and Attractions

Sisters Folk Festival, second weekend in September, Sisters; (541) 549-4979; sistersfolkfestival.org

Sisters Rodeo and Parade, second weekend in June, Sisters; (541) 549-0121; sistersrodeo.com

Restaurants

Angeline's Bakery, 121 W. Main Ave., Sisters; (541) 549-9122; angelinesbakery.com

32 Black Butte

This trail leads to the top of one of central Oregon's best-known landmarks, 6,436-foot Black Butte. The summit includes three historic fire lookouts and fantastic views of several Cascade peaks to the west. Interpretive signs en route to the summit point out native plant and tree species.

Start: The trailhead is located 15.1 miles northwest of Sisters off OR 20.
Distance: 3.8 miles out and back
Hiking time: 2 to 3 hours
Difficulty: Difficult; very steep ascent to the summit of Black Butte
Best season: June through Oct
Other trail users: Hikers only
Canine compatibility: Dogs permitted
Land status: National forest
Nearest town: Sisters

Fees and permits: Northwest Forest Pass (small fee) required. Purchase a pass online at www.fs.usda.gov/main/r6/passes-permits/recreation or by calling (800) 270-7504.
Schedule: Late May through Oct
Maps: Maptech CD: Coos Bay/Eugene/Bend, OR; USGS: Black Butte, OR
Trail contact: Deschutes National Forest, Sisters Ranger District, Pine Street and Highway 20, Sisters, OR 97759; (541) 549-7700; fs.usda.gov/main/centraloregon/home

Finding the trailhead: Travel 6 miles west of Sisters on OR 20 and turn right onto Green Ridge Road (FR 11). Go 3.8 miles to FR 1110. Turn left onto FR 1110 and travel 4.2 miles to the junction with FR 700. Turn right and continue 1.1 miles to a large parking area and the trailhead. *DeLorme: Oregon Atlas & Gazetteer:* Page 50 A4. GPS: N44 23.679 / W121 38.839

The Hike

Black Butte rises 6,436 feet above the central Oregon landscape. This well-known geological landmark, a 1.5-million-year-old stratovolcano, was created by numerous basaltic lava flows over hundreds of years. Because Black Butte stands in the rain shadow of the Cascade Mountains, it has not been exposed to the eroding forces of wind and water like its neighboring peaks and has therefore managed to maintain its conical shape.

Black Butte is located approximately 10 miles east of the village of Sisters, a typical western town established in 1888. The town's name was inspired by the Three Sisters Mountains—known to early settlers as Faith, Hope, and Charity—which rise impressively from the pine-filled valley surrounding Sisters. Before 1900 Sisters was the only settlement between Prineville and the Cascade Mountains and was an important stopping point for people traveling through the state. It was also the local supply center for farmers and ranchers. In the early 1900s the town began to grow and soon hosted a sawmill, hotel, saloon, blacksmith shop, real estate office, schoolhouse, and mercantile store.

TRAIL TIP

Black Butte's summit can be windy and cold—be sure to pack extra layers of warm clothing.

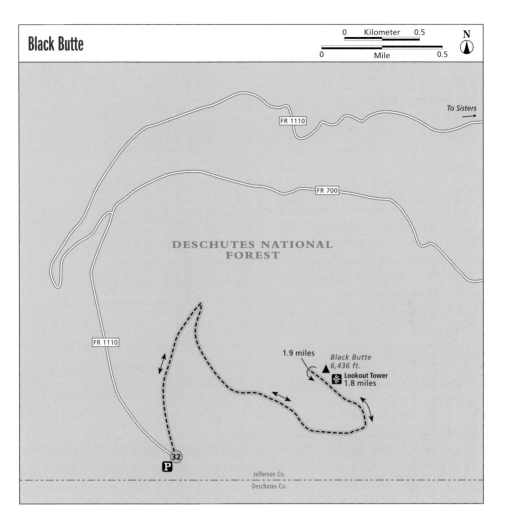

Black Butte

To Sisters

FR 1110

FR 700

DESCHUTES NATIONAL
FOREST

FR 1110

1.9 miles

Black Butte
6,436 ft.

Lookout Tower
1.8 miles

32

P

Jefferson Co.
Deschutes Co.

Some of the first explorers to pass through the Sisters area mentioned Black Butte in their journals. That old trail has most likely faded away, but today there is a relatively new path to Black Butte's summit. The 1.9-mile trail begins at the end of FR 1110 and winds through a dry, open forest of ponderosa and whitebark pine and Douglas, subalpine, and grand fir. Signposts along the trail point out these tree species as well as other indigenous plants including squaw currant, bitterbrush, and pinemat manzanita. Small groves of quaking aspens have also staked out territory along the trail. These silvery, shimmering trees have one of the largest footholds in the West and can be found from the Atlantic to the Pacific Coast. French-Canadian trappers believed that Christ's crucifix was made of aspen, which accounted for why the trees are still trembling today.

◀   *The old lookout tower at Black Butte*

After about a mile the trail becomes steeper, and soon there are gorgeous, sweeping views of Mount Washington and other Cascade peaks rising majestically to the west. At the butte's summit there are signs indicating the names and elevations of the prominent peaks. Enjoy views of Broken Top (9,175 feet), South Sister (10,350 feet), North Sister (10,085 feet), Belknap Crater (6,872 feet), and Mount Washington (7,794 feet) to the southwest; and to the northwest, views of Haystack Butte (5,523 feet), Three Fingered Jack (7,841 feet), Mount Jefferson (10,497 feet), Mount Hood (11,235 feet), and Mount Adams (12,326 feet). There are also historic fire towers you can view. Soak up the sun and the views before you turn around and head back to your vehicle.

Miles and Directions

0.0 Start hiking on the signed trail.

0.2 Check out the greenleaf manzanita (*Arctostaphylos patula*). Proceed approximately 15 yards to a sign indicating snowbrush (*Ceanothus velutinus*).

0.4 Pass a sign indicating chinquapin (*Castanopsis chrysophylla*). There's a great view of Mount Washington to the left.

0.5 Arrive at a grand fir tree (*Abies grandis*).

0.8 Notice the whitebark pine (*Pinus albicaulis*).

0.9 Walk through a grove of aspen trees (*Populus tremuloides*). Notice the grand view of Mount Washington.

1.0 Notice the Squaw currant, which is a bushy plant with geranium-like leaves.

1.1 A sign on the right points out bitter cherry (*Prunus emarginata*), a bushy plant with white, feathery tufts.

1.2 That's bitterbrush (*Purshia tridentata*) on the left.

1.5 A sign on the right points out pinemat manzanita. This ground-hugging plant resembles a green-leafed mat. A few yards up the trail, there's a subalpine fir (*Abies lasiocarpa*).

1.7 Turn right at the trail fork.

1.8 Pass the old cupola and lookout tower on your right. This historic tower, built in 1934, took more than 1,000 packhorse-loads of material to build.

1.9 Arrive at the 6,436-foot summit of Black Butte and the turnaround point.

3.8 Arrive back at the trailhead.

Hike Information

Local Information
Sisters Area Chamber of Commerce, 291 E. Main Ave., Sisters, OR 97759; (866) 549-0252

Local Events and Attractions
Sisters Folk Festival, second weekend in September, Sisters; (541) 549-4979; sistersfolkfestival.org

Sisters Rodeo and Parade, second weekend in June, Sisters; (541) 549-0121; sistersrodeo.com

Restaurants
Angeline's Bakery, 121 W. Main Ave., Sisters; (541) 549-9122; angelinesbakery.com

33 Little Belknap Crater

This stretch of the Pacific Crest Trail traverses rock-strewn, moonlike terrain on its way to the summit of Little Belknap Crater. But the effort is worth it. Along the way you pass lava rock, lava tubes, and fascinating caves. And from the summit you can enjoy views of the Three Sisters, Mount Washington, Black Crater, and many other Cascade peaks.

Start: The trailhead is located 14.9 miles west of Sisters off the McKenzie Highway (OR 242).
Distance: 7.2 miles out and back
Hiking time: 3 to 4 hours
Difficulty: Difficult; rough trail surface and significant elevation gain
Best season: July through Oct
Other trail users: Hikers only
Canine compatibility: Not dog friendly because of very sharp lava scree that can cut your dog's feet and very hot conditions with no shade or water

Land status: Wilderness area
Nearest town: Sisters
Fees and permits: A free wilderness permit required
Schedule: Open late June through Oct
Maps: Mount Washington, OR; Maptech CD: Coos Bay/Eugene/Bend, OR; USGS: Mount Washington, OR
Trail contact: Deschutes National Forest, Sisters Ranger District, Pine Street and Highway 20, Sisters, OR 97759; (541) 549-7700; fs.usda.gov/main/centraloregon/home

Finding the trailhead: From Sisters travel 14.9 miles west on the McKenzie Highway (OR 242) to the Pacific Crest Trail 2000 trailhead, located on the right (north) side of the road. (A very small "hiker" sign marks the trailhead.) **Note:** Depending on winter snow conditions, the McKenzie Highway may not open until July. *DeLorme: Oregon Atlas & Gazetteer:* Page 50 B2. GPS: N44 15.589 / W121 48.305

The Hike

The rugged character of central Oregon's lava country is nowhere better represented than on this hike to the summit of Little Belknap Crater. The rich history of the area begins with the highway to the trailhead. The McKenzie Highway (OR 242) is a gorgeous scenic byway with spectacular views of mountains, lava fields, and endless blue sky—a great introduction to the hike you're about to take.

When gold was discovered in eastern Oregon and Idaho in the 1860s, settlers made a push to find a route that connected the Willamette Valley on the west side of the Cascades to the land on the east. In 1862 Felix Scott and his brother Marion led a party of forty men, sixty oxen, and 900 head of cattle and horses across McKenzie Pass, blazing what would later become the Scott Trail. An extremely rough trail, the Scott Trail required almost five days to travel from Eugene in the Willamette Valley to the small town of Sisters in central Oregon. For future travelers, a toll road was built

Ken Sheen hiking to the summit of Little Belknap Crater

in 1872 that traveled up Lost Creek Canyon, traversed the rough lava beds, and ended at the Deschutes River.

Today the road is paved and toll-free. It also happens to pass the Dee Wright Observatory (11 miles west of Sisters), built by the Civilian Conservation Corp and named for an early 1900s Forest Service packer and mountain guide. The observatory's arched windows frame eleven Cascade peaks. A paved half-mile walkway offers an easy means to explore the eerie moonscape of the Belknap lava flow. The trail is complemented by interpretive signs detailing the area's unique geology. Signs of the old McKenzie Highway, which once crossed the flow, are visible from this vantage point.

When you've had enough of the observatory, continue on to the trailhead for Little Belknap Crater. The trail (95 percent of which is the Pacific Crest Trail), leads through the heart of the Mount Washington Wilderness and its rugged lava formations, craters, and extinct volcanoes. The route begins rather innocently as it winds through an open forest. But within a mile, things change drastically. Soon the forest is replaced by a grayish-black lava flow practically devoid of life, except for the rare hardy tree that has managed to sink its roots through the jumbled basalt rocks.

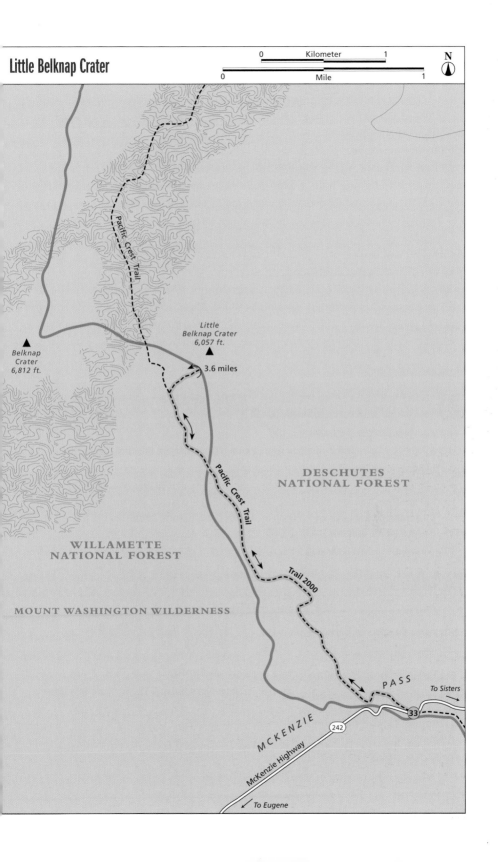

0   Kilometer   1

0   Mile   1

N

Pacific Crest Trail

Little
Belknap Crater
6,057 ft.

3.6 miles

Belknap
Crater
6,812 ft.

Pacific Crest Trail

DESCHUTES
NATIONAL FOREST

WILLAMETTE
NATIONAL FOREST

Trail 2000

MOUNT WASHINGTON WILDERNESS

PASS

To Sisters

33

MCKENZIE

242

McKenzie Highway

To Eugene

The flow was created more than 2,900 years ago when hot liquid basalt poured from Belknap Crater, the large cinder cone to the west. Approximately twenty years later a second eruption sprung out of Little Belknap Crater, located directly north of the trailhead. A third phase of eruptions occurred a little more than a thousand years later from the northeast base of Belknap Crater, releasing lava 9 miles west into the McKenzie River Valley.

After 3 miles of hiking through this mysterious maze of rock, you come to a trail junction and go right. In 0.3 mile you pass a deep lava tube on your left. If you approach the edge of the tube and look in (be careful—it's quite a drop-off), you can feel the cool air escaping from deep within the earth.

From the lava tube, hike a steep and dramatic 0.1 mile to the top of Little Belknap Crater. The trail surface is loose and crumbly, and piles of gray rock mingle with the bright-red cinders that form much of the crater. When you reach the top, you can enjoy magnificent views of Belknap Crater, Mount Washington, Black Crater, and the Three Sisters Mountains. The summit of Little Belknap Crater is your turnaround point. If you're backpacking, continue on the Pacific Crest Trail as it winds its way north through the magnificent lava country of the Mount Washington Wilderness.

Miles and Directions

0.0 Start hiking on the signed Pacific Crest Trail 2000. (**Note:** Be sure to fill out the free self-issue wilderness permit at the trailhead.)

1.0 Begin walking on the lava flow.

3.2 Come to a trail junction and turn right to hike to the summit of Little Belknap Crater.

3.5 Pass a lava tube on your left.

3.6 Reach the summit and enjoy sweeping views of Belknap Crater, Mount Washington, Black Crater, and the Three Sisters. Turn around here and retrace your route back to the trailhead. **Option:** Continue north on the Pacific Crest Trail and explore more of the Mount Washington Wilderness.

7.2 Arrive back at the trailhead.

Hike Information

Local Information

Sisters Area Chamber of Commerce, 291 E. Main Ave., Sisters, OR 97759; (866) 549-0252

Local Events and Attractions

Sisters Folk Festival, second weekend in September, Sisters; (541) 549-4979; sistersfolkfestival.org

Sisters Rodeo and Parade, second weekend in June, Sisters; (541) 549-0121; sistersrodeo.com

Restaurants

Angeline's Bakery, 121 W. Main Ave., Sisters; (541) 549-9122; angelinesbakery.com

34 Black Crater

This trail winds its way through a mountain-hemlock forest to the craggy red-cinder summit of Black Crater. At the prominent summit you can enjoy sweeping views of the snow-topped Three Sisters Mountains, Mount Washington, and the surrounding lava flows and craters that make up the Mount Washington Wilderness. The walk to the top is tough, but the view of the surrounding central Oregon volcanic landscape is well worth the effort.

Start: The trailhead is located 11.5 miles west of Sisters on the McKenzie Highway (OR 242).
Distance: 8.4 miles out and back
Hiking time: 4 to 6 hours
Difficulty: Difficult; very strenuous climb to the summit of Black Crater
Best season: July through Oct
Other trail users: Hikers only
Canine compatibility: Dogs permitted
Land status: Wilderness area
Nearest town: Sisters

Fees and permits: Wilderness permit (free) required. Wilderness permits are self-issued and can be found at the trailhead.
Schedule: Open late June through Oct
Maps: Maptech CD: Coos Bay/Eugene/Bend, OR; USGS: Black Crater, OR; Mount Washington, OR
Trail contact: Deschutes National Forest, Sisters Ranger District, Pine Street and Highway 20, Sisters, OR 97759; (541) 549-7700; fs.usda.gov/main/centraloregon/home

Finding the trailhead: From Sisters travel 11.5 miles west on the McKenzie Highway (OR 242) to the Black Crater trailhead, on the left (south) side of the road. **Note:** Depending on winter snow conditions, the McKenzie Highway may not open until July. *Delorme: Oregon Atlas & Gazetteer:* Page 50 B2. GPS: N44 17.085 / W121 45.947

The Hike

Central Oregon is truly the land of volcanoes, and the Sisters vicinity is perhaps its most shining example. One incredible hike is along the Black Crater Trail, which leads to the summit of 7,251-foot Black Crater. The difficult path, which climbs to the craggy, double-pinnacled summit, is a test of both strength and endurance.

The trail begins as a series of switchbacks through a mountain-hemlock forest. Mountain hemlock can be found growing at elevations of 3,500 to 6,000 feet and is often confused with western hemlock. The hardy tree is differentiated from the western hemlock by its thick needles that fan out in bushy clusters. It also has 2-inch-long cones and blue-green foliage. In contrast, the western hemlock has flat needles that are shaped in an open spray, cones that are an inch or less in length, and yellow-green foliage. Mountain hemlocks are also characterized by their deep, furrowed bark and are usually the first trees to grow at timberline. It's not uncommon for a mature branch to touch the ground and take root as a new tree. The parent tree then shelters the new tree from the harsh high-altitude environment.

Nice views of the Three Sisters Mountains from the summit of Black Crater

As you hike up this trail, bright-purple lupine and vibrant-red Indian paintbrush decorate the grassy hillside meadows. After about 3 miles the trail emerges from the thick forest for great views to the north of Mount Jefferson and Mount Hood. As you climb higher notice the crooked whitebark pine trees (shaped by the prevailing southeasterly winds). Inhabiting elevations above 5,500 feet, these tough trees are sprinkled across hundreds of miles of high-country landscape from central British Columbia to California and as far east as Wyoming. At the edge of the tree line, these trees grow 40 to 80 feet tall and have thick, stout trunks with widespread branches. Above timberline, whitebark pines take on a totally different appearance. Growing to heights of only 5 to 12 feet, the trees become more shrublike. The branches and trunk are often twisted and bent and are known as krummholzes—German for "crooked wood." At higher elevations the trees become even smaller and are often referred to as alpine scrub.

As the trail nears the summit, it crosses an alpine-like meadow sprinkled with purple, yellow, and white bouquets of wildflowers. At the summit are two prominent pinnacles that rise above the crater. From these spires you can enjoy a panoramic view of the Three Sisters to the south and Belknap Crater and Mounts Washington, Jefferson, and Hood to the north. The spectacular scenery makes it obvious why so many other hikers are attracted to this spot. If you're looking for solitude, hike the trail on a weekday.

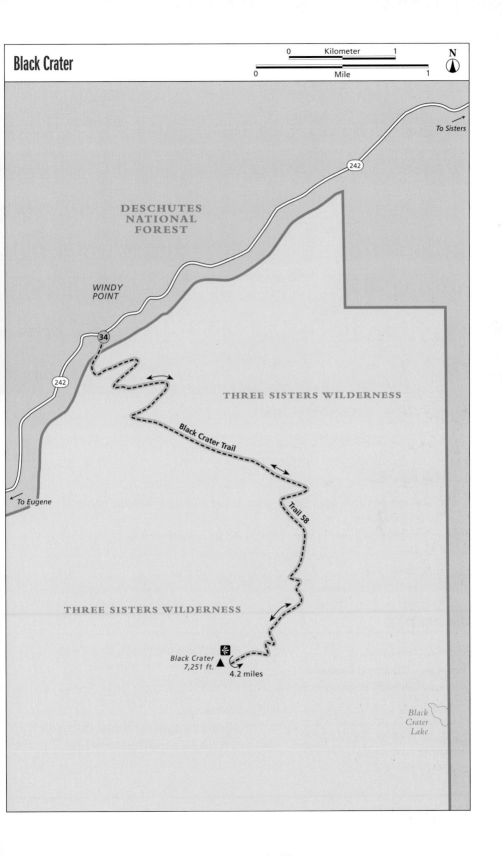

Black Crater

0   Kilometer   1

0   Mile   1

N

DESCHUTES
NATIONAL
FOREST

To Sisters

242

WINDY
POINT

34

242

THREE SISTERS WILDERNESS

Black Crater Trail

To Eugene

Trail 58

THREE SISTERS WILDERNESS

Black Crater
7,251 ft.

4.2 miles

Black
Crater
Lake

View of the Black Crater trail from the summit

Miles and Directions

0.0 Start hiking on Black Crater Trail 58. (**Note:** Be sure to fill out a free wilderness permit at the trailhead sign.)

3.3 Enjoy spectacular views of Mount Jefferson and Mount Hood to the north.

4.2 Reach the summit and your turnaround point. Retrace the same route back to your starting point.

8.4 Arrive back at the trailhead.

Hike Information

Local Information

Sisters Area Chamber of Commerce, 291 E. Main Ave., Sisters, OR 97759; (866) 549-0252

Local Events and Attractions

Sisters Folk Festival, second weekend in September, Sisters; (541) 549-4979; sistersfolkfestival.org

Sisters Rodeo and Parade, second weekend in June, Sisters; (541) 549-0121; sistersrodeo.com

Restaurants

Angeline's Bakery, 121 W. Main Ave., Sisters; (541) 549-9122; angelinesbakery.com

35 Tam McArthur Rim

Tam McArthur Rim is a wide-open ridge that captures the true beauty of the high alpine country of the Three Sisters Wilderness. From a vantage point high on this prominent ridge, you'll have a lifetime's worth of views of many well-known Cascade peaks such as the Three Sisters Mountains and Broken Top to the west, Mount Washington and Mount Jefferson to the northwest, and Mount Bachelor to the south.

Start: The trailhead is located 15.6 miles south of Sisters on FR 16.
Distance: 5.0 miles out and back
Hiking time: 2.5 to 3.5 hours
Difficulty: Difficult; steep ascent on multiple switchbacks
Best season: July through Oct
Other trail users: Hikers only
Canine compatibility: Dogs permitted
Land status: National forest and wilderness area

Nearest town: Sisters
Fees and permits: Wilderness permit (free) required. Wilderness permits are self-issued and available at the trailhead.
Schedule: Open late June through Oct
Maps: Maptech CD: Coos Bay/Eugene/Bend, OR; USGS: Tumalo Falls, OR; Broken Top, OR
Trail contact: Deschutes National Forest, Sisters Ranger District, Pine Street and Highway 20, Sisters, OR 97759; (541) 549-7700; fs.usda.gov/main/centraloregon/home

Finding the trailhead: From US 20 in Sisters, turn south onto Elm Street (FR 16). Head 15.6 miles south (the road becomes gravel after 14 miles) to the trailhead parking area located on the left side of the road at Three Creek Lake. *DeLorme: Oregon Atlas & Gazetteer:* Page 50 C4. GPS: N44 06.064 / W121 37.250

The Hike

Located south of Sisters and east of Broken Top, Tam McArthur Rim is a windswept ridge offering outstanding views of Three Sisters country. This broad ridge is home to twisted whitebark pines that somehow manage to survive the brutal winds and harsh winters that frequent this moonlike landscape.

The Tam McArthur Rim Trail begins adjacent to Three Creek Lake, which resides in a basin carved by Ice Age glaciers and is a popular summer recreation spot for those living and visiting central Oregon. It's stocked with rainbow and brook trout raised at the Wizard Falls Fish Hatchery northwest of Sisters. To the west of Three Creek Lake is Little Three Creek Lake, which can be reached via a 2.2-mile round-trip trail from Driftwood Campground. Mountain bikes are allowed on the trail to Little Three Creek Lake but not on the Tam McArthur Rim Trail.

Tam McArthur Rim takes its name from Lewis A. "Tam" McArthur, author of *Oregon Geographic Names.* Interest in Oregon ran deep in the McArthur family. Both of Tam's grandfathers were involved in surveying Oregon and in Oregon politics.

You can enjoy many nice views of the Central Cascade Mountains from Tam McArthur Rim.

Born in The Dalles, Oregon, on April 27, 1883, McArthur worked for the Pacific Power & Light Company from 1923 to 1946. He also served as secretary to the Oregon Geographic Board from 1914 to 1949. It was during this time that the idea of writing a book about Oregon's geographic names took shape. The first edition of *Oregon Geographic Names* was published in 1928. Today the book is in its sixth edition and is edited by McArthur's son, Lewis L. McArthur. After McArthur passed away in 1951, Robert W. Sawyer, a good friend of McArthur, named the prominent ridge above Three Creeks Lake in his honor.

Begin this hike by heading south on steep switchbacks through a fir forest lined with grassy meadows and purple lupine. As the trail climbs, there are many opportunities to view the Three Creek Lake basin to the east. When the path reaches the ridge crest, at mile 1.8, it forks. At this point the landscape is wide open, with occasional groups of tough whitebark pines. The views are endless. Go right at the intersection and hike another mile to a high point on the ridge. From there you can enjoy spectacular views of the Three Creek Lake basin to the east, the Three Sisters

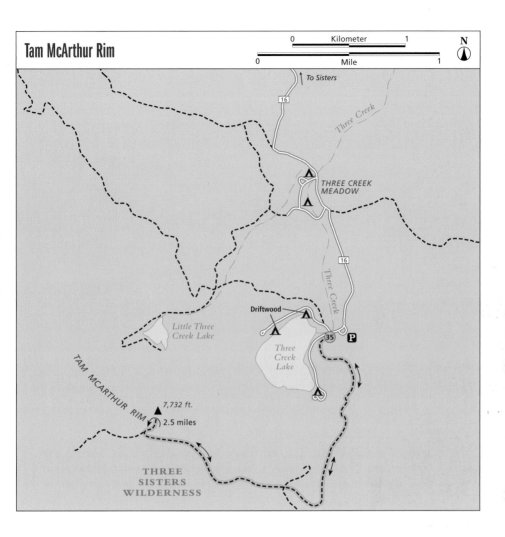

Tam McArthur Rim

To Sisters

16

Three Creek

THREE CREEK
MEADOW

16

Three Creek

Driftwood

Little Three
Creek Lake

35

P

Three
Creek
Lake

TAM MCARTHUR RIM

▲ 7,732 ft.
2.5 miles

THREE
SISTERS
WILDERNESS

Mountains and Broken Top to the west, Mount Washington and Mount Jefferson to the northwest, and Mount Bachelor to the south. From here it's all downhill. Turn around and head back to the trailhead the same way you came.

Miles and Directions

0.0 Start hiking on a steep uphill at the wooden trailhead sign for Tam McArthur Rim 4078. The sign indicates that it is 2.5 miles to the summit viewpoint. (**Note:** This trail climbs steeply the first 0.8 mile through a high alpine forest. Open meadows, old tree logs, and bright-purple lupine line the trail. The trail leads you to the top of the wide-open, windswept ridge where whitebark pine thrives. Follow the trail west along the dramatic ridgeline. Along the way spur trails will head off the trail. Continue on the main trail, ignoring these spurs.)

Sweeping views of the high country from the Tam McArthur Rim Trail

1.8 At the trail fork, turn right.

2.3 Turn right at an unmarked trail intersection.

2.5 Arrive at a spectacular viewpoint. From this gorgeous vantage point, you'll have views of the Three Creek Lake Basin to the east, Broken Top and the Three Sisters Mountains to the west, Mount Washington and Mount Jefferson to the northwest, and Mount Bachelor to the south. After enjoying the mesmerizing view, head back on the same route to your starting point.

5.0 Arrive back at the trailhead.

Hike Information

Local Information
Sisters Area Chamber of Commerce, 291 E. Main Ave., Sisters, OR 97759; (866) 549-0252

Local Events and Attractions
Sisters Folk Festival, second weekend in September, Sisters; (541) 549-4979; sistersfolkfestival.org

Sisters Rodeo and Parade, second weekend in June, Sisters; (541) 549-0121; www.sistersrodeo.com

Restaurants
Angeline's Bakery, 121 W. Main Ave., Sisters; (541) 549-9122; angelinesbakery.com

36 South Sister

This is a hike of a lifetime—long, tough, and with high alpine scenery and spectacular summit views. The trek up 10,358-foot South Sister, the crown jewel of the Three Sisters Wilderness, is well worth the hard work. The trail starts out by heading through the high, open Wickiup Plain on the way to Lewis Glacier and, finally, the summit crater. At the peak you'll find gorgeous views of Middle and North Sister to the north and Green Lakes, Mount Bachelor, and Broken Top to the southeast. The weather on South Sister is notoriously erratic, so be prepared for anything. If the skies look threatening, don't attempt to reach the summit. Keep in mind that you may find snow on the summit as late as mid-July. If you climb the peak before the snow melts, you'll need waterproof mountaineering boots and an ice ax.

Start: The trailhead is at Devils Lake, located 28.5 miles west of Bend on the Cascade Lakes Highway (OR 46).
Distance: 11.0 miles out and back
Hiking time: 7 to 9 hours
Difficulty: Difficult; a steep, unrelenting climb to the summit of South Sister
Best season: Aug through Oct
Other trail users: Hikers only
Canine compatibility: Dogs permitted. However it is not dog friendly because of the lava scree at the top of the mountain that is very sharp and will cut your dog's feet. If you do take your dog, be sure that he has foot protection.

Land status: Wilderness area
Nearest town: Bend
Fees and permits: A free wilderness permit is required. A Northwest Forest Pass (small fee) is required. You can purchase a pass online at www.fs.usda.gov/main/r6/passes-permits/recreation or by calling (800) 270-7504.
Schedule: Open late June through Oct
Maps: Maptech CD: Coos Bay/Eugene/Bend, OR; USGS: South Sister, OR
Trail contact: Deschutes National Forest Supervisor's Office, 63095 Deschutes Market Rd., Bend, OR 97701; (541) 383-5300; fs.usda.gov/main/centraloregon/home

Finding the trailhead: From Bend travel 28.5 miles west on the Cascade Lakes Highway (OR 46) to the Devils Lake Trailhead located on the left side of the highway. *DeLorme: Oregon Atlas & Gazetteer:* Page 50 D2. GPS: N44 02.066 / W121 45.924

The Hike

The Deschutes National Forest encompasses 1.6 million acres in central Oregon. The diverse woodland is home to lofty volcanic peaks, interesting lava formations, alpine lakes and forest, and sagebrush- and juniper-covered plateaus and canyons. Some of Oregon's highest peaks are found in this area, including the centerpieces of the 242,400-acre Three Sisters Wilderness: 10,085-foot North Sister, 10,047-foot Middle Sister, and 10,358-foot South Sister. More than 260 miles of trails, including 40 miles of the Pacific Crest Trail, wind through this scenic wilderness area.

You can enjoy a stunning view of Middle and North Sister as well as the rest of the cascade range from the summit of South Sister.

Early settlers to the area called the North, Middle, and South Sister Mountains Faith, Hope, and Charity, but these names never gained official recognition. Geologists believe each peak is a separate volcano. Some mountaineers have dubbed the oldest mountain, North Sister, "the Black Beast of the Cascades" because of the difficult route to its summit. The eroding mountain was once a broad shield volcano almost 20 miles wide and 8,000 feet tall. Eruptions added another 3,000 feet, but over the past 300,000 years it has suffered serious erosion. Middle Sister is the second oldest of the three. Though it's the smallest of the three peaks, it has the most symmetrical cone. Situated on the peak's western slope is the impressive Collier Glacier, a 1.5-mile-long ice sheet that has been shrinking for the past hundred years.

Its cone still filled with ice and snow, South Sister is the baby of the trio. It's thought to date back to the late Pleistocene era. During the warmer months of the summer, portions of the summit's ice and snow melt into a brilliant aqua-blue lake called Teardrop Pool. South Sister is also home to Oregon's largest glacier, Prouty, named for climber Harley Prouty, who served as president of the Mazamas, a Portland-based mountaineering group. He was the first person to ascend Prouty Pinnacles on

North Sister in August 1910 and is thought to be the first person to reach the summit of North Sister.

It's possible to reach South Sister's summit on a very strenuous out-and-back day hike, but most people like to take it slow and camp along the way. Whatever you decide, begin at the Devils Lake trailhead and start out climbing a steep series of switchbacks through a thick fir forest. After 2 miles you arrive at a junction. If you're climbing to the summit (on a day hike), continue straight. If you're planning to camp for the night, turn right and continue half a mile to Moraine Lake and its twenty-three designated campsites. Watch your step here—the land is very delicate and vulnerable to misuse. Practice zero-impact camping, and make every effort to preserve the integrity of the area.

A spur trail leads around the lake and up a canyon and then rejoins the South Sister Trail. Back at the junction (2 miles from the trailhead), continue across the wide-open Wickiup Plain—*wickiup* is the Native American term for a wigwam or tepee. This open alpine landscape is characterized by small islands of trees, long lava ridges, and smooth, glacier-carved basins.

At mile 4.4 you'll arrive at the southern tip of Lewis Glacier, named for explorer Meriwether Lewis, who traveled through Oregon in 1805 with his famous partner, William Clark. Stay to the left of the small lake at the base of the glacier and follow a steep and rocky trail a little over a mile to the south rim of South Sister Crater. From there continue 0.2 mile on the Rim Trail to the true summit. Or, if there is still snow in the crater, access the summit by traversing the snowfield. On the way you'll pass Teardrop Pool, the state's highest lake.

The scenery at the summit is fantastic. On a clear day Mount Rainier is visible 180 miles to the north in Washington. There are also inspiring views of the Chambers Lakes and Middle and North Sisters to the north and of Green Lake, Mount Bachelor, and Broken Top to the southeast. It's often cold and windy at the summit, so bring extra clothing, plenty of food and water, and aspirin if you are prone to altitude sickness.

Miles and Directions

0.0   Start at the Devils Lake trailhead.

0.1   The trail intersects the Cascade Lakes Highway (OR 46). Cross the highway and continue on the singletrack trail on the other side.

2.0   Continue straight (left) at the trail junction. (**Note:** If you turn right, you'll arrive at Moraine Lake in 0.5 mile. Moraine Lake has designated campsites if you want to stay overnight.)

TRAIL TIP

If you're planning to camp overnight at Moraine Lake, bring mosquito repellent to ward off the swarms.

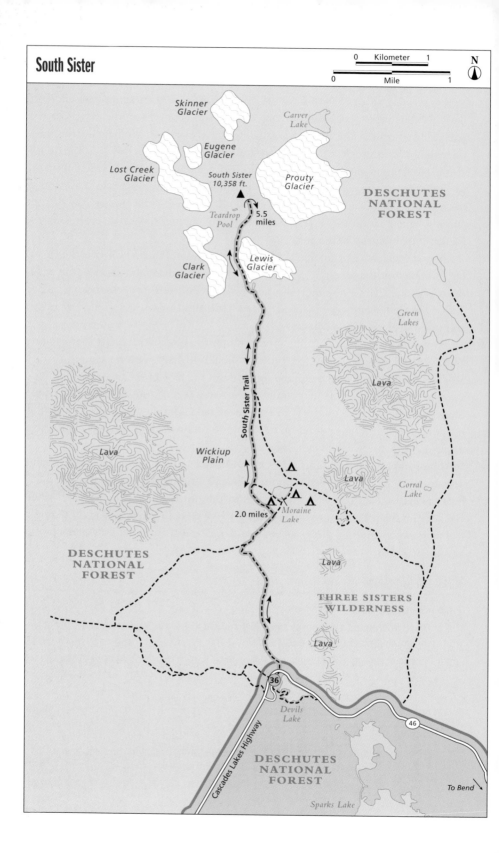

South Sister

Snow on the summit crater

4.4 Arrive at the southern tip of Lewis Glacier. From this point stay to the left of the glacier on an unofficial trail. The trail is very steep, and as you near the summit, it becomes loose scree.

5.3 Arrive at the south rim of South Sister Crater. Hike another 0.2 mile on the rim trail to reach the true summit.

5.5 Reach the true summit of South Sister and your turnaround point. Enjoy views of 10,047-foot Middle Sister, 10,085-foot North Sister, and Chambers Lakes to the north and 9,152-foot Broken Top and Green Lakes to the southeast. Retrace the same route back to the trailhead.

11.0 Arrive back at the trailhead.

Hike Information

Local Information

Visit Bend, 750 NW Lava Rd., Suite 160, Bend, OR 97701; (877) 245-8484; visitbend.com

Local Events and Attractions

High Desert Museum, 59800 S. Highway 97, Bend, OR 97702; (541) 382-4754; highdesertmuseum.org

Restaurants

Deschutes Brewery Bend Public House, 1044 NW Bond St., Bend; (541) 382-9242; deschutesbrewery.com

37 Benham Falls to Slough Meadow

This route follows the southern segment of the Deschutes River Trail. It takes you through a magnificent old-growth ponderosa pine forest along the banks of the moody Deschutes River. Highlights of the route include a spectacular viewpoint of Benham Falls, grand views of South Sister and Broken Top, and opportunities to see osprey and other wildlife.

Start: The trailhead is located 15.2 miles northwest of Bend off US 97.

Distance: 4.6 miles out and back (with longer options)

Hiking time: 2 to 3 hours

Difficulty: Easy; smooth trail surface and minimal elevation gain

Best season: May through Oct

Other trail users: Mountain bikers (on the multiuse trail only)

Canine compatibility: Leashed dogs permitted

Land status: National forest

Nearest town: Bend

Schedule: Year-round

Maps: Maptech CD: Coos Bay/Eugene/Bend, OR; USGS: Benham Falls, OR

Fees and permits: A Northwest Forest Pass is required. You can purchase a pass online at www.fs.usda.gov/main/r6/passes-permits/recreation or by calling (800) 270-7504.

Trail contact: Deschutes National Forest Supervisor's Office, 63095 Deschutes Market Rd., Bend, OR 97701; (541) 383-5300; fs.usda.gov/main/centraloregon/home

Finding the trailhead: From the intersection of Northwest Franklin and US 97 in Bend, travel 11.2 miles south on US 97 to a sign that indicates Lava Lands Visitor Center. Turn right (west) onto the entrance road and then take an immediate left onto FR 9702 where a sign indicates Deschutes River 4/Benham Falls 4. Continue 4 miles to a gravel parking area at the road's end at the Benham Falls Day-Use Area. DeLorme: Oregon Atlas & Gazetteer: Page 45 A5. GPS: N43 55.815 / W121 24.720

The Hike

This route starts at the picturesque Benham Falls day-use picnic area that is set among towering old-growth ponderosa pine trees. The day-use area has picnic tables, fire rings, and restrooms. You'll begin the hike by walking on a forested path along the shores of the Deschutes River. The river is very quiet and wide along this section because of a man-made logjam that is present above the wooden bridge that crosses the river. This logjam was built in the 1920s to help protect bridge pilings from debris floating down the river. Plants and grass have grown on top of the logs, creating an "almost" natural dam on the river. At 0.1 mile you'll cross the river over a long wooden bridge. Over the next 0.5 mile you'll walk on a wide multiuse path that is popular with mountain bikers. At 0.7 mile you'll turn off the multiuse path onto a hiking trail that follows the contours of the river.

As you approach Benham Falls, the character of the river changes from slow and meandering to fast and furious as the river channel narrows. At 0.8 mile you'll arrive

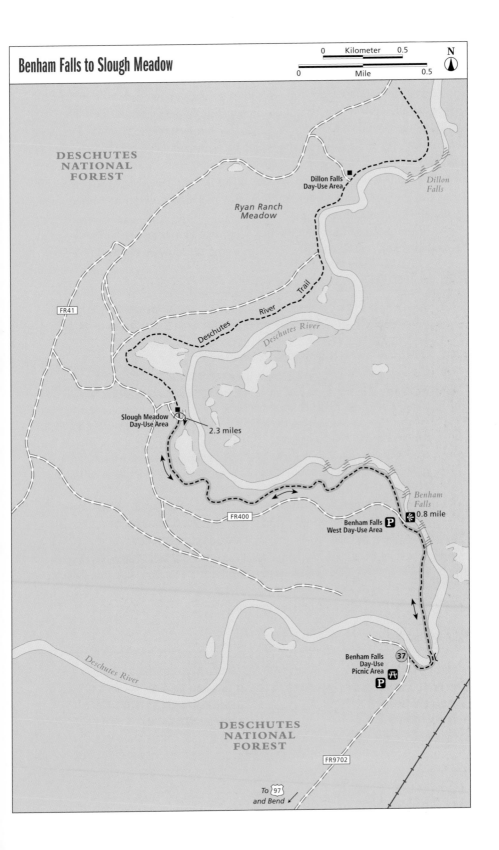

0   Kilometer   0.5

0   Mile   0.5

N

DESCHUTES
NATIONAL
FOREST

Dillon Falls
Day-Use Area

Dillon
Falls

Ryan Ranch
Meadow

Trail

River

Deschutes

Deschutes River

FR41

Slough Meadow
Day-Use Area

2.3 miles

FR400

Benham
Falls

0.8 mile

Benham Falls
West Day-Use Area

Deschutes River

Benham Falls
Day-Use
Picnic Area

37

DESCHUTES
NATIONAL
FOREST

FR9702

To 97
and Bend

at a spectacular viewpoint of Benham Falls. The river roars over jagged lava through a narrow canyon. From here the route continues along the shores of the river, where you'll have views of a magnificent lava flow on the opposite side of the river and spectacular views of South Sister and Broken Top. Osprey feed and nest along this section of the river. Also known as "fish hawks," they feed on the large stocks of trout present in the river. You can identify osprey by their predominantly white undersides and black markings on the top of their wings. Their heads are white, with a distinctive black band across their eyes and cheeks. Look for their nests, which are usually located in the tops of dead trees. At 2.3 miles you'll arrive at your turnaround point at Slough Meadow Day-Use Area.

If you are interested in a longer hike, you have the option of continuing on the Deschutes River Trail for another 6.2 miles to the Meadow Picnic Area.

Miles and Directions

0.0   Start by hiking on the trail signed DESCHUTES RIVER TRAIL NO. 2.1, which begins at the river's edge opposite the picnic area. Another sign indicates BENHAM FALLS ½ / DILLON FALLS 3½ / LAVA ISLAND FALLS 7, MEADOW DAY USE 8½.

0.1   Cross a long wooden bridge over the Deschutes River.

0.6   Veer right on the hiking trail, indicated by a hiker symbol.

0.7   The hiking trail intersects the wide biking trail. Turn right and continue on the narrower hiking trail. Proceed about 200 yards to a T intersection. Turn right and descend to a viewpoint of Benham Falls. (If you go left at this junction, you'll arrive at the Benham West Day-Use Area, which has restrooms).

0.8   Arrive at a scenic viewpoint of Benham Falls. After enjoying the view, turn around and head uphill on the same trail to a trail junction. Turn right where a sign indicates SLOUGH MEADOW 1.5 MILES.

0.9   Arrive at an interpretive sign on the right that describes the geology of this area. At this point you'll also have spectacular views of Broken Top and South Sister.

1.1   Turn right and continue on the hiking trail, indicated by a hiker symbol.

2.3   Arrive at the Slough Meadow Day-Use Area (your turnaround point). **Option:** You can continue another 6.2 miles on the Deschutes River Trail to the Meadow Picnic Area. Retrace the same route back to the trailhead.

4.6   Arrive back at the Benham Falls Day-Use Area.

Hike Information

Local Information

Visit Bend, 750 NW Lava Rd., Suite 160, Bend, OR 97701; (877) 245-8484; visitbend.com

Local Events and Attractions

High Desert Museum, 59800 S. Highway 97, Bend, OR 97702; (541) 382-4754; highdesertmuseum.org

38 Paulina Peak

This hike to the top of Paulina Peak begins with an easy jaunt through a beautiful pine and fir forest. But don't be deceived. After half a mile things get steep and you'll have to shift gears for the thigh-burning ascent to the summit. There, 7,984 feet above sea level, you'll be rewarded with gorgeous views of Paulina and East Lakes, Newberry Caldera, and the Big Obsidian lava flow.

Start: From the Crater Rim Trail 57 trailhead, located 36.2 miles southeast of Bend off Paulina Lake Road (FR 21).
Distance: 6.0 miles out and back
Hiking time: 3.5 to 4.5 hours
Difficulty: Difficult; steep ascent to summit of Paulina Peak and significant elevation gain
Best season: July through Oct
Other trail users: Hikers only
Canine compatibility: Leashed dogs permitted
Land status: National monument
Nearest town: Bend

Schedule: Open late June through Oct
Fees and permits: There is a day-use entrance fee to the national monument. You can also purchase 3-day Newberry National Volcanic Monument Pass.
Maps: Maptech CD: Coos Bay/Eugene/Bend, OR; USGS: Paulina Peak, OR
Trail contact: Deschutes National Forest Supervisor's Office, 63095 Deschutes Market Rd., Bend, OR 97701; (541) 383-5300; fs.usda.gov/main/centraloregon/home

Finding the trailhead: From the intersection of Greenwood Avenue and US 97 in Bend, travel south on US 97 for 23 miles to a sign for Newberry National Volcanic Monument and Paulina and East Lakes. Turn left on Paulina Lake Road (FR 21) and drive 13.2 miles to the visitor center. The trailhead is 50 feet before the visitor center on the right side of the road. *DeLorme: Oregon Atlas & Gazetteer:* Page 45 C7. GPS: N43 42.675 / W121 16.463

The Hike

Established in 1990, the 55,000-acre Newberry National Volcanic Monument showcases Newberry Caldera, a 500-square-mile volcanic crater. This area is absolutely teeming with geologic history. You'll find hot springs, lava flows, and cinder cones, all of which can be explored on well-established trails.

One particularly noteworthy trail is the 3.0-mile path to the summit of 7,984-foot Paulina Peak, the highest point in the monument. The trail begins just to the right of the visitor center in a lodgepole pine forest—the straight and slender lodgepole pines grow in thick stands and are distinguished by their prickly cones and pairs of 2-inch-long needles. After half a mile over fairly flat terrain, the path begins a steep climb. The higher it gets, the better the views become, and soon you'll see Paulina and East Lakes below. At the summit you'll find restrooms and, sadly for some, a large parking lot. Yes, you can choose to drive to the top via FR 500.

Summit views of Paulina Lake (on the left) and East Lake (on the right)

Rising prominently from Paulina Lake, Paulina Peak offers spectacular views of the mountains and high desert country of central Oregon. The peak is what remains of ancient Mount Newberry, which, at 10,000 feet above sea level, was once the highest volcano in the Paulina Mountains. About 200,000 years ago Newberry erupted and collapsed. The huge caldera left in its place eventually filled with water to create an enormous lake. Thousands of years later, more eruptions split the water into two separate lakes (Paulina and East) and left a central cone and several obsidian flows. The most recent eruption, which occurred about 1,300 years ago, resulted in the Big Obsidian lava flow (see Hike 39), visible to the east.

Despite the area's remarkable geologic history, it's the wildlife that often proves to be the biggest draw here. Each year the Oregon Fish and Wildlife Service stocks more than 200,000 trout and salmon in Paulina and East Lakes to satisfy the annual onslaught of 60,000 anglers. Campers must fend off black bears in search of edible delicacies in coolers and trailers. Other wild critters include badgers, deer, elks, and pine martens, as well as a variety of chipmunks and squirrels.

Before you trek to the top of Paulina Peak, stop in at the visitor center near the trailhead. There you'll find informative brochures (including advice on what to do about the bears), the lowdown on camping, and ideas on other things to see and do while in the monument. Other recommended hikes in the monument are the 7.5-mile Paulina Lakeshore Trail (you can access the trail from Paulina Lake Campground) and the Big Obsidian Flow Trail (see Hike 39).

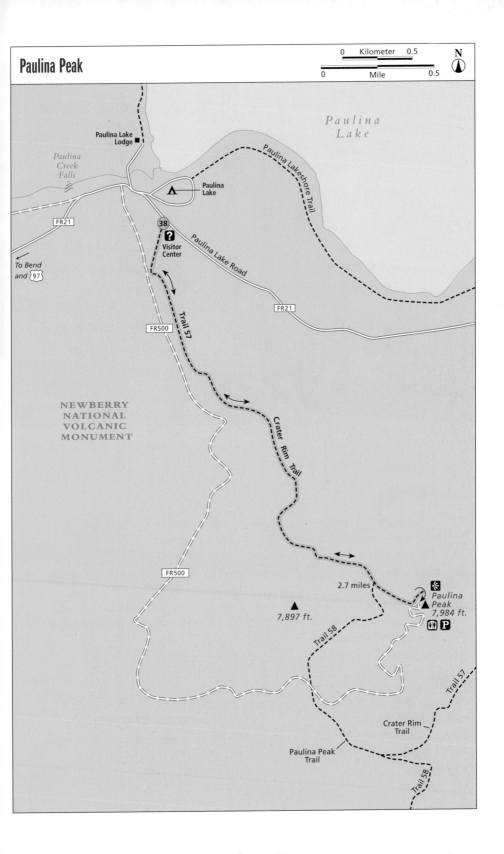

Paulina Peak

Paulina Lake

Paulina Lake Lodge

Paulina Creek Falls

Paulina Lake

FR21

Visitor Center

38

Paulina Lake Road

To Bend and 97

FR500

Trail 57

FR21

Paulina Lakeshore Trail

NEWBERRY NATIONAL VOLCANIC MONUMENT

Crater Rim Trail

FR500

2.7 miles

7,897 ft.

Paulina Peak
7,984 ft.

Trail 58

Trail 57

Crater Rim Trail

Paulina Peak Trail

Trail 58

Paulina Creek Falls

Miles and Directions

0.0 Start at the Paulina Peak trailhead sign, located approximately 50 feet to the right of the visitor center. The sign reads CRATER RIM TRAIL #57, PAULINA PEAK 3 MILES.

1.5 Enjoy good views of Paulina and East Lakes.

2.7 Continue straight toward Paulina Peak. (**Note:** If you go right, you'll intersect FR 500 in 0.5 mile on Trail 58.)

3.0 Arrive at the top of Paulina Peak. This is your turnaround point. A viewpoint and restrooms are located here. (**Note:** You can also drive to this viewpoint on FR 500.) Retrace the same route back to the trailhead.

6.0 Arrive back at the trailhead.

Hike Information

Local Information
Visit Bend, 750 NW Lava Rd., Suite 160, Bend, OR 97701; (877) 245-8484; visitbend.com

Local Events and Attractions
High Desert Museum, 59800 S. Highway 97, Bend, OR 97702; (541) 382-4754; highdesertmuseum.org

39 Big Obsidian Flow Trail

The Big Obsidian Flow Trail is an easy and convenient way to check out Oregon's youngest lava flow. Located in Newberry National Volcanic Monument, this fascinating path crosses the lava flow and highlights the volcanic history of the area. Interpretive signs along the way explain how Native Americans visited the area to collect obsidian for making jewelry and tools.

Start: The Big Obsidian trailhead is located 38.4 miles southeast of Bend off Paulina Lake Road (FR 21).
Distance: 0.7-mile lollipop
Hiking time: 30 minutes to 1 hour
Difficulty: Easy; flat terrain
Best season: July through Oct
Other trail users: Hikers only
Canine compatibility: Leashed dogs permitted
Land status: National monument
Nearest town: Bend

Fees and permits: There is a day-use entrance fee for the national monument. You can also purchase a 3-day Newberry National Volcanic Monument Pass.
Maps: Maptech CD: Coos Bay/Eugene/Bend, OR; USGS: East Lake, OR
Schedule: Open late June through Oct
Trail contact: Deschutes National Forest Supervisor's Office, 63095 Deschutes Market Rd., Bend, OR 97701; (541) 383-5300; fs.usda.gov/main/centraloregon/home

Finding the trailhead: From the intersection of Greenwood Avenue and US 97 in Bend, travel south on US 97 for 23 miles to a sign for Newberry Caldera National Monument and Paulina and East Lakes. Turn left onto Paulina Lake Road (FR 21) and drive 15.4 miles to the Big Obsidian trailhead parking area on the right side of the road. *DeLorme: Oregon Atlas & Gazetteer: Page 45 C7. GPS: N43 42.386 / W121 14.134*

The Hike

One of the main attractions at the 55,000-acre Newberry National Volcanic Monument is the Big Obsidian Flow Trail, which provides a fascinating tour of Oregon's youngest lava flow. The trail, which begins as a flat, paved path, offers panoramic views of the flow and includes interpretive signs intended to make understanding the landscape easy. The lava rock is very sharp, so be sure to wear sturdy shoes.

After a short distance the path ascends a steep set of metal stairs and, at the top, arrives at the flow itself, a vast spread of gray pumice interspersed with shiny glass–like boulders of obsidian. Just past the stairs, the trail comes to a T intersection. From here you can go right or left to begin a 0.3-mile loop. The loop offers outstanding views of 7,984-foot Paulina Peak and the Paulina and East Lakes, located at the center of 500-square-mile Newberry Crater.

The 1,300-year-old flow, which covers 1.1 square miles and has an average thickness of 150 feet, began as extremely hot magma (up to 1,600 degrees Fahrenheit) trapped by the earth's crust 2 to 4 miles underground. The magma eventually

Huge glass-like boulders of black, shiny obsidian can be seen along the trail.

found weak points in the earth's surface, and a violent eruption ensued. Later, as the eruption slowed, the sticky magma began oozing out of the earth and crawling over the landscape.

One of the more interesting features of the present-day rough-and-jumbled flow is the glass-like obsidian found on its surface. Due to the way obsidian is formed (through rapid cooling of the lava), it is very hard and extremely sharp. These properties were highly valued by Native Americans, who called the rock Isukws (pronounced "eshookwsh"). They made arrowheads, knives, jewelry, ornaments, sculptures, ceremonial objects, and tools out of the obsidian to trade with other tribes for fish, shells, and roots. Artifacts dating back 10,000 years have been found in the monument and surrounding areas. You can read about these relics of the past as you walk the trail.

◀ *Hikers enjoying the views on the Big Obsidian Flow Trail*

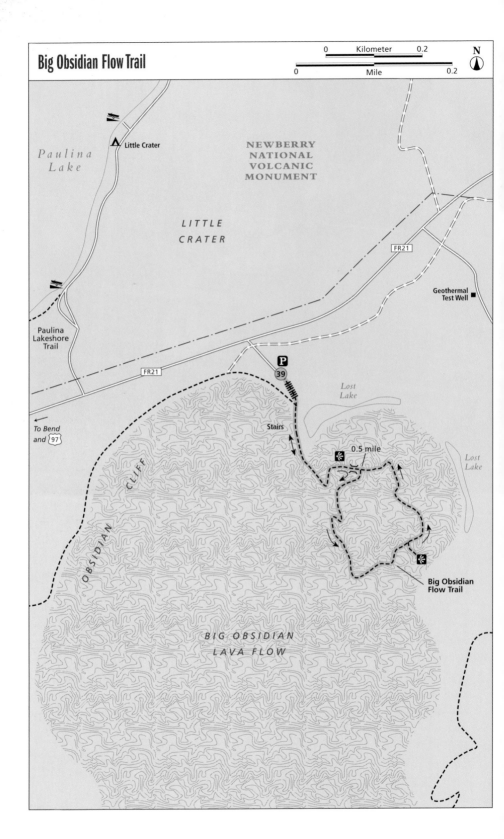

Big Obsidian Flow Trail

0 — Kilometer — 0.2

0 — Mile — 0.2

N

Paulina Lake

Little Crater

NEWBERRY NATIONAL VOLCANIC MONUMENT

LITTLE CRATER

FR21

Geothermal Test Well

Paulina Lakeshore Trail

FR21

P 39

To Bend and 97

Stairs

Lost Lake

0.5 mile

Lost Lake

CLIFF

OBSIDIAN

Big Obsidian Flow Trail

BIG OBSIDIAN LAVA FLOW

The moonlike landscape along the Big Obsidian Flow Trail

Miles and Directions

0.0 Start hiking on the paved path by the parking area.

0.1 Ascend a set of metal stairs to the lava flow.

0.2 Turn right to begin the loop portion of the trail.

0.5 Turn right (this is the end of the loop).

0.7 Arrive back at the parking area.

Hike Information

Local Information

Visit Bend, 750 NW Lava Rd., Suite 160, Bend, OR 97701; (877) 245-8484; visitbend.com

Local Events and Attractions

High Desert Museum, 59800 S. Highway 97, Bend, OR 97702; (541) 382-4754; highdesertmuseum.org

Restaurants

Deschutes Brewery Bend Public House, 1044 NW Bond St., Bend; (541) 382-9242; deschutesbrewery.com

40 Smith Rock State Park

This scenic loop explores the volcanic landscapes of Smith Rock State Park. A world-class climbing area, it is packed with challenging multipitch routes, miles of hiking trails, and gorgeous scenery. The route takes you into a scenic river canyon carved by the Crooked River and then ascends to the top of Misery Ridge, where you'll have outstanding views of the Central Cascade Peaks and a magnificent rock formation called Monkey Face.

Start: The park is located about 8 miles north-east of Redmond off US 97.
Distance: 4.0-mile loop (with other options)
Hiking time: 3 to 4 hours
Difficulty: Moderate; steep ascent to the summit of Misery Ridge and steep descent back into the Crooked River Canyon
Best season: Apr through Oct
Other trail users: Mountain bikers and equestrians
Canine compatibility: Leashed dogs permitted
Land status: State park

Nearest town: Terrebonne
Fees and permits: Day-use parking pass (small fee) required
Schedule: Year-round
Maps: Maptech CD: Coos Bay/Eugene/Bend, OR; USGS: Gray Butte, OR; O'Neil, OR; Redmond, OR
Trail contact: Oregon State Parks and Recreation, 725 Summer St. NE, Suite C, Salem, OR 97301; (800) 551-6949; oregonstateparks.org/park_51.php

Finding the trailhead: From Redmond travel 5 miles north on US 97 to the small town of Terrebonne. At the flashing yellow light, turn right onto B Avenue (this becomes Smith Rock Way after the first stop sign). Continue 3.3 miles northeast, following the signs to Smith Rock State Park. *DeLorme: Oregon Atlas & Gazetteer:* Page 51 B7. GPS: N44 21.898 / W121 08.284

The Hike

Smith Rock is one of central Oregon's most popular state parks. At the main parking area, you'll see climbers sorting through their gear and chatting about the routes they've planned for the day. You'll also see families, photographers, mountain bikers, hikers, and dogs (keep yours on a leash or you'll be slapped with a hefty fine). Before you even leave your car, you'll enjoy spectacular views of the park's colorful 400-foot-tall cliffs. These volcanic masterpieces started to take shape in the Miocene period, seventeen million to nineteen million years ago, when hot steam and ash spewed from the ground. Traces of basalt can be found from the Newberry Volcano eruption 1.2 million years ago that formed Paulina and East Lakes. Since this volcanic activity the Crooked River has eroded the rock to form the columnar shapes that you see in the upper gorge today.

This 4.0-mile loop route begins with a steep descent to the canyon floor. A maintained viewpoint along the way is an excellent place to snap a photo and includes an interpretive sign describing the park's geologic history.

Smith Rock State Park is a popular destination for hikers and can get crowded on weekends during the spring and summer months.

Upon reaching the canyon floor, the path crosses a bridge, turns left, and parallels the Crooked River. Along this stretch of the trail, watch for Canada geese, whose striking white throat patch and black head and neck make them easy to spot. The geese feed on the riverside vegetation and are apt to honk in alarm as you approach. Also keep an eye out for river otters, which are sometimes seen along this stretch of the river.

After following the Crooked River for 1.6 miles on the River Trail over relatively flat terrain, the trail begins ascending a series of steep switchbacks on the Mesa Verde Trail near the base of Monkey Face—a 350-foot-tall volcanic monolith with multiple climbing routes and an enormous cave. Look for climbers clinging to the wall's features as they attempt to reach the top of this amazing rock formation. After 2.1 miles you'll arrive at the top of the ridge. Look west to view several prominent Cascade volcanoes including Mount Bachelor, North Sister, Middle Sister, South Sister, Mount Washington, Mount Jefferson, and, to the far north, Mount Hood. You'll continue following the Misery Ridge Trail along the ridge for 0.2 mile until you begin a steep descent on a series of steps at switchbacks that take you back to the canyon

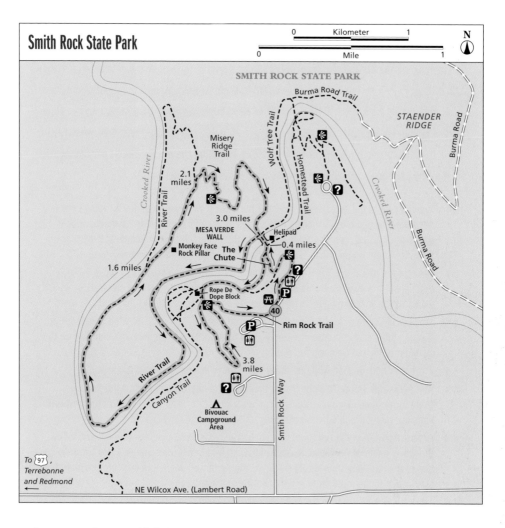

0   Kilometer   1

0   Mile   1

N

SMITH ROCK STATE PARK

Burma Road Trail

STAENDER RIDGE

Burma Road

Wolf Tree Trail

Misery Ridge Trail

Crooked River

Homestead Trail

Crooked River

Burma Road

2.1 miles

River Trail

3.0 miles

MESA VERDE WALL

Monkey Face Rock Pillar

The Chute

Helipad

0.4 miles

1.6 miles

Rope De Dope Block

P

40

P   Rim Rock Trail

River Trail

Canyon Trail

3.8 miles

Bivouac Campground Area

Smtih Rock Way

To 97, Terrebonne and Redmond

NE Wilcox Ave. (Lambert Road)

floor. From here you'll follow a series of park trails that lead you back to the canyon rim and your starting point at 4.0 miles.

Miles and Directions

0.0   From the parking area head toward the canyon and take a right onto an asphalt trail. Follow this to the canyon rim, where it begins its rough and raggedy spiral into Crooked River Canyon. After about 50 yards of careful descent, turn right onto the Chute foot trail. Hike down this steep and slick trail to the canyon floor.

0.4   Cross a footbridge over the Crooked River. After you cross the bridge, turn left and continue on the River Trail.

Rock climbers testing their skills at Smith Rock State Park

PEREGRINE FALCONS

Peregrines are the high-speed flyers of the raptor world. With their sharp, pointed wings, they can dive up to 275 miles per hour. In addition to their stunning speed and agility, peregrines have remarkably keen eyes. Their eyesight is eight times sharper than ours, and two times that of golden eagles. They can spot a bird up to 5 miles away. Peregrines feed primarily off small to medium-size birds, which they carefully pick from the air. The flocks of pigeons that nest in the park are a favorite meal of the resident clan of peregrines.

1.6   Turn right on to the Mesa Verde Trail near the base of Monkey Face. This amazing pillar is host to some of the most difficult rock climbs in the world. From this intersection you'll continue up steep switchbacks to the top of the ridge. The trail forks near the top of the ridge. Veer right on the Misery Ridge Trail and continue your ascent.

2.1   Arrive at the top of the ridge. Once you reach the top, stay on the Misery Ridge Trail. Continue along the ridge for 0.2 mile until you begin descending on a very steep, loose trail. (**Note:** Watch your footing on this hill as you head down switchbacks and multiple stairs.)

3.0   Arrive at the canyon floor. Continue straight and cross a footbridge over the Crooked River. The trail forks after you cross the bridge. Turn right on the Canyon Trail and continue on the wide dirt track that parallels the river.

3.1   Arrive at a trail junction with the Chute Trail. Stay to the right on the Canyon Trail.

3.4   Turn left on the Rope-De-Dope Trail at the base of a large basalt rock called Rope-De-Dope Block. Begin climbing stairs to the left side of this large basalt rock. At the next trail junction, veer left and continue climbing to the top of the ridge.

3.8   Arrive at the top of the ridge and the junction with the Rim Rock Trail. Turn left and follow the gravel trail that parallels the edge of the rim and offers awesome views in every direction of the park and Crooked River Gorge. After about 50 yards turn left onto the path that leads back to the main parking area and the trailhead.

4.0   Arrive back at the parking area and your starting point.

Hike Information

Local Information

Visit Bend, 750 NW Lava Rd., Suite 160, Bend, OR 97701; (877) 245-8484; visitbend.com

Local Events and Attractions

Redpoint Climber's Supply, 8283 11th St., Terrebonne, OR 97760; (541) 923-6207; redpointclimbing.com

Restaurants

Cascade Lakes Brewery, 2141 SW First St., Redmond; (541) 923-3110; cascadelakes.com

Terrebonne Depot, 400 NW Smith Rock Way, Terrebonne; (541) 548-5030; terrebonne depot.com

41 Steins Pillar

If peace and solitude are what you need, this uncrowded trail through the heart of central Oregon's Ochoco National Forest is your answer. The trail starts out fairly flat as it winds its way through a Douglas fir and ponderosa pine forest. It then descends an open high-desert ridge covered with juniper and sagebrush, eventually arriving at the base of 350-foot-tall Steins Pillar. The hike can be completed in a couple hours and is a great introduction to the diverse landscapes present in this part of the state.

Start: The trailhead is located 17.9 miles east of Prineville off US 26.
Distance: 5.2 miles out and back
Hiking time: 2 hours
Difficulty: Moderate; some short hill climbs and moderate descents
Best season: June through Oct
Other trail users: Equestrians
Canine compatibility: Dogs permitted
Land status: National forest

Nearest town: Prineville
Fees and permits: None
Schedule: Open May through Oct
Maps: Maptech CD: Hermiston/Prineville/ Canyon City, OR; USGS: Salt Butte, OR; Steins Pillar, OR
Trail contact: Ochoco National Forest, 3160 NE Third St., Prineville, OR 97754; (541) 416-6500; fs.usda.gov/centraloregon

Finding the trailhead: Travel 9.1 miles east of Prineville on US 26. Turn left (north) onto Mill Creek Road (FR 33). Travel 6.7 miles on Mill Creek Road (the road becomes gravel after 5.2 miles) to the junction with FR 500. Turn right onto FR 500 and continue 2.1 miles to the trailhead on the left side of the road. *DeLorme: Oregon Atlas & Gazetteer:* Page 80 C2. GPS: N44 23.693 / W120 37.463

The Hike

Steins Pillar is a fascinating rock formation located in the heart of the Ochoco National Forest in the Ochoco Mountains. The 350-foot pillar is an important geologic remnant of the area's rich volcanic history.

Nearly fifty million years ago, this was volcano land. Eruptions layered the area in volcanic tuff, andesite, and ash. The Clarno and John Day Formations, world famous for their many fossil remains, were created as a result of these eruptions. James Condon, a young Congregational minister and naturalist, first discovered fossils in the area in the 1860s. His first find was an ancient tortoise shell in Picture Gorge in the John Day Valley. Over the next several years, Condon and others uncovered many more plant and animal fossils. This became the precursor to research and cataloging of hundreds of specimens in the area over the next century. Examples of fossils that have been discovered include amynodonts and brontotheres of the Clarno Formation period (thirty-seven million to fifty-four million years ago) and dogs, cats, camels, oreodonts, swine, rhinoceroses, and rodents of the John Day Formation period (twenty million to thirty-nine million years ago).

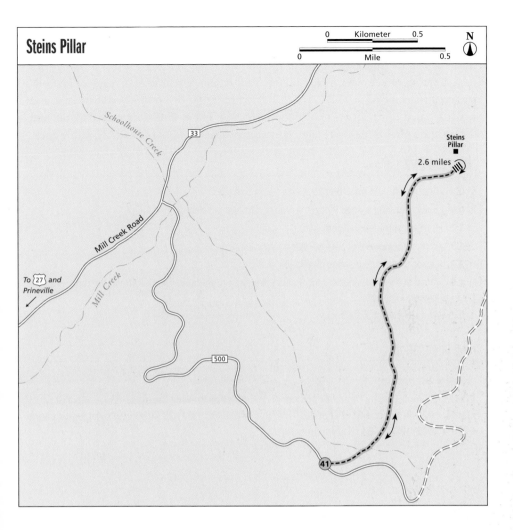

A great way to get a feel for the geologic history of the area is by hiking the moderate 2.6-mile trail to the base of Steins Pillar. The trail starts out fairly flat through a dry, open forest of Douglas fir trees and then transitions into an open rocky landscape filled with sagebrush and western juniper trees. The small, fragrant, bluish berries of the juniper are a favorite food of small birds and small mammals. In spring and summer, wildflowers are scattered along the trail—bright-red Indian paintbrush, bluish-purple lupine, and bright-yellow mule's ears are just a few of the varieties you'll see.

After 1.2 miles the trail begins to descend the ridge, and the landscape shifts back to Douglas fir and ponderosa pine. Tree debris scattered on the forest floor along this section of trail appears to be the result of an old burn and frequent winter storms.

◀ *Steins Pillar*

Another mile up the trail, you'll catch your first glimpse of Steins Pillar as it rises prominently above the Mill Creek Valley and Steins Ranch. To reach the base of the pillar, descend a long series of steps for the remaining 0.3 mile. While at the pillar's base, look up to see why rock climbers find it such a tempting challenge. The pillar was first climbed in 1950. A 5.11A rated route heads up the northeast face, and a 5.10D rated route shoots up the southeast face. These climbs are very difficult, and some of the pitches are overhanging, with crossover sections of crumbly, rotten rock.

Miles and Directions

0.0 Start on the dirt track next to a STEINS PILLAR trail sign.

0.3 Begin climbing a ridge through a Douglas fir and ponderosa pine forest.

1.2 The trail starts descending.

2.3 Reach a viewpoint of Steins Pillar on your left.

2.4 Descend on a long series of wooden steps.

2.6 Arrive at the base of 350-foot Steins Pillar (your turnaround point). Retrace the route back to the trailhead.

5.2 Arrive back at the trailhead.

Hike Information

Local Information
Prineville-Crook County Chamber of Commerce, 102 NW Second St., Prineville, OR 97754; (541) 447-6304; visitprineville.org

Restaurants
Solstice Brewing Company, 234 N. Main St., Prineville; (541) 233-0883; solsticebrewing.com

42 Twin Pillars

The first 3 miles of this hike, a beautiful and peaceful walk through the Mill Creek Wilderness, includes wildlife, wildflowers, and a meandering stream. The remaining portion of the trail traverses a ponderosa pine forest interspersed with grassy meadows before arriving at the base of Twin Pillars, the eroded remnant of a volcano that erupted forty million to fifty million years ago.

Start: The trailhead is located 19.8 miles northeast of Prineville off US 26.
Distance: 10.6 miles out and back
Hiking time: 4 to 6 hours
Difficulty: Easy for the first 3 miles along Mill Creek; difficult for the final 2.3 miles due to a very steep ascent on a series of switchbacks to the base of Twin Pillars
Best season: June through Oct
Other trail users: Equestrians

Canine compatibility: Dogs permitted
Land status: Wilderness area
Nearest town: Prineville
Fees and permits: None
Schedule: May through Oct
Maps: Maptech CD: Hermiston/Prineville/Canyon City, OR; USGS: Steins Pillar, OR
Trail contact: Ochoco National Forest, 3160 NE Third St., Prineville, OR 97754; (541) 416-6500; fs.usda.gov/centraloregon

Finding the trailhead: From Prineville drive 9.1 miles east on US 26 to Mill Creek Road. Turn left (north) and travel 10.6 miles to a fork in the road. Turn right at the sign for Wildcat Campground. Drive 0.1 mile and turn right into a gravel parking area at the trailhead. Wildcat Campground is another 0.3 mile past the parking area. *DeLorme: Oregon Atlas & Gazetteer:* Page 80 B2. GPS: N44 26.468 / W120 34.572

The Hike

Located in the 17,000-acre Mill Creek Wilderness of Ochoco National Forest, the Twin Pillars Trail is a 10.6-mile out-and-back path along bubbling Mill Creek. The route passes through a forest of ponderosa pine, grand fir, and Douglas fir and up a steep ridge to the base of Twin Pillars, the double-spiked rock formation that constitutes the trail's namesake.

The trail begins with a series of creek crossings, so be sure to bring an old pair of tennis shoes or sandals to wear in the water. As you walk along the creek, you'll hear the cries of kingfishers protesting your presence on their home turf. Other birds in the area include pileated woodpeckers, wild turkeys, and northern goshawks. Pileated woodpeckers are the largest species of woodpecker and can be identified by their prominent red crests, black feathers, and white undersides. Northern goshawks, which weigh between six and eight pounds and live up to ten years, have slate-gray feathers and bright orange-red eyes outlined in white. You'll most likely see them weaving in and out of the woodlands with great speed and finesse as they hunt for small birds and mammals. If you don't first see a northern goshawk, you may hear

Twin Pillars is an interesting rock formation.

its distinctive "ca-ca-ca" hunting cry. Other wildlife in this pristine wilderness area includes Rocky Mountain elk, mule deer, bobcats, cougars, and black bears.

As you continue on the trail, you'll pass green meadows of daisies, delicate purple aster, crimson penstemon, and bright-purple thistle. Tall stalks of woolly mullein with their bright bunches of yellow flowers are also common. Shimmering green aspen trees grow in clusters along the banks of the creek, and cutthroat trout hang out in shady rock pools.

Three miles from the trailhead, the path turns away from Mill Creek and climbs steeply in a series of long and winding switchbacks for 2 miles up a ridge to the base of the 200-foot-tall Twin Pillars rock formation. Towering stands of Douglas fir and ponderosa pine grace the slopes of this ridge; below, wildflowers sprinkle open meadows with splashes of color.

Because of the length of this hike, you may want to complete the trail as an overnight backpack. There are many potential camping spots overlooking Mill Creek. Once you set up camp, you can wade in the creek, fish for trout, or just relax. The following day a light daypack is all you'll need for the remaining climb to the pillars'

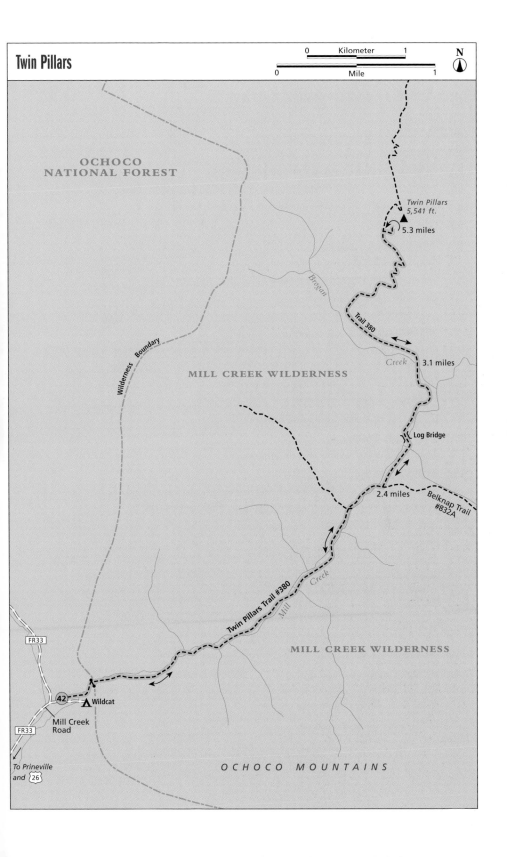

Twin Pillars

0 Kilometer 1

0 Mile 1

N

OCHOCO
NATIONAL FOREST

Twin Pillars
5,541 ft.
5.3 miles

Brogan

Trail 380

Creek

3.1 miles

MILL CREEK WILDERNESS

Log Bridge

Wilderness Boundary

2.4 miles

Belknap Trail
#832A

Twin Pillars Trail #380

Mill

Creek

MILL CREEK WILDERNESS

FR33

42

Wildcat

Mill Creek
Road

FR33

To Prineville
and 26

OCHOCO MOUNTAINS

base. If you don't want to backpack, complete the trail in a day, then pitch your tent at Wildcat Campground. The camping area is located just 0.3 mile northeast of the trailhead; there is a small per-night fee to camp here.

Miles and Directions

0.0   Start hiking on the signed Twin Pillars Trail 380.

0.1   Cross Mill Creek Road (FR 33) and continue straight.

0.2   Proceed through a green metal gate and enter the Mill Creek Wilderness.

0.3   Wade across Mill Creek. After the creek the trail forks. Turn left.

0.8   Cross the creek.

0.9   Cross the creek.

1.1   Navigate another stream crossing.

1.2   Cross the creek. Proceed approximately 100 yards and cross again.

1.5   Cross the creek.

2.2   Arrive at another stream crossing. Logs are in place to help you cross. Walk another 50 yards and cross the stream again.

2.4   Cross the creek and arrive at a trail junction. Continue straight (left). (**Note:** Belknap 832A Trail goes right.)

2.5   Pass a sign on the left that reads TWIN PILLARS 2 MILES.

2.7   Cross the creek on a log bridge.

2.9   The trail climbs steeply, then veers away from the creek.

3.1   Cross Brogan Creek.

3.4   Enjoy a view of the Twin Pillars rock formation.

3.6   Cross a side creek.

4.0   Cross a very small side creek. As you hike this section, you'll pass open slopes of tall bunch grass filled with purple aster, Indian paintbrush, and wild iris.

5.1   Turn right at the trail junction and scramble up a steep rock-strewn slope to the base of the pillars.

5.3   Arrive at the base of Twin Pillars and your turnaround point. Enjoy a scenic view of the surrounding Ochoco Mountains, then retrace the same route back to the trailhead.

10.6   Arrive back at the trailhead.

Hike Information

Local Information

Prineville-Crook County Chamber of Commerce, 102 NW Second St., Prineville, OR 97754; (541) 447-6304; visitprineville.org

Restaurants

Solstice Brewing Company, 234 N. Main St., Prineville; (541) 233-0883; solsticebrewing.com

The author hikes along Mill Creek on the Twin Pillars Trail. ▶

PHOTO KEN SKEEN

Honorable Mentions

Central Oregon

KK Green Lakes Loop

This difficult 11.6-mile route travels uphill for more than 1,175 feet, paralleling enchanting Fall Creek and then entering the Green Lakes Basin. The return loop takes you on the Soda Creek Trail through the even more gorgeous Three Sisters Wilderness. To get there from the intersection of US 97 and Franklin Avenue in downtown Bend, turn west onto Franklin Avenue. Proceed 1.2 miles (Franklin Avenue becomes Riverside Boulevard) to the intersection with Tumalo Avenue. Turn right onto Tumalo Avenue (which turns into Galveston Avenue). Go 0.5 mile and turn left onto Fourteenth Street. This street soon turns into Century Drive, also known as the Cascade Lakes Highway (OR 46). Continue about 27 miles on the highway to the Green Lakes trailhead parking area on the right side of the road. Start hiking on Trail 17, which parallels Fall Creek.

A sign indicates MORAINE LAKE 2 MILES / GREEN LAKES 4.5 MILES / PARK MEADOW 9 MILES / SCOTT PASS 21 MILES. At 2 miles continue straight (right) on the smooth track as it parallels Fall Creek. (The trail that goes left at this junction heads toward Moraine Lake.) At 4.3 miles turn right toward Park Meadow/Soda Creek. Continue 10 yards and then take another quick right turn toward Soda Creek/Broken Top. Continue on the trail as it skirts the south edge of 9,175-foot Broken Top. Here you'll have spectacular views of the Green Lakes to the north. At 7.1 miles turn right toward Soda Creek/Todd Lake. (The Broken Top Trail continues left at this junction.) At 7.9 miles turn right where a sign indicates SODA CREEK. (The trail that goes left heads toward Todd Lake.) From here you'll continue downhill. Be ready to negotiate water crossings at Crater and Soda Creeks. At 11.6 miles you'll arrive back at the Green Lakes trailhead.

A Northwest Forest Pass is required for this hike. You can purchase a pass online at www.fs.usda.gov/main/r6/passes-permits/recreation or by calling (800) 270-7504. For more information, contact the Deschutes National Forest Supervisor's Office, 63095 Deschutes Market Rd., Bend, OR 97701; (541) 383-5300; fs.usda.gov/main/central oregon/home. *DeLorme: Oregon Atlas & Gazetteer:* Page 50 D3.

LL Ray Atkeson Memorial Loop Hike

This easy 2.3-mile loop hike, named for the famed nature photographer, takes you along the shore of Sparks Lake and travels through a thick lodgepole pine forest and past interesting lava flows. Along the way you'll have wonderful views of the Central Cascades. To get there from Bend, travel 26 miles west on the Cascade Lakes Highway

(OR 46) to the turnoff for FR 400 at the Sparks Lakes Recreation Area sign. Turn left (south) onto FR 400 and go 0.1 mile to a road junction. Turn left onto FR 100 toward the signed Sparks Lake boat ramp and trailheads. Go 1.7 miles and turn left into the signed Ray Atkeson Memorial trailhead parking area.

A Northwest Forest Pass is required for this hike. You can purchase a pass online at www.fs.usda.gov/main/r6/passes-permits/recreation or by calling (800) 270-7504. For more information, contact the Deschutes National Forest Supervisor's Office, 63095 Deschutes Market Rd., Bend, OR 97701; (541) 383-5300; fs.usda.gov/main/centraloregon/home.

MM Lava Lands Visitor Center Trails

This 1.1-mile route combines two trails: the Trail of the Molten Land and the Trail of the Whispering Pines. The first trail takes you on a journey through an amazing lava flow to a viewpoint with spectacular views of the Central Cascade Mountains. The second trail winds through a second-growth ponderosa pine forest and has interpretive signs explaining the plants, animals, and history of the area. To get there, from the intersection of Northwest Franklin and US 97 (Business) in Bend, travel 11.2 miles south on US 97 to a Lava Lands Visitor Center sign. Turn right (west) and park in the main parking area.

A Northwest Forest Pass is required for this hike. You can purchase a pass online at www.fs.usda.gov/main/r6/passes-permits/recreation or by calling (800) 270-7504. For more information, contact the Deschutes National Forest Supervisor's Office, 63095 Deschutes Market Rd., Bend, OR 97701; (541) 383-5300; fs.usda.gov/main/centraloregon/home.

NN Jefferson Park

This difficult 11.4-mile round-trip takes you through the high alpine country of Jefferson Park in the Mount Jefferson Wilderness. It's highly recommended that you complete this hike as an overnight backpack so that you can fully explore the area. To get there from Detroit, drive east on FR 46 for 11 miles to the junction with FR 4685. Turn right onto FR 4685 and drive 4 miles to the trailhead parking area.

Start the hike on the South Breitenbush Trail, located above the South Breitenbush River. The climb is steep and scenic and will give your quads a workout. After 1.7 miles you come to the Bear Point Trail junction. Stay to the right and follow the trail as it ascends through a fir forest, past picturesque meadows. Your turnaround point is at 5.7 miles—the junction with the Pacific Crest Trail.

A wilderness permit is required for day hikes and overnight trips, and in order to park at this trailhead, you'll need a Northwest Forest Pass. You can purchase a pass online at www.fs.usda.gov/main/r6/passes-permits/recreation or by calling (800) 270-7504. For more information, contact the Willamette National Forest, Detroit Ranger Station, 44125 N. Santiam Hwy. SE, Detroit, OR 97342; (503)

You will learn a lot about the geologic history of central Oregon when you visit the Lava Lands Visitor Center.

854-3366; fs.usda.gov/main/willamette/home. *DeLorme: Oregon Atlas & Gazetteer:* Page 56 C1.

◯◯ Pamelia Lake

Take a step back in time when you hike on this easy 4.4-mile out-and-back route that travels through towering old-growth trees to Pamelia Lake. Mossy coated logs, wild rhododendrons, and picturesque Pamelia Creek are added bonuses to this near-perfect-10 trail—the only drawback is its popularity and having to deal with the hassle of getting a permit.

After 2.2 miles you'll arrive at the inviting shores of Pamelia Lake. If you hike this trail in autumn, you'll find more solitude and you'll get to enjoy the brilliant end-of-the-season colors. If you are up for a longer route, you may want to continue another 4 miles past Pamelia Lake on a steep uphill trek to scenic Hunts Cove, or you can continue 3 miles past the lake on a grueling climb to the summit of Grizzly Peak.

The author walking through towering old growth on the Pamelia Lake Trail ▶

To get there from Salem, travel 62 miles east of Salem on North Santiam Highway 22 to Pamelia Lake Road (FR 2246). Turn left and travel 3.7 miles on Pamelia Lake Road to the parking area and trailhead.

A Northwest Forest Pass is required. You can purchase a pass online at www.fs.usda .gov/main/r6/passes-permits/recreation or by calling (800) 270-7504. A special-use permit is required to access this trail. You can obtain a permit at the Detroit Ranger Station, 44125 N. Santiam Hwy. SE, Detroit, OR 97342; (503) 854-3366; www.fs .usda.gov/main/willamette/home. *DeLorme: Oregon Atlas & Gazetteer: Page 56 C2.*

PP Hand Lake

This easy 1.0-mile out-and-back route travels to picturesque Hand Lake and offers breathtaking views of Mount Washington and the Three Sisters Mountains. To get there from Sisters, turn west onto the McKenzie Highway (OR 242) and travel 19.3 miles to a gravel pullout on the left side of the road, marked by a brown "hiker" symbol.

Begin the hike by crossing the highway (use caution here!) to the signed trailhead. Begin walking on the trail as it descends through a thick lodgepole pine forest dotted with bunches of purple lupine. At 0.5 mile emerge out of the forest into a scenic, high alpine meadow. You can explore an old three-sided wooden shelter. From here a side trail leads down to the lakeshore. Retrace the route back to the trailhead.

A free wilderness permit is required. Permits are available at the trailhead. Note that OR 242 is closed in winter and is sometimes not open until early July. For more information, contact Deschutes National Forest, Sisters Ranger District, Pine Street and Highway 20, Sisters, OR 97759; (541) 549-7700; fs.usda.gov/main/centraloregon/ home. *DeLorme: Oregon Atlas & Gazetteer: Page 50 C1.*

QQ Canyon Creek Meadows Loop

This 5.5-mile loop trail takes you through spectacular wildflower meadows with stunning views of Three Fingered Jack's craggy spires. To get there from Sisters, head west on US 20 for 12 miles to Jack Lake Road (FR 12). Turn right and travel 4.3 miles on Jack Lake Road to the junction with FR 1230. Turn left onto FR 1230 and go 1.7 miles. Turn left onto FR 1234 (the road becomes gravel here) and travel about 6.2 miles on FR 1234 to Jack Lake and the trailhead.

Start hiking on the smooth singletrack trail signed for Canyon Creek Meadows. This fast trail sails past quiet Jack Lake. At 0.2 mile turn left toward Canyon Creek. The trail leads you into an amazing high alpine meadow filled with bubbling creeks and colorful wildflowers. At 1.7 miles turn left at the trail fork. After 2 miles you'll

Nice mountain views on the Canyon
Creek Meadows Loop ▶

View of majestic South Sister

reach a high alpine meadow with a stunning view of 7,841-foot Three Fingered Jack. This is your turnaround point. At 2.3 miles turn left. At 3.2 miles turn right. Continue walking through gorgeous high alpine scenery to another trail junction at 5.3 miles. Continue straight (left) toward Jack Lake and the trailhead. Reach the trailhead at 5.5 miles.

A wilderness permit is required for day hikes and overnight trips, and in order to park at this trailhead, you'll need a Northwest Forest Pass. You can purchase a pass online at www.fs.usda.gov/main/r6/passes-permits/recreation or by calling (800) 270-7504. For more information, contact Deschutes National Forest, Sisters Ranger District, Pine Street and Highway 20, Sisters, OR 97759; (541) 549-7700; fs.usda .gov/main/centraloregon/home. *DeLorme: Oregon Atlas & Gazetteer:* Page 50 A2.

RR Three Sisters Loop

The Three Sisters Loop is a splendid backpack tour around the magnificent Three Sisters Mountains in the wilderness area of the same name. This loop travels about 43 miles and can easily be completed in four days. It begins at the Lava Lakes trailhead off OR 242 (McKenzie Pass Highway). On this loop trail you follow the Pacific Crest Trail as it heads southwest past South Matthieu Lake, Yapoah Crater, Collier Cone, Glacier Creek, and the Obsidian area.

To get there from Sisters, drive 11 miles west on OR 242 (the McKenzie Highway) to the gravel road junction with signs to Lava Camp Lake. Turn left and drive about a half mile to the Pacific Crest Trail parking area, located on the right side of the road. (Note that OR 242 is closed in winter and is sometimes not open until early July.)

Along the first half of this loop, there are many opportunities to gaze at the spectacular Three Sisters Mountains. After about 20 miles turn left and hook up with the Moraine Lake Trail and follow it to Moraine Lake—which you'll reach in about another 1.7 miles. From Moraine Lake, follow the trail east for another mile to Fall Creek—stay to the left. After another 2 miles heading northwest, you hook up with the Green Lakes Trail, at which point you pass through the Green Lakes Basin. Three miles later you find yourself at Park Meadow, an open grassy alpine meadow with superb views of Broken Top. From Park Meadow turn left on the Pole Creek Trail (which heads north), and after about 31 miles you cross the south fork of Squaw Creek.

Continue heading north and cross the north fork of Squaw Creek and Alder Creek. When you reach the Scott Trail junction—at about 38.7 miles—turn left (west). Follow this trail to the top of Scott Pass and the intersection with the Pacific Crest Trail. Turn right onto the Pacific Crest Trail and continue straight until you hook back up with the Lava Lakes Trail and follow it another 0.2 mile where you will arrive back at the Lava Lakes Trailhead.

There are many trail intersections on this loop trail, and it's highly recommended that you obtain a Three Sisters Wilderness map (available from the Sisters Ranger Station) before heading out. You'll also need a wilderness permit to hike in the Three Sisters Wilderness. Call ahead for information about obtaining an overnight permit. In order to park at this trailhead, you'll need a Northwest Forest Pass. You can purchase a pass online at www.fs.usda.gov/main/r6/passes-permits/recreation or by calling (800) 270-7504.

For more information, contact Deschutes National Forest, Sisters Ranger District, Pine Street and Highway 20, Sisters, OR 97759; (541) 549-7700; fs.usda.gov/main/centraloregon/home. *DeLorme: Oregon Atlas & Gazetteer:* Page 49 A7.

SS Tam-a-Lau Trail

This moderate 6.8-mile loop trail takes you to the top of a high peninsula above Lake Billy Chinook in Cove Palisades State Park. From there you have grand views

Striking Chimney Rock formation in central Oregon

of the vast reservoir below and the snowcapped Central Cascade peaks, including Mount Hood, Mount Jefferson, Broken Top, Mount Bachelor, and the Three Sisters. The Crooked, Deschutes, and Metolius Rivers feed this giant lake, which is popular with boaters.

To get there from Redmond, travel 19 miles north on US 97 to a turnoff for Cove Palisades State Park and Culver/Round Butte Dam. Turn left (west) onto the Culver Highway and follow the state park signs 6 miles to the park entrance. (From Madras travel 15 miles southwest on US 97, following signs to the park.) Follow the entrance road down into the canyon to a road junction. At the bottom of the canyon, turn left toward Deschutes Campground and day-use areas. Continue 3.7 miles to another road junction. Turn left toward the signed Deschutes Campground. Proceed 0.6 mile to a TAM-A-LAU TRAIL sign. Turn right, go 0.3 mile, and turn right into the single car parking area.

Begin by walking on the paved path at the northeast corner of the day-use parking area. You'll travel a short distance and arrive at a grassy picnic area and swimming beach. From the picnic area, follow a paved path that heads uphill on the right side of the restrooms. At 0.3 mile turn right at the trail fork and continue, ascending a flight of steps. At 0.4 mile turn left at the trail fork and continue, ascending the paved trail. Cross a paved road and walk through an opening in a fence around Deschutes Campground A. At 0.5 mile turn right onto a dirt path adjacent to a large interpretive sign. Over the next 1.1 miles, the trail ascends steeply to a high plateau above the lake.

The hillside is blanketed with bunch grass, yellow balsamroot, and purple lupine. At 1.4 miles turn left onto a wide doubletrack road. At 1.6 miles turn left and begin the loop portion of the hike. Follow the dirt path as it parallels the edge of the rimrock and offers outstanding views of the lake canyon and the Central Cascade peaks. After 2.7 miles you'll arrive at the tip of the peninsula, which serves as a good lunch spot. At 5.2 miles you'll end the loop portion of the hike and descend on the same route back to your starting point at 6.8 miles. Avoid this hike during July and August, when temperatures can exceed one hundred degrees F.

For more information, contact Oregon State Parks and Recreation, 725 Summer St. NE, Suite C, Salem, OR 97301; (800) 551-6949; oregonstateparks.org/park_32.php.

TT Chimney Rock

This 2.6-mile route takes you to the base of Chimney Rock—a prominent formation located high above the Crooked River. Along the way, you'll walk through a high desert ecosystem of sage and juniper and enjoy views of the Crooked River Canyon and Cascade Mountains.

To get there from US 26 in Prineville, turn south onto Main Street. Continue south for 17.1 miles to a gravel parking area on the left side of the road marked RIM TRAIL. The trailhead is located across from the Chimney Rock Recreation area.

For more information, contact the Bureau of Land Management, Prineville District Office, 3050 NE Third St., Prineville, OR 97754; (541) 416-6700; blm.gov/or/index .php.

Northeast Oregon

Northeast Oregon has a rich pioneer history and is dotted with farms, ranches, imposing mountain ranges, deep river gorges, and picturesque canyons filled with fossilized treasures. The rugged country is bordered by the Wallowa Mountains and Hells Canyon, which, at over a mile deep, is the deepest canyon in North America.

Your first stop in this wide-open country should be the Sheep Rock Unit of the John Day Fossil Beds National Monument, located about 11.7 miles northwest of Dayville off OR 19. Here you can examine fossilized evidence of the prehistoric life that roamed the hills and valleys of the John Day area more than forty million years ago. For a good introduction to this national treasure, stop by the Sheep Rock Unit Visitor Center, 2 miles northwest of the intersection of US 26 and OR 19. After touring the visitor center, try hiking the short Island in Time Trail, which winds through an intricately carved canyon embedded with fossils.

Don't miss the Painted Hills Unit of the John Day Fossil Beds. This spot is filled with color-splashed hills that vary from red and pink to bronze and tan—occasionally even black. Several trails wander through the Painted Hills Unit, located 52 miles northeast of Prineville off US 26.

The Wallowa Mountains in the far northeast corner of Oregon contain some of Oregon's highest peaks. These jagged granite peaks resemble California's Sierra Nevada and contain hundreds of miles of trails to high alpine lakes and glacier-carved meadows. These peaks are part of the Eagle Cap Wilderness, just south of the small towns of Lostine, Enterprise, and Joseph off OR 82. Lakes Basin is one popular destination. To see this unique area, you can backpack into the lakes and take a very long day hike on the Lakes Basin Trail. This difficult 20.2-mile trail leads you along the east fork of the Lostine River, through a spectacular glacial valley, and then loops through the scenic Lakes Basin at the base of 9,595-foot Eagle Cap. There is also a hiking trail to the top of Eagle Cap if you want to enjoy the spectacular views from the top of this peak (see Honorable Mention Hike ZZ).

Cant Ranch Historical Museum in the
John Day Fossil Beds Sheep Rock Unit

An old wagon at the Cant Ranch Historical Museum in the John Day Fossil Beds Sheep Rock Unit

The Blue and Strawberry Mountains are part of the immense 1,460,000-acre Malheur National Forest, a rolling expanse of ponderosa pine, lodgepole pine, and a variety of firs.

You can take a jaunt to two high alpine lakes in the Strawberry Mountain Wilderness on the Strawberry Lakes hike. This 6.8-mile out-and-back route takes you past Strawberry Lake and Strawberry Falls. Prairie City, located on US 26, is one major access point into this area.

Hells Canyon is a must. The Snake River has been hard at work over the past two million years carving out the deepest river gorge in North America (over a mile deep). It flows swiftly through the canyon, past high cliffs, grassy plateaus, ancient petroglyphs, and lava flows and serves as the dividing line between Oregon and Washington. If you want to get down into the canyon, try the 14.0-mile McGraw Creek Loop, which parallels the mighty Snake River and McGraw Creek. Keep in mind, however, that the temperatures in Hells Canyon vary by as much as thirty degrees from the canyon's rim to the canyon floor, rising as you descend. During the summer months temperatures in the seventies on the rim may translate to temperatures in the nineties—sometimes topping one hundred degrees—on the floor. Heatstroke is a big concern on trails in the canyon; so always carry at least a gallon of water per person per day (or carry a water filter). In addition, the trails in the canyon are isolated, rough, and poorly maintained. Other concerns include black bears and rattlesnakes. They don't call it Hells Canyon for nothing.

43 Painted Hills Unit
(John Day Fossil Beds National Monument)

The short hikes in the Painted Hills Unit of the John Day Fossil Beds National Monument provide a close-up look at the area's beautiful color-splashed hills and fascinating fossil beds. The Painted Hills Overlook Trail is a 1.0-mile out-and-back route that takes you to the top of an overlook with views of the colorful surrounding hills. If you want more of an adventure, trek 1.5 miles to the top of Carroll Rim, where you'll have a sweeping view of the painted hills and surrounding high-desert country. If you want to see one of these hills up close, stroll the quarter-mile Painted Cove Trail. To view fossils of plants that dominated this area thirty-three million years ago, walk the Leaf Hill Trail. It's possible to complete all four of the established trails in just a day.

Start: The trailhead is located about 52 miles northeast of Prineville off US 26.
Distance:
A. Carroll Rim Trail: 1.5 miles out and back
B. Painted Hills Overlook Trail: 0.5 mile out and back
C. Painted Cove Trail: 0.25-mile loop
D. Leaf Hill Trail: 0.25-mile loop
E. Red Hill Trail: 0.4 mile out and back
Hiking time: Varies depending on the trails selected
Difficulty: The Carroll Rim Trail is moderate; the other trails are easy.

Best season: May through Oct
Other trail users: Hikers only
Canine compatibility: Leashed dogs permitted
Land status: National monument
Nearest town: Mitchell
Fees and permits: None
Schedule: Year-round
Maps: Maptech CD: Hermiston/Prineville/ Canyon City, OR; USGS: Painted Hills, OR
Trail contact: John Day Fossil Beds National Monument, 32651 Highway 19, Kimberly, OR 97848-9701; (541) 987-2333, ext. 1240; nps.gov/joda/planyourvisit/index.htm

Finding the trailhead: From Prineville travel 45.2 miles east on US 26 to the junction with Burnt Ranch Road, where a sign indicates JOHN DAY FOSSIL BEDS NATIONAL MONUMENT—PAINTED HILLS UNIT. Turn left (north) and go 5.7 miles. Turn left onto Bear Creek Road and proceed 0.9 mile to the turnoff for the Carroll Rim trailhead. Turn left and then take an immediate right into the gravel parking area on the right. The Carroll Rim Trail begins on the opposite side of the road from the parking area. Follow the road signs to reach the Painted Cove Trail, Leaf Hill Trail, and the Red Hill Trail.
DeLorme: Oregon Atlas & Gazetteer: Page 80 B3. GPS: N44 39.251 / W120 15.115

The Hike

The Painted Hills Unit of the John Day Fossil Beds National Monument has several hikes offering glimpses of the area's rich geologic history. The hikes are easy to moderately difficult, and each provides a different perspective on the unique formations in this national monument.

The Painted Hills Overlook Trail offers some of the best viewpoints of the Painted Hills.

The most striking features you'll notice are the round, multicolored hills of colorful claystone. Thirty million years ago layers of ash were deposited in this area from volcanoes erupting to the west. Over millions of years the forces of nature have carved and shaped the hills that you see today. Different elements such as aluminum, silicon, iron, magnesium, manganese, sodium, calcium, titanium, and others have combined to produce minerals that have unique properties and colors.

To get a bird's-eye view of these interesting hills, take a short jaunt on the 0.5-mile out-and-back Painted Hills Overlook Trail, which takes you up a gentle ridge and includes several viewpoints along the way. If you want a close-up view of one of these unique painted hills, take a walk on the 0.25-mile Painted Cove Trail loop.

The Painted Cove Trail gives you a close-up view of the impenetrable red clay particles that make up the scenic red hills in the park. ▷

Interesting mud formation on the Red Hill Trail

A brochure and corresponding trail markers offer an in-depth look at these geologic formations. For instance, the colors of the hills change with the weather. When it rains the clay absorbs water, causing more light reflection and changing the color of the hills from red to pink and from light brown to yellow-gold. As the hills dry out, the soil contracts, causing surface cracking that diffuses the light and makes the color of the hills deepen. The purple layer in the hill is the weathered remains of a rhyolite lava flow. Other colored bands in the hillside are due to differences in mineral content and weathering. Plants can't grow on the painted hills because the clay is so dense that moisture can't penetrate the surface. Also, the clay soil is nutritionally poor.

Another distinguishing landmark of the Painted Hills Unit is Carroll Rim, a high ridge consisting of John Day ignimbrite, better known as "welded tuff." More than twenty-eight million years ago, a volcano to the west erupted and hurled hot ash, debris, and gases into the air, which then landed and cooled to form a glass-like layer.

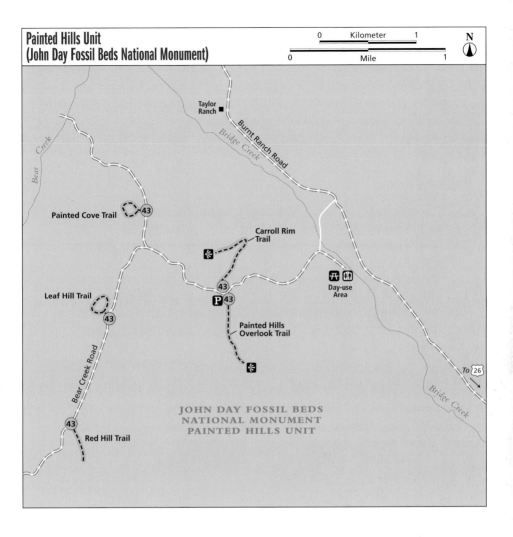

To reach the top of this landmark and excellent views of the surrounding hills and valleys, hike up the 1.5-mile out-and-back Carroll Rim Trail. From the top you'll be able to see Sutton Mountain, which rises prominently to the east.

For fossils, check out the 0.25-mile-long Leaf Hill Trail and its collection of ancient plants. The trail circles a small hill of loose shale deposits. While at first the hill seems somewhat unremarkable, a closer look reveals secrets to the plants that once dominated here. The shales present in this hill were formed about thirty-three million years ago from lake-deposited volcanic ash. Thirty-five species of fossilized plants can be found at Laurel Hill, with alder, beech, maple, and the extinct hornbeam most prevalent. Other specimens include elm, rose, oak, grape, fern, redwood, and pine. Scientists have analyzed these plant fossils and concluded that this group of plants closely resembles two types of modern forests found in China—the mixed northern hardwood forest and the mixed mesophytic forest. Comparing the mix of plant species to these two modern forests indicates that this area had a much higher rainfall (up to 40 inches), milder temperatures, and a warmer climate than that found here today. (Today the area receives about 12 to 15 inches of rain a year and experiences more extreme temperature variations.) In addition, the vegetation that grows here today is made up of high desert–type plants—juniper, sagebrush, and grasses.

The 0.4-mile Red Hill Trail gives you another interesting perspective of the striking red clay that makes up this unique landscape.

Miles and Directions

A. **Carroll Rim Trail:** 1.5-mile out-and-back trek to the top of Carroll Rim that offers sweeping views of the surrounding hills and valleys.

B. **Painted Hills Overlook Trail:** 0.5-mile out-and-back path with a panoramic view of the Painted Hills.

C. **Painted Cove Trail:** 0.25-mile loop that circles a painted hill and gives you a close-up look at the unique properties that make up these interesting geologic formations.

D. **Leaf Hill Trail:** 0.25-mile loop that circles a hill where ancient plant fossils are abundant.

E. **Red Hill Trail:** 0.4-mile out-and-back trail that takes you past an interesting, bright-red clay hill.

Hike Information

Local Information
Prineville-Crook County Chamber of Commerce, 102 NW Second St., Prineville, OR 97754; (541) 447-6304; visitprineville.org

Restaurants
Solstice Brewing Company, 234 N. Main St., Prineville; (541) 233-0883; solsticebrewing.com

44 Island in Time (John Day Fossil Beds—Sheep Rock Unit)

The Island in Time Trail leads you on a beautiful tour through a desert canyon filled with intricate rock terraces and high cliff walls that have been molded and shaped by wind and water. Interpretive signs posted along the trail describe different ancient fossils and offer interesting details about what the region's climate and landscape were like more than thirty million years ago.

Start: The trailhead is located 11.7 miles west of Dayville off OR 19.
Distance: 1.4 miles out and back
Hiking time: 30 to 45 minutes
Difficulty: Easy; gentle grade
Best season: May through Oct
Other trail users: Hikers only
Canine compatibility: Leashed dogs permitted. If you are hiking with your dog during July and Aug, the trail surface can be very hot. Use caution.

Land status: National monument
Nearest town: Dayville
Fees and permits: None
Schedule: Year-round
Maps: Maptech CD: Hermiston/Prineville/ Canyon City, OR; USGS: Picture Gorge East, OR; Picture Gorge West, OR
Trail contact: John Day Fossil Beds National Monument, 32651 Highway 19, Kimberly, OR 97848-9701; (541) 987-2333, ext. 1240; nps.gov/joda/planyourvisit/index.htm

Finding the trailhead: From Dayville travel 6.6 miles west on US 26. At the junction with OR 19, turn right and drive 5.1 miles (you'll pass the Sheep Rock Unit Visitor Center after 2 miles) to the Blue Basin trailhead and parking area on the right side of the road. There are restrooms and interpretive signs at the trailhead. *DeLorme: Oregon Atlas & Gazetteer:* Page 81 B6. GPS: N44 35.726 / W119 37.930

The Hike

Two paths can be accessed from the Blue Basin trailhead: the Blue Basin Overlook Trail and the Island in Time Trail. The 0.7-mile Island in Time Trail, described here, is located in the Sheep Rock Unit of the John Day Fossil Beds National Monument and highlights some of the species that roamed the area's hills and valleys more than thirty million years ago. The Sheep Rock Unit is one of three units in the national monument that cover a total of 14,000 acres—the other two units are Clarno, located 18 miles west of Fossil off OR 218; and Painted Hills, 9 miles northwest of Mitchell off US 26. Established in 1975, this vast preserve offers a glimpse at the plants and animals that lived between the extinction of the dinosaurs and the Ice Age.

Before you embark on the Island in Time Trail, or any trail in the national monument, stop by the park's two interpretive centers: the Thomas Condon Paleontology Center and the Cant Ranch Historical Museum. The Thomas Condon Paleontology Center is located 2 miles northwest of the intersection of US 26 and OR 19, and the

Dramatic rock formations on the Island in Time Trail

Cant Ranch Historical Museum is located another 0.25 mile past the Paleontology Center on OR 19. The Thomas Condon Paleontology Center has exhibits on the geology, fossils, and processes of paleontology in the area, and it also has a short hiking trail that ends at a nice viewpoint of the valley. The Cant Ranch Historical Museum has displays that tell the story of life on the ranch. It also has displays of antique farm equipment, two easy hiking trails, and a shady picnic area. Restrooms and water are available at both interpretive centers.

After soaking up the fun facts at the interpretive centers, proceed about 3 miles northwest on OR 19 to the Blue Basin trailhead and the start of the Island in Time

A family learning about the ancient inhabitants of the John Day Valley ▶

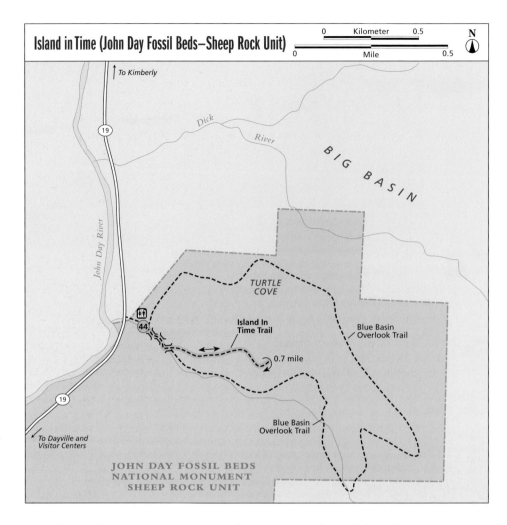

Island in Time (John Day Fossil Beds–Sheep Rock Unit)

Kilometer
0   0.5
Mile
0   0.5

N

To Kimberly

19

Dick River

BIG BASIN

John Day River

TURTLE COVE

Island In Time Trail

44

0.7 mile

Blue Basin Overlook Trail

19

Blue Basin Overlook Trail

To Dayville and Visitor Centers

JOHN DAY FOSSIL BEDS
NATIONAL MONUMENT
SHEEP ROCK UNIT

Trail. According to an interpretive sign located just up the trail, the volcanic eruptions that occurred here millions of years ago covered the native plants and animals with windblown silt and washed them into ash-filled streams and ponds. Subsequent years of wind and rain have eroded the greenish clay rock in the basin to expose the fossils. The trail passes several of these fossils, now enclosed in glass.

At 0.3 mile you can view a glass-encased fossil of an ancient tortoise; at 0.4 mile you can gaze at the interesting fossil of an oreodont, a sheep-size leaf-eater that was once abundant in this area. You can also see the fossil remains of a stabbing cat, which the park describes as a "saber-toothed cat" that preyed on "slow-moving and thick-skinned animals." What is especially interesting about these displays is that you are seeing the fossils as they were actually discovered in the claystone rock.

If you're in the mood for a steeper, more challenging hike, try the Blue Basin Overlook Trail, a 3.0-mile loop to a scenic vista overlooking the John Day River

Valley. Still more trails, including the quarter-mile Flood of Fire Trail, which ascends a ridge for a view of the John Day Valley, and the wheelchair-accessible Story in Stone Trail, which features more fossils, are located to the northwest in the national monument's Foree Area.

Miles and Directions

0.0 Start at the large trailhead sign at the Blue Basin parking lot. Go right to begin the Island in Time Trail (the Blue Basin Overlook loop is to the left). Cross a bridge and pass an interpretive sign.

0.1 Pass a bench on your right.

0.2 Cross two wooden bridges and pass an interpretive sign on your right. (An intersection with the Blue Basin Overlook Trail is on your right.)

0.3 Cross two more bridges and arrive at an interpretive sign and bench on the right side of the trail. Next to the sign is a glass-enclosed fossil of an ancient tortoise. Continue past the fossil and cross three more bridges.

0.4 Cross two more bridges and ascend a set of stone steps. Arrive at an interpretive sign on your right and a glass-enclosed fossil of an oreodont.

0.5 Arrive at another interpretive sign and a stabbing-cat fossil. Continue along the trail and cross a bridge.

0.7 Arrive at the end of the trail and the turnaround point.

1.4 Reach the Blue Basin parking lot and your car.

Hike Information

Local Information

Grant County Chamber of Commerce, 301 W. Main St., John Day, OR 97845; (800) 769-5664; gcoregonlive.com

45 Black Canyon Trail

The Black Canyon Trail takes you on a tour of the outback in the Black Canyon Wilderness. The trail follows Black Canyon Creek through a deep, rocky canyon filled with ponderosa pine and Douglas fir and numerous stream crossings. If you hike the trail during the midsummer months, don't miss the opportunity to feast on the wild red raspberries. If you are up for an adventure and want to get away from it all, backpack the entire 11.6-mile trail (not just the 2.6 miles described below). Set up a shuttle by leaving a car at the Wolf Mountain trailhead.

Start: The trailhead is located 13.5 miles south of Dayville off South Fork John Day Road (FR 47).
Distance: 5.2 miles out and back (11.6-mile shuttle option)
Hiking time: 3 to 4 hours
Difficulty: Difficult; many stream crossings and thick brush
Best season: July through Oct
Other trail users: Equestrians
Canine compatibility: Dogs permitted

Land status: Wilderness area
Nearest town: Dayville
Fees and permits: None
Schedule: June through Nov
Maps: Maptech CD: Hermiston/Prineville/ Canyon City, OR; USGS: Wolf Mountain, OR; Aldrich Gulch, OR
Trail contact: Paulina Ranger Station, 77803 Beaver Creek Rd., Paulina, OR 97751; (541) 549-7700; fs.usda.gov/main/centraloregon/ home

Finding the trailhead: From Dayville travel south 0.5 mile on South Fork John Day Road (FR 47), from US 26. Turn right and continue on South Fork John Day Road for another 13 miles until you reach a dirt pullout on the right side of the road. A sign reads BLACK CANYON TRAILHEAD. *DeLorme: Oregon Atlas & Gazetteer:* Page 81 C6. GPS: N44 20.022 / W119 33.910

The Hike

The Black Canyon Trail cuts right through the heart of the 3,400-acre Black Canyon Wilderness. The area is a haven for more than 300 species of wildlife—black bears, elk, deer, cougars, rattlesnakes, and raptors, to name a few. It's a true wilderness hike, guaranteed to make you feel as though you're away from it all.

The trail is fraught with numerous stream crossings and lots of poison oak, so carry extra shoes and wear long pants to combat these obstacles. Also carry a sturdy walking stick in case you need to sweep a rattlesnake from your path. Check the trailhead for sticks used by previous hikers.

The first mile of trail leads through a thick layer of streamside plants, trees, and raspberry bushes. Begin by fording the South Fork of the John Day River. Cross the slippery rocks, using a walking stick for balance if you need it. In spring the river can be swift and high, so be careful. After the trail crosses the river, it seems to disappear in a mass of streamside vegetation, but if you turn left and walk up the bank about 30

Black Canyon Trail

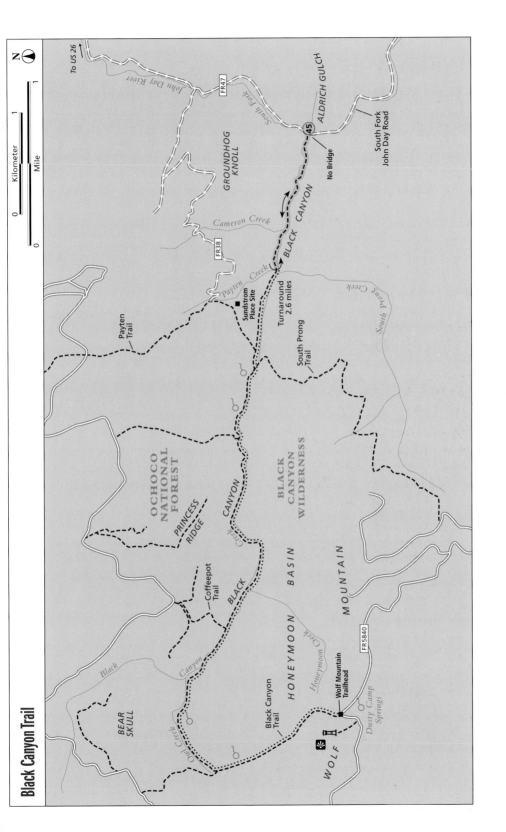

N

0 Kilometer 1

0 Mile 1

To US 26

John Day River

South Fork

FR47

45

ALDRICH GULCH

No Bridge

South Fork
John Day Road

GROUNDHOG
KNOLL

BLACK CANYON

Cameron Creek

FR38

Payten Creek

Sundstrom
Place Site

Turnaround
2.6 miles

South Prong
Trail

South Prong Creek

Payten
Trail

OCHOCO
NATIONAL
FOREST

PRINCESS
RIDGE

CANYON

Creek

BLACK CANYON
WILDERNESS

BASIN

MOUNTAIN

Coffeepot
Trail

BLACK

HONEYMOON

Honeymoon Creek

FR5840

Black

Canyon

Owl Creek

Black Canyon
Trail

Wolf Mountain
Trailhead

Dusty Camp
Springs

BEAR
SKULL

WOLF

TRAIL TIP

This trail is infamous for its rattlesnakes, poison oak, and range cows. Wear long nylon pants and boots. Bring an extra pair of tennis shoes or sandals for the multiple stream crossings.

yards, you'll find the path again. In no time, you'll become an expert at fording the creek. In just 2.6 miles you'll get your feet wet fifteen times. Tennis shoes (without socks) seem to work best for these crossings, but bring along a pair of sandals to wear during breaks.

Don't be surprised if you see range cows munching grass along the stream bank. Cows aren't supposed to be in the wilderness area, but the fence along the border is in disrepair. If you do see cows, let the Forest Service know they're in the area so that they can be safely returned to their owners, the fences can be mended, and the wilderness can recuperate.

As the trail continues up the canyon, it zigzags through thick brush and follows grassy ridges through a ponderosa pine, fir, and tamarack forest. Interspersed among the tangles of bushes are sprinkles of crimson penstemon, bright-purple lupine, and vibrant Indian paintbrush. It's a beautiful place indeed.

If you want to complete the entire 11.6-mile trail through the canyon, you can set up a car shuttle. To get to the trailhead near Wolf Mountain, drive 14 miles west of Dayville (63 miles east of Prineville) on US 26. Turn south onto FR 12 and drive 15.6 miles. Turn left onto FR 1250 and drive 3.9 miles to a road junction. Continue driving straight on FR 090 for 3.6 miles. (The road becomes very rough here, but it's passable with a passenger car.) Turn left onto FR 5820 and drive 0.4 mile to a junction with FR 5840. Continue driving 2.5 miles on FR 5840 to the trailhead.

Miles and Directions

0.0 Start the hike at the Black Canyon trailhead. (**Note:** Be sure to look for walking sticks left by other hikers. These sticks will help you navigate the many stream crossings and are useful to probe the trail ahead of you for rattlesnakes.) Immediately cross the South Fork of the John Day River. This river can be very high in spring, but it's only usually calf deep beginning in July. After crossing the river, walk 30 feet to your left to hook up with the trail.

0.1 Cross Black Canyon Creek.

0.2 Cross the creek.

0.3 Navigate another stream crossing; walk 25 yards and cross the creek again.

0.7 Cross the creek; walk 20 yards and cross the creek again.

0.9 Navigate another stream crossing.

1.0 Cross the creek three times.

1.2 Cross the creek.

1.3 Cross the creek again.

1.5 Cross the creek again.

1.9 Navigate another stream crossing.

2.4 Cross a side stream.

2.6 Cross a side stream and arrive at the turnaround point. Retrace the same route back to the trailhead. **Option:** You can continue another 9 miles one-way to the end of the trail.

5.2 Arrive back at the trailhead.

Hike Information

Local Information

Grant County Chamber of Commerce, 301 W. Main St., John Day, OR 97845; (800) 769-5664; gcoregonlive.com

46 Strawberry Lakes Trail

This trail takes you on a tour of the scenic Strawberry Mountain Wilderness. Your tour begins at Strawberry Campground and takes you to a high glacial cirque that is home to Strawberry Lake. The trail then leads around the lake, taking you to the spectacular cascade of Strawberry Falls and ultimately to charming Little Strawberry Lake.

Start: The trailhead is located 11.5 miles south of Prairie City on CR 60.
Distance: 6.8 miles out and back
Hiking time: 3 to 4 hours
Difficulty: Moderate; a challenging ascent to Strawberry and Little Strawberry Lakes
Best season: July through Oct
Other trail users: Hikers only
Canine compatibility: Leashed dogs permitted
Land status: Wilderness area

Nearest town: Prairie City
Fees and permits: Free wilderness permit required
Schedule: Open July through Oct
Maps: Maptech CD: Hermiston/Prineville/Canyon City, OR; USGS: Strawberry Mountain, OR
Trail contact: Malheur National Forest, Prairie City Ranger District, 327 SW Front St., Prairie City, OR 97869; (541) 820-3800; www.fs.usda.gov/malheur/

Finding the trailhead: From Prairie City turn off US 26 onto Bridge Street (CR 60) and head south. Continue approximately 11.5 miles to Strawberry Campground. (The road becomes gravel after 3.3. miles.) *Delorme: Oregon Atlas & Gazetteer:* Page 82 C2. GPS: N44 19.152 / W118 40.490

The Hike

The vast Malheur National Forest, in the northeast corner of the state, encompasses nearly 1.5 million acres of the Blue Mountain Range, drawing together elevations from 4,000 to more than 9,000 feet. Ponderosa and lodgepole pines and many different species of fir dominate the region's forests. The area supports five different ecozones and a diverse cast of animals—elk, mule deer, antelope, bighorn sheep, beaver, and pine marten. Among its notable raptors are bald and golden eagles and sharp-shinned and red-tailed hawks.

Within Malheur National Forest is the 68,700-acre Strawberry Mountain Wilderness—characterized by its rugged high alpine country with lakes, jagged mountain peaks, and U-shaped glacial valleys. Old and young mountains make up the impressive peaks of the Strawberry Range. More than 200 million years ago, when the North American continent drifted westward, it pushed up a large section of the Pacific seafloor, creating the western half of the Strawberry Range. The eastern half, created only sixteen million years ago, took form when lava erupted from vents and spread east from John Day to Unity.

A nice creek-side view on the Strawberry Lakes Trail ▶

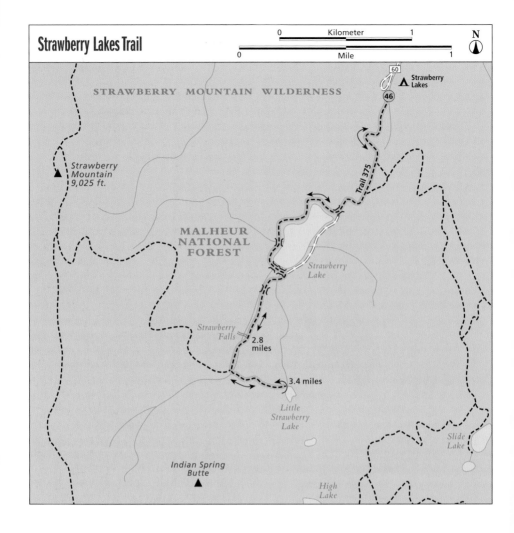

0   Kilometer   1

0   Mile   1

N

STRAWBERRY MOUNTAIN WILDERNESS

60
Strawberry Lakes
46

Strawberry Mountain 9,025 ft.

Trail 375

MALHEUR NATIONAL FOREST

Strawberry Lake

Strawberry Falls
2.8 miles

3.4 miles

Little Strawberry Lake

Slide Lake

Indian Spring Butte

High Lake

Strawberry Mountain, the forest's tallest point and star attraction, is the remnant of a much larger stratovolcano that once existed here. Nathan Wills Fisk, one of the area's first settlers, gave the 9,025-foot mountain its name because of the abundance of wild strawberries found in the area.

More than 100 miles of trail run through the Strawberry Mountain Wilderness. Trail 375 offers a good introduction to the trail network and to this special wilderness. The route begins at Strawberry Lakes Campground in an aromatic fir forest and travels 1.4 miles to Strawberry Lake. It then loops around the lake, past shimmering groves of aspen trees, and follows a creek through thick forest for half a mile to Strawberry Falls before coming to an end at Little Strawberry Lake, a great place to rest and enjoy lunch before turning back for the trek home.

Miles and Directions

0.0 Start from Strawberry Lakes Campground at the Trail 375 trailhead. Voluntary registration cards are available at the trailhead.

1.0 Turn right at the trail fork. (The trail heading left goes to Slide Lake.)

1.3 Turn right toward Strawberry Lake. (The trail heading left goes to Slide Lake.)

1.4 Reach Strawberry Lake and arrive at a trail junction. Turn right and cross a log bridge over Strawberry Creek; continue on the trail as it parallels Strawberry Lake.

2.3 Turn right toward Little Strawberry Lake. Walk a short way and then come to another trail junction. Stay to the right.

2.8 Reach Strawberry Falls.

3.0 Turn left toward Little Strawberry Lake.

3.4 Arrive at Little Strawberry Lake and your turnaround point. Retrace the same route back to the trailhead.

6.8 Arrive back at the trailhead.

Hike Information

Local Information

Grant County Chamber of Commerce, 301 W. Main St., John Day, OR 97845; (800) 769-5664 gcoregonlive.com

47 Lakes Basin

The Lakes Basin hike is an adventure into Oregon's Little Switzerland. The jagged granite peaks of the Wallowa Mountains, high alpine lakes, and scenic glacial valleys are just a few of the spectacular natural landmarks on this classic trail. The route begins at the Two Pan trailhead and then parallels the East Fork of the Lostine River. Passing through an alpine valley, the hike then climbs to reveal the many beautiful lakes of the Lakes Basin area. Keep in mind that this is a very popular trail. If you're seeking solitude, come in early fall, after the summer crowds (and mosquitoes) have gone.

Start: The Two Pan trailhead is located 17.8 miles south of Lostine on Lostine River Road.
Distance: 20.2 miles lollipop
Hiking time: 10 to 12 hours
Difficulty: Difficult; steep ascent and length of hike
Best season: Aug through Oct
Other trail users: Hikers only
Canine compatibility: Dogs permitted
Land status: Wilderness area
Nearest town: Lostine

Fees and permits: A Northwest Forest Pass is required. You can purchase a pass online at www.fs.usda.gov/main/r6/passes-permits/recreation or by calling (800) 270-7504. A free wilderness permit is also required.
Schedule: Mid-July through Oct
Maps: Maptech CD: Pendleton/Northeast, OR; USGS: Eagle Cap, OR
Trail contact: Wallowa-Whitman National Forest, 1550 Dewey Ave., Baker City, OR 97814; (541) 523-6391; www.fs.usda.gov/wallowa-whitman/

Finding the trailhead: From Lostine turn south off OR 82 onto Lostine River Road (FR 8210). Drive 17.8 miles (the road becomes gravel after 7 miles) to the Two Pan trailhead. *DeLorme: Oregon Atlas & Gazetteer:* Page 87 D7. GPS: N45 15.011 / W117 22.592

The Hike

The 358,461-acre Eagle Cap Wilderness is one of northeast Oregon's most treasured areas. The centerpiece of this magnificent area is the Wallowa Mountains, whose jagged granite peaks and ridges resemble California's Sierra Nevada range. Seventeen peaks here, including the 9,826-foot marble-topped Matterhorn and 9,595-foot Eagle Cap, top out at more than 9,000 feet.

The limestone and marble rocks found here today are the remnants of an ancient sea floor. Yes, 200 million years ago this mountain range was entirely underwater. When the North American continent shifted, this sea floor was pushed upward. About one hundred million years ago, hot lava intruded into the surrounding underground sedimentary layers. It then cooled slowly over a long period of time to form granite. Millions of years of glacial erosion have since carved the Wallowa Mountains and their valleys and lake basins into spectacular granite masterpieces.

Gorgeous Mirror Lake is a popular destination in the Wallowa Lakes Basin.

The Wallowa Mountains take their name from the Nez Percé word *wallowa,* meaning "fish trap." For hundreds of years the Wallowa band of the Nez Percé gathered plants, fished, and hunted game here in the summer months and then traveled to the warmer Hells Canyon country in winter.

When gold was discovered in the region in the mid-1860s and settlers began to arrive, the federal government decided to take back land that was originally promised to the Nez Percé in treaties from a decade earlier. In 1863 a newly proposed treaty asked the Nez Percé to return more than 6 million acres of their tribal land to the government. Nez Percé chiefs felt that the new treaty was unfair and refused to allow government officials to force their people to move. Eventually the government agreed and announced that white settlers could not remain in the area. The land would continue to belong to the Nez Percé.

Unfortunately, settlers and politicians refused to accept the decision. To avoid trouble, several bands of Nez Percé decided to relocate to a reservation in Idaho.

But things didn't go smoothly. On their way to the reservation, young braves from one of the bands killed four white settlers, kicking off the Nez Percé War of 1877.

As the war began, the leader of the Wallowa band, In-mut-too-yah-lat-lat (translated as "Thunder Coming up Over the Land from the Water"), decided to lead his people to Canada. There, he thought, they would find freedom from persecution by the US Army. He led 800 of his people on a 1,400-mile trek through Idaho and Montana, eluding and fighting US soldiers until they were caught just 40 miles from the Canadian border in the Bear Paw Mountains of Montana. After their surrender, In-mut-too-yah-lat-lat and his people were moved to a reservation in Oklahoma.

Sadly, In-mut-too-yah-lat-lat's wishes were never realized: In 1885 he and the rest of the Nez Percé were relocated to the Colville Reservation in Washington State. It is said that the wise and peaceful chief died of a broken heart because he was never allowed to return to his homeland. Today visitors to the Lakes Basin area of the Eagle Cap Wilderness understand why the Nez Percé wished to remain in this stunning area.

The Two Pan Trail leads to the heart of the wilderness through a glaciated valley and an alpine lake basin. The trail begins by paralleling the East Fork of the Lostine River and ascends steeply through a thick forest of Engelmann spruce and western larch. To the east is a good view of Hurricane Divide. After 3 miles the trail arrives at a high, rock-strewn glacial valley. The trail skirts the

OREGONIAN TONGUE TWISTERS

Having trouble pronouncing your latest destination? This handy key should help:

Aloha—Uh-LO-uh

Belknap—BELL-nap

Cape Arago—Cape AIR-uh-go

Celilo Falls—Seh-LIE-lo Falls

Champoeg—Sham-POO-ee

Chemult—Sheh-MULT

Chiloquin—CHILL-oh-quin

Clatskanie—KLATS-kuh-ni

Coquille—Ko-KEEL

Deschutes—Deh-SHOOTS

Gleneden—Glen-EE-den

Grand Ronde—Grand Rond

Heceta—Heh-SEE-tah

La Grande—La GRAND

Madras—MAD-Russ

Ochoco—O-CHOH-ko

Owyhee—O-WHY-he

Paulina—Paul-I-nah

Siuslaw—Sigh-OO-slah

The Dalles—The DALS

Tillamook—TILL-uh-muk

Wallowa—rhymes with Ka-POW-uh

Willamette—Will-LAM-it

Winema—Why-NEE-mah

Yachats—YAW-Hots

Yaquina—Ya-QUIN-uh

Horse packers on the East Fork of Lostine River Trail in the Lakes Basin

western side of the valley for the next 4 miles and includes magnificent views of Eagle Cap rising prominently in the distance.

At the southern end of the valley, the trail begins to switchback steeply through a lodgepole pine and alpine fir forest to the upper Lakes Basin. At mile 7.3 you come to a junction and veer left. You pass Mirror Lake on your right and have a spectacular view of 9,595-foot Eagle Cap to the south. At mile 7.6 you begin a 5.0-mile loop, during which you pass Moccasin, Douglas, and Sunshine Lakes. After the loop it's another 7.6 miles back to the trailhead. Snow is present on the trail until early August. Be sure to bring plenty of mosquito repellent. The mosquitoes can be very bad during July and August.

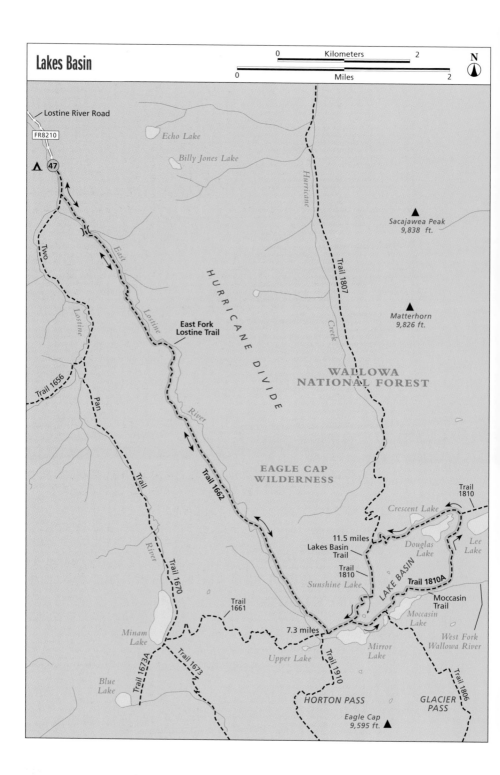

Lakes Basin

0 — Kilometers — 2

0 — Miles — 2

N

Lostine River Road

FR8210

47

Echo Lake

Billy Jones Lake

Hurricane

Two

East

Lostine

Lostine

Trail 1656

Pan

Trail

River

East Fork
Lostine Trail

H U R R I C A N E   D I V I D E

River

Trail 1662

Sacajawea Peak
9,838 ft.

Trail 1807

Creek

Matterhorn
9,826 ft.

WALLOWA
NATIONAL FOREST

EAGLE CAP
WILDERNESS

Trail
1810

Crescent Lake

Douglas
Lake

Lee
Lake

11.5 miles
Lakes Basin
Trail

Trail
1810

Trail 1810A

LAKE BASIN

Sunshine Lake

Moccasin
Trail

Trail
1670

River

Trail
1661

Moccasin
Lake

West Fork
Wallowa River

Minam
Lake

7.3 miles

Upper Lake

Trail 1910

Mirror
Lake

Trail 1806

Trail 1673A

Trail 1673

Blue
Lake

HORTON PASS

GLACIER
PASS

Eagle Cap
9,595 ft.

Miles and Directions

0.0   Start hiking at the Two Pan trailhead. (**Note:** Fill out a free self-issue wilderness permit at the trailhead.)

0.1   Turn left at the trail fork. A sign indicates EAST FORK LOSTINE TRAIL 1662. Cross a stream and enter the Eagle Cap Wilderness.

0.3   Turn right and cross a log bridge over the East Fork of the Lostine River.

3.0   Begin walking through a high, scenic glacial meadow.

7.3   Turn left where the sign indicates LAKES BASIN TRAIL 1810. Pass Mirror Lake on your right. (**Note:** If you are backpacking, this is a great place to set up base camp.)

7.6   Turn right where a sign indicates MOCCASIN TRAIL 1810a. (**Note:** The Lakes Basin Trail 1810 turns to the left here.) Begin the loop portion of the trail. Pass Moccasin Lake on your right.

8.3   Turn left where a sign indicates WEST FORK OF THE WALLOWA RIVER. (The trail heading right goes toward Glacier Pass.)

10.1   Walk by picturesque Douglas Lake and then come to a trail junction. Turn left where the sign reads HURRICANE CREEK. (The trail that heads right goes toward the West Fork of the Wallowa River.)

11.5   Turn left where a sign indicates LAKES BASIN TRAIL 1810. (The trail that goes right heads toward Hurricane Trail 1807.)

12.4   Pass Sunshine Lake on your left.

12.6   Complete the loop portion of the hike. Turn right onto the East Fork Lostine Trail and proceed 7.6 miles back to the trailhead.

20.2   Arrive back at the Two Pan trailhead.

Hike Information

Local Information

Wallowa County Chamber of Commerce, 936 W. North St., Enterprise, OR 97828; (800) 585-4121; wallowacountychamber.com

Restaurants

Terminal Gravity Brewing Public House, 803 SE School St., Enterprise; (541) 426-3000; terminalgravitybrewing.com/index.html

Honorable Mentions

Northeast Oregon

UU   Sumpter Valley Dredge State Heritage Area

You can explore the rich history of Sumpter Valley by visiting the Sumpter Valley Dredge State Heritage Area. The main attraction at this heritage site is the Sumpter Valley Dredge that was used to extract gold from the Powder River. This impressive vessel weighs 1,240 tons and was in operation until 1954. You can explore the dredge and learn about its history as well as hike on 3.5 miles of trails. The park also has a visitor center that has more opportunities to learn about the history of this area.

The Sumpter Valley Dredge weighs 1,240 tons and has a 52-foot-wide hull.

The old union oil wagon was used to carry lube and fuel oil for the D7 cat the dredge used for pulling rigging and assisting the test drill running ahead of the dredge.

The park is open May through October and is located in Sumpter, which is 30 miles west of Baker City off of OR 7. For more information, contact Oregon State Parks and Recreation, 725 Summer St. NE, Suite C, Salem, OR 97301; (800) 551-6949; oregonstateparks.org/park_239.php. *DeLorme: Oregon Atlas & Gazetteer:* Page 82 A4.

VV North Fork John Day River to Trout Creek

You'll love this easy 5.2-mile out-and-back route along the North Fork of the John Day River. To get there from Baker City, head north on I-84 for 19 miles; take exit 285 for North Powder. Follow Anthony Lake signs for 21 miles to the Anthony Lake Recreation Area. From here continue on FR 73 for 17 miles to a stop sign. Continue straight and enter the North Fork of the John Day Campground. Proceed through the campground to the trailhead on the left.

Follow the trail as it wanders through a shady Douglas fir forest along this Wild and Scenic River. At 2.6 miles you'll arrive at a footbridge crossing lively Trout Creek (your turnaround point). For a longer adventure or backpack, continue on the trail for several more miles. A campground is located at the trailhead.

For more information, contact the Wallowa-Whitman National Forest, 1550 Dewey Ave., Baker City, OR 97814; (541) 523-6391; www.fs.usda.gov/wallowa-whitman. *DeLorme: Oregon Atlas & Gazetteer:* Page 82 A3.

WW Hells Canyon

This easy 2.4-mile out-and-back hike begins at the Hells Canyon Dam visitor center, which has displays that describe the history of the dam. Start the hike here by heading down a set of stairs to a boat launch area. Pick up the path on the far side of the boat launch. Follow the trail past rugged high-walled cliffs as it parallels the shores of the impressive Snake River. At 1 mile you'll reach tumbling Stud Creek. From the creek continue another 0.2 mile to the trail's end at a rocky beach next to the river (your turnaround point). Retrace the route back to your car. Watch for poison oak on this trail. To get there from Baker City, head 65 miles east on OR 86 to Oxbow. From Oxbow follow signs for 24 miles to the visitor center at Hells Canyon Dam.

For more information, contact the Wallowa-Whitman National Forest, 1550 Dewey Ave., Baker City, OR 97814; (541) 523-6391; www.fs.usda.gov/wallowa-whitman. *DeLorme: Oregon Atlas & Gazetteer:* Page 88 A4.

XX Echo/Traverse Lakes

This difficult 16.6-mile trail blazes through the high country of the Wallowa Mountains to offer stunning views of Echo and Traverse Lakes—lakes that rest in spectacular glacial-carved basins. To get there from La Grande, take I-84 to OR 203 exit 265. Drive south on OR 203 for 11 miles to downtown Union. In Union take a sharp left and continue following OR 203 south for 13.8 miles to the junction with FR 77 (a gravel road). Turn left onto FR 77 and drive 15 miles to West Eagle Creek. The trailhead is located on the left side of the road. (**Note:** The road becomes very rough after 9.6 miles. A sign warns that the road is not suitable for passenger cars; however, if you go slowly, the road is passable in a passenger car.)

Make sure you don't start the trail at the wooden trailhead sign. Instead, start by walking up the dirt road at the north end of the parking lot. Follow this dirt road as it passes some walk-in campsites for about 0.2 mile. It then turns into the dirt path. At mile 0.3 cross a wooden bridge. The trail parallels an open grassy valley where you may see cows grazing. At mile 0.5 come to a fork and stay left. (Going right puts you on Fake Creek Trail 1914.) After another 1.2 miles you cross a stream. At mile 1.3 you'll have to ford a stream. You can either wade through the stream or walk across thin logs to get across. Do not continue following the trail as it parallels the stream. Pick the trail up on the other side.

After 1.4 miles you enter the Eagle Cap Wilderness. Another 3 miles and you cross Eagle Creek on a log bridge. The trail begins climbing steeply up an enormous granite canyon on a long series of switchbacks. After 3.8 miles the trail comes to a fork. Go right, where the sign indicates TRAIL CREEK. (If you turn left, you'll be headed toward Elk Creek.) After 6.1 miles cross Eagle Creek again. At mile 6.3 there's a spectacular view of Echo Lake on your right. You can turn around here or, for an even more spectacular view, continue another 2 miles to Traverse Lake.

This trail requires a free wilderness permit. For more information, contact the Wallowa-Whitman National Forest, La Grande Ranger District, 3502 Highway 30, La Grande, OR 97850; (541) 963-7186; www.fs.usda.gov/wallowa-whitman. *DeLorme: Oregon Atlas & Gazetteer:* Page 87 D7.

The 9,595-foot Eagle Cap Mountain is the centerpiece of the Lakes Basin in the Wallowa Mountains.

The author and her dogs, Tiz and Bear, on the summit of Eagle Cap Mountain.

YY Historic Oregon Trail

This easy 4.2-mile trail takes you back in time as it weaves through the old wagon ruts of the famous Oregon Trail, which during the 1800s brought thousands of settlers to Oregon. This route offers historic and natural wonders: You'll be able to check out historic pioneer homesites and defunct mines, as well as reward yourself with grand views of the Powder River Valley and the majestic Elkhorn Mountains. While you're here, be sure to take the time to visit the National Historic Oregon Trails Interpretive Center, which provides a wealth of displays about those who traveled the Oregon Trail, as well as the history and culture of the Native Americans impacted by this westward migration. To get there from Baker City, drive east on OR 86 for 6 miles to the National Historic Oregon Trails Interpretive Center. The trailhead is in the back of the center.

For more information, contact the National Historic Oregon Trail Interpretive Center, 22267 Highway 86, P.O. Box 987, Baker City, OR 97814-0987; (541) 523-1843; oregontrail.blm.gov. *DeLorme: Oregon Atlas & Gazetteer:* Page 83 A5.

ZZ Eagle Cap Mountain

If you like to hike to the top of peaks, you should try hiking to the top of 9,595-foot Eagle Cap Mountain. It is a 20-mile strenuous out-and-back hike from the Two Pan trailhead with about 4,000 feet of elevation gain. It is highly recommended that you backpack in, camp overnight, and then attempt to hike up the summit the next day. You will follow Trail 1662 along the East Fork of the Lostine River for 7.3 miles to the junction with the Minam Lake/Mirror Lake Trail 1661. Follow Trail 1661 a short distance to the junction with Trail 1910. Follow trail 1910 for 1.2 miles to the junction with Trail 1805 (East Fork Eagle Creek Trail). Continue straight (left) on Trail 1805 and follow it another 1.5 strenuous miles to the summit of 9,595-foot Eagle Cap Mountain. It is recommended that you try this hike during mid- to late August when all of the snow has melted. Be forewarned that the mosquitoes are very bad in this area from June through August.

A Northwest Forest Pass is required for this hike. You can purchase a pass online at www.fs.usda.gov/main/r6/passes-permits/recreation or by calling (800) 270-7504. A free wilderness permit is also required and is available at the trailhead. For more information, contact the Wallowa-Whitman National Forest, 1550 Dewey Ave., Baker City, OR 97814; (541) 523-6391; www.fs.usda.gov/wallowa-whitman/.

Southeast Oregon

No place celebrates the beauty, remoteness, and ruggedness of southeast Oregon like the nearby Hart Mountain National Antelope Refuge, located approximately 60 miles northeast of Lakeview. This distinct refuge comprises sagebrush, hot springs, rugged canyons and ridges, and aspen-filled valleys. The refuge was established in 1936 by President Franklin Roosevelt to protect the pronghorn antelope. Today it supports a healthy antelope population as well as coyotes, jackrabbits, raptors, bighorn sheep, and mule deer. You'll also have to contend with rattlesnakes and mosquitoes—always wear leather boots and carry mosquito repellent. You can hike through this open sagebrush country along Poker Jim Ridge as it rises dramatically above the Warner Basin and the Warner Wetlands. These wetlands support dozens of species of migrating birds, including Canada geese, whistling swans, and white pelicans—keep an eye out.

Head northeast from Lakeview to the natural wonder of Steens Mountain, a fault-block mountain that showcases U-shaped, glacier-carved gorges and supports a variety of ecozones. Take the summit hike to the top of 9,733-foot Steens Mountain for fantastic views of the surrounding lakes and mountains. Bring binoculars to spot the golden eagles riding the thermals and bighorn sheep grazing the slopes of the glacial gorges.

Backpackers and day hikers will enjoy trekking into the Gearhart Mountain Wilderness, located 18 miles northeast of Bly off OR 140. This area is characterized by old-growth ponderosa, lodgepole, and whitebark pines. Take a walk to the top of Gearhart Mountain for magnificent views of the Three Sisters, Steens Mountain, and California's Mount Lassen.

The weather in this part of Oregon can hover in the eighties and nineties at the lower elevations and drop thirty degrees at the higher elevations. Some trailheads around this area are remote and often off roads that are in poor condition. Always carry extra water with you in your car, as well as tools and a spare gallon of gas.

When you are visiting this part of Oregon, it's recommended that you carry a well-stocked first-aid kit, at least one gallon of water per person per day, sunscreen, a wide-brimmed hat, and sunglasses.

Cattle ranches are a common site in southeast Oregon. ▶

48 Gearhart Mountain

If you truly want to experience the beauty and solitude of pristine wilderness, this hike is for you. Old-growth ponderosa, lodgepole, and whitebark pines fill the Gearhart Mountain Wilderness with their stately beauty. This hike also takes you through the Palisades, a unique area of oddly shaped rock formations, and ends at a high pass with magnificent views of Steens Mountain to the east, the Three Sisters Mountains to the west, and California's Mount Lassen. Backpackers have the option of continuing another 3.4 miles to Blue Lake, a high alpine lake stocked with rainbow trout.

Start: The trailhead is located 17.7 miles northeast of Bly off OR 140.
Distance: 11.2 miles out and back (with a longer backpacking option to Blue Lake)
Hiking time: 5 to 7 hours
Difficulty: Difficult; steep ascent of Gearhart Mountain
Best season: July to Oct
Other trail users: Hikers only
Canine compatibility: Dogs permitted

Land status: Wilderness area
Nearest town: Bly
Schedule: June through Oct
Fees and permits: None
Maps: Maptech CD: Malheur Lake/Southeast, OR; USGS: Gearhart Mountain, OR
Trail contact: Fremont National Forest, Supervisor's Office, 1301 S. G St., Lakeview, OR 97630; (541) 947-2151; www.fs.usda.gov/fremont-winema/

Finding the trailhead: From Bly (54 miles east of Klamath Falls and 42 miles west of Lakeview on OR 140), head 1.3 miles east on OR 140 to Campbell Road. Turn left and travel 0.5 mile. Turn right onto FR 34, where a sign indicates GEARHART WILDERNESS 17 MILES. Drive 14.3 miles on FR 34. At the road fork stay left. Continue another 0.2 mile and then turn left onto Corral Creek Road (FR 212), a rough and narrow dirt road. Continue 1.4 miles to Gearhart Mountain Trail 100 (you'll pass Corral Creek Campground in 0.3 mile). *Delorme: Oregon Atlas & Gazetteer:* Page 72 B1. GPS: N42 27.700 / W120 47.996

The Hike

The bulk of Fremont National Forest lies in Lake County, one of Oregon's least populated areas. Though it's filled with scenic trails that offer both solitude and magnificent scenery, the 1,198,301-acre reserve is one of Oregon's most overlooked outdoor playgrounds. The forest borders California to the south, the Warner Range to the east, and the Deschutes and Winema National Forests to the north and west. The dry, high-desert ecosystem can be both harsh and unpredictable, with temperatures varying from thirty to one-hundred-plus degrees Fahrenheit and precipitation ranging from 16 to 40 inches. At the lower elevations, sagebrush and juniper trees dominate the landscape; at higher elevations you'll find thick stands of white fir, ponderosa pine, white pine, sugar pine, incense cedar, and lodgepole pine.

FREMONT NATIONAL FOREST

Fremont National Forest takes its name from John C. Frémont (1813-90), a topographical engineer for the US Army who led many explorations throughout the West, among them an expedition through Oregon in 1843. One of Frémont's more notable assignments was to find a railroad route over the Rocky Mountains. In his later years Frémont took to politics, becoming one of California's first senators in 1851. In 1856 Fremont showed up on the Republican Party ticket for president of the United States.

More than 300 species of fish, birds, and mammals flourish in this region. Among the large mammals you might be lucky enough to spot while hiking are Rocky Mountain elk, mule deer, and pronghorn antelope. Mountain lions, black bears, and bobcats also roam the hills and valleys of this seemingly endless expanse of national forest. Mallard ducks, whistling swans, and Canada geese are commonly found in the wetlands, and bald eagles and peregrine falcons nest here.

One of this national forest's hidden treasures is the 22,823-acre Gearhart Wilderness, the only wilderness area in the forest. The centerpiece of this wilderness area is Gearhart Mountain (8,364 feet), a shield-type volcano with glacier-carved valleys and well-known craggy cliffs (such as the Dome and Haystack Rock). Gearhart Mountain Trail 100 takes you right through the heart of this pristine wilderness. The trail described here begins at the Gearhart Mountain Trail 100 trailhead and leads you through an open old-growth ponderosa pine forest scattered with wildflowers in spring and summer. In short order, you come to the Palisades, a miniature rock city. Here you'll find balanced rocks, stacked rocks, and rocks in all sorts of unusual shapes. Next up is the Dome, a huge rock cliff that shoots skyward. Nearing the turnaround point, you'll reach an overlook with magnificent views of California's Mount Lassen to the south, Steens Mountain to the east, and the Three Sisters Mountains to the west. At the high pass and turnaround point, those backpacking may want to continue on the trail as it descends another 3.4 miles to the only lake in this wilderness area, Blue Lake. The lake is stocked with rainbow trout and makes a nice campsite after the 9-mile hike from the trailhead.

Miles and Directions

0.0 Start the hike at the wooden trailhead sign. Voluntary registration cards are available to fill out at the trailhead. Begin walking on Gearhart Mountain Trail 100. Shortly you'll pass a sign on your left that reads PALISADES ¾ MILE/THE NOTCH 6 MILES/BLUE LAKE 10 MILES.

0.7 Arrive at an area called the Palisades. Walk through interesting rock formations for about 0.3 mile and then continue on the trail as it descends on switchbacks for about 0.2 mile.

3.6 Pass the Dome—an impressive wall of rock cliff that shoots skyward on your right.

4.9 Turn right at the trail fork.

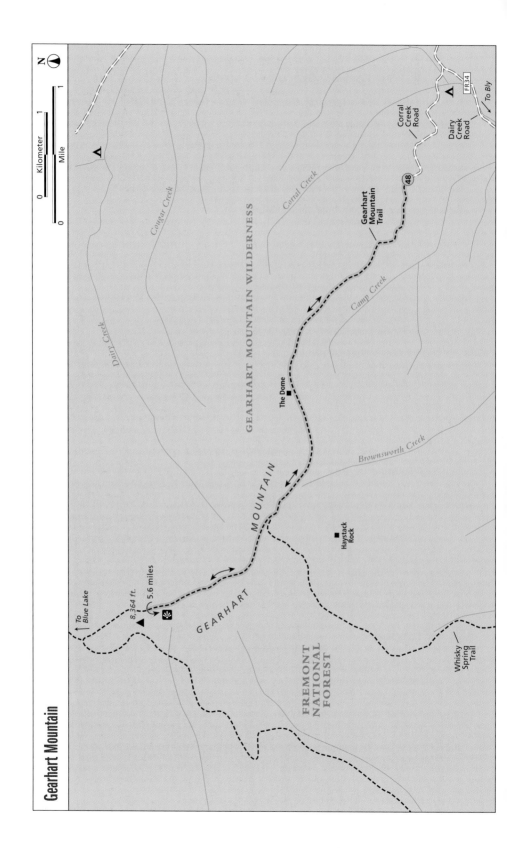

Gearhart Mountain

N

0 Kilometer 1

0 Mile 1

To
Blue Lake

8,364 ft.

5.6 miles

GEARHART

MOUNTAIN

Cougar Creek

Dairy Creek

GEARHART MOUNTAIN WILDERNESS

Corral Creek

Camp Creek

The Dome

Gearhart
Mountain
Trail

48

Corral
Creek Road

Dairy
Creek Road

FR34

To Bly

Brownsworth Creek

Haystack
Rock

FREMONT
NATIONAL
FOREST

Whisky
Spring Trail

5.5 Reach a spectacular view of the Gearhart Wilderness, California's Mount Lassen to the south, Steens Mountain to the east, and the Three Sisters Mountains to the west.

5.6 Reach a high pass and your turnaround point. Retrace the same route back to the trailhead. **Option:** Backpackers may want to continue another 3.4 miles to Blue Lake.

11.2 Arrive back at the trailhead.

Hike Information

Local Information

Lake County Chamber of Commerce, 126 N. E St., Lakeview, OR 97630; (541) 947-6040; lakecountychamber.org

49 Poker Jim Ridge

Escape to the wild expanse of the southeast Oregon desert and the Hart Mountain National Antelope Refuge, home to more than 330 species of animals, including the elusive pronghorn antelope. This hike takes you on a cross-country adventure along the edge of Poker Jim Ridge. Loaded with magnificent views of dozens of seasonal lakes that dot the Warner Basin, the hike culminates in a relaxing soak in a hot springs.

Start: The trailhead is located about 60 miles northeast of Lakeview off Hart Mountain Road (CR 212).
Distance: 4.0 miles out and back
Hiking time: 2 to 3 hours
Difficulty: Moderate; uneven, rocky terrain
Best season: June through Oct
Other trail users: Equestrians
Canine compatibility: Not dog friendly. The rocky trail is rough on dog paws. Also, there are rattlesnakes and foxtails.

Land status: National antelope refuge
Nearest town: Plush
Fees and permits: None
Schedule: Year-round
Maps: Maptech CD: Malheur Lake/Southeast, OR; USGS: Campbell Lake, OR
Trail contact: Hart Mountain National Antelope Refuge, Highway 40, 65 miles northeast of Lakeview, OR 97630; (541) 947-2731; fws.gov/sheldonhartmtn/Hart/index.html

Finding the trailhead: From Lakeview travel 4.6 miles north on US 395 to the OR 140 junction. Turn right (east) and drive 15.6 miles to the junction with Plush Cutoff Road (CR 313). Turn left (north) and drive 18.5 miles to the town of Plush. Continue driving through town for about a mile and turn right onto Hart Mountain Road (CR 212). Drive 20 miles (the road becomes to gravel at mile 13.1) and park in the dirt pullout on the right side of the road where a sign reads RESTRICT OFF-ROAD TRAVEL TO FOOT OR HORSEBACK. UNLOAD AND CASE OR DISMANTLE ALL GUNS. *Delorme: Oregon Atlas & Gazetteer:* Page 73 B6. GPS: N42 33.897 / W119 41.828

The Hike

Hidden away in the southeast corner of Oregon is the lake-filled Warner Basin. This remote and sparsely populated part of Oregon is covered with miles of sagebrush, beveled fault-block mountains, and alkaline lakes. Near the end of the last ice age, a 500-square-mile lake covered the Warner Basin. This lake eventually receded, leaving a succession of smaller lakes that rise and fall, appear and disappear with the level of rainfall. Among them are Bluejoint, Stone Corral, Campbell, Flagstaff, Swamp, and Anderson—with Crump, Hart, and Pelican Lakes sticking around on a more permanent basis. These lakes make up the Warner Wetlands, which support many species of migrating birds, including Canada geese, pied-billed grebes, white pelicans, snowy egrets, a variety of ducks, and whistling swans. This hike takes you along Poker Jim Ridge, where you'll have far-reaching views of these numerous lakes and the vast landscape that make up the Warner Basin.

Ken Skeen soaks in the views on Poker Jim Ridge.

Poker Jim Ridge is located in the Hart Mountain National Antelope Refuge, a 430-square-mile preserve of sagebrush, hot springs, rugged canyons and ridges, and aspen-filled valleys. This vast high-desert landscape supports more than 330 species of animals, including coyotes, jackrabbits, raptors, pronghorn antelope, bighorn sheep, mule deer, and many others. The 275,000-acre refuge was established in 1936 by President Franklin D. Roosevelt to protect the pronghorn antelope—the fastest land mammal in North America. With a huge heart, powerful lungs, padded hooves, and keen eyesight, the pronghorn is built for speed. It can storm across the desert at speeds up to 35 miles per hour and can even manage short power surges of up to 70 mph. The antelope can spot these predators up to 3 miles away; at the slightest sign of trouble, they're off in a flash.

The number of pronghorn in the West once numbered more than forty million in the 1800s, but the animals were nearly wiped out by hunting. Now several million pronghorns wander the high-desert plains of southeast Idaho, eastern Washington, central and eastern Oregon, and Nevada and other western states, with one of the largest herds (about 1,700 animals) living in the Hart Mountain National Antelope

Stunning views from Poker Jim Ridge

Refuge. When hiking on Poker Jim Ridge, it's highly recommended that you carry a pair of binoculars and scan the horizon for these magnificent creatures. You can identify them by the two white chest bands on their light-brown coat, the striking white rump, and the black, spiked horns. Pronghorn are very observant and terribly skittish, so if you see a cloud of dust form, more than likely it's from a pronghorn that spotted you.

This hike begins just off Hart Mountain Road, at the base of a broad plateau that forms the better part of the Hart Mountain National Antelope Refuge. From your car you'll walk east along Hart Mountain Road for about 0.1 mile and then turn left and walk north over rough, sagebrush-covered terrain along Poker Jim Ridge.

Be forewarned that you'll be hiking cross-country, which makes hiking here more challenging, if not more alluring. As you hike along the edge of the ridge, watch your footing on the numerous loose lava rocks. To the west is a magnificent expanse of blue lakes that stretch for miles.

Wear long pants and tough footwear for this hike, and remember that rattlesnakes are found here. The boots will help protect your feet and ankles, and long pants will

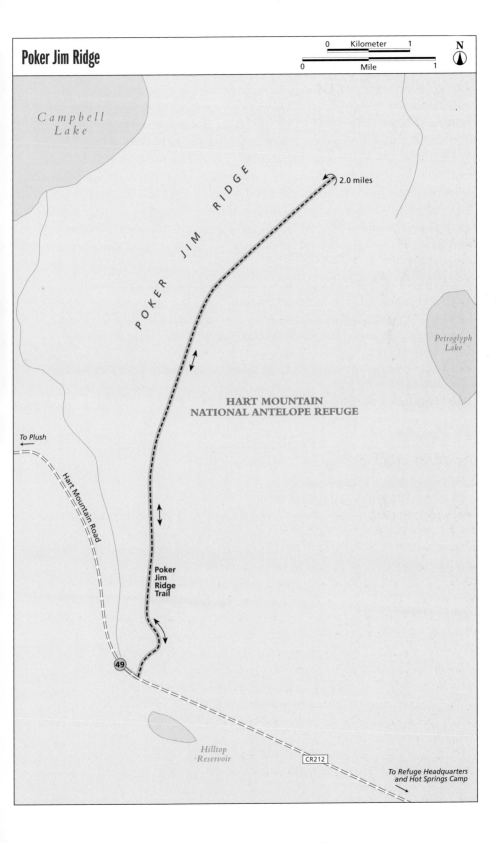

Poker Jim Ridge

0   Kilometer   1
0   Mile   1

N

Campbell
Lake

POKER JIM RIDGE

2.0 miles

Petroglyph
Lake

HART MOUNTAIN
NATIONAL ANTELOPE REFUGE

To Plush

Hart Mountain Road

Poker
Jim
Ridge
Trail

49

Hilltop
Reservoir

CR212

To Refuge Headquarters
and Hot Springs Camp

shield your legs from the scratchy sagebrush. A dozen species of sagebrush thrive in this high-desert environment. In spring and early summer, you'll also catch glimpses of larkspur and bright-red Indian paintbrush dotting this expansive ridge.

Before or after your hike, be sure to stop by the refuge headquarters to learn about the region's plants and wildlife and to soak in the hot springs at Hot Springs Camp. To reach the refuge headquarters, continue driving east on Hart Mountain Road for approximately 3 miles. To reach Hot Springs Camp, drive south on Hart Mountain Road from the refuge headquarters to a fork, where you'll veer right and drive 1.7 miles to another fork. Stay to the right and drive 2.5 miles to a Hot Springs Camp sign. Turn right here; the hot springs are sheltered in a not-so-pretty concrete building. If you plan on camping here, be sure to come prepared with insect repellent—the mosquitoes are ruthless in this part of the state.

Miles and Directions

0.0 Start walking east on the doubletrack dirt road.

0.1 Turn left (north) and head cross-country along the edge of Poker Jim Ridge, where you'll have glorious views of Stone Corral, Campbell, Flagstaff, Swamp, Anderson, and many other lakes.

2.0 Turn around here and retrace your tracks. **Option:** You can continue farther if you like, and turn around at any point.

4.0 Arrive back at the trailhead.

Hike Information

Local Information

Lake County Chamber of Commerce, 126 N. E St., Lakeview, OR 97630; (541) 947-6040; lakecountychamber.org.

50 Steens Mountain Trails

Take a tour through the Wild West in Oregon's southeast desert. The star attraction of your tour is 9,733-foot Steens Mountain, a magnificent geologic wonder located approximately 60 miles southeast of Burns. There are several ways to explore this amazing mountain. You can start your tour in the tiny town of Frenchglen and head up to the summit using Steens Mountain Loop. Along the way you may see wild horses roaming the hills around you. You'll be surrounded by expansive views and pure solitude. At different viewpoints along the route, you'll see magnificent glacier-carved gorges and sweeping views of Winter Rim, Summer Lake, Lake Abert, Abert Rim, the Warner Basin, Hart Mountain, and the Alvord Basin.

Start: All 4 hikes start on Steens Mountain, located about 60 miles southeast of Burns off OR 205.
Distance and Difficulty:
A. Kiger Gorge Viewpoint: 0.4 mile out and back, easy
B. East Rim Viewpoint: 0.1 mile out and back, easy
C. Wildhorse Lake Trail: 3.0 miles out and back, moderate
D. Steens Summit Trail: 1.0 mile out and back, moderate
Hiking time: Varies depending on the trail selected
Best season: Aug through Oct

Other trail users: Hikers only
Canine compatibility: Dogs permitted
Land status: National recreation lands
Nearest town: Frenchglen
Fees and permits: None
Schedule: July through Oct
Maps: Maptech CD: Malheur Lake/Southeast, OR; USGS: Frenchglen, OR; Page Springs, OR; Tombstone Canyon, OR; Roaring Springs, OR; Fish Lake, OR; McCoy Ridge, OR; Wildhorse Lake, OR
Trail contact: Bureau of Land Management, Burns District Office, 28910 Highway 20 W., Hines, OR 97738; (541) 573-4400; blm.gov/or/districts/burns/recreation/steens-mtn.php

Finding the trailhead: From Frenchglen drive south on OR 205 and turn left onto Steens Mountain Loop. Drive 3 miles to a T intersection and turn left. (If you turn right here, you'll arrive at Page Spring Campground in 1 mile). Drive 19.2 miles and turn left at the Kiger Gorge Viewpoint and drive 0.5 mile to the parking area. To continue on your tour, drive back to Steens Mountain Road and turn left and drive 2.7 miles to a three-way road junction. Turn left at the junction and drive 0.5 mile to the East Rim Viewpoint. When you're finished enjoying the East Rim, drive back to the junction and take the middle fork of the road where a sign indicates Wildhorse Lake 2¼ / Steens Summit 2½. Drive 2 miles to the parking area and trailheads for the Wildhorse Lake and the Steens Summit Trails. *DeLorme: Oregon Atlas & Gazetteer:* Page 74 A2. GPS: N42 42.510 / W118 34.512.

The Hike

Hidden away in the southeast Oregon desert is the natural wonder of Steens Mountain. This impressive 9,733-foot fault-block mountain rises dramatically from the sagebrush-covered Blitzen and Catlow Valleys on its west side and the Alvord Desert

Sheep grazing on Steens Mountain

on its east side. At more than 30 miles wide and 60 miles long, this mountain is a store of startling geologic and ecologic diversity. The mountain's complex evolution began about twenty-five million years ago when the east side of Steens Mountain surged upward along the Alvord Fault, creating a steep-sloping east face and a gently sloping west face. Roughly ten million years later, basalt lava flows (known as Steens basalts) erupted from fissures in the earth, creating almost two-thirds of the mountain you see today.

Managed by the Bureau of Land Management, this geologic masterpiece is part of the Burns District, which covers an immense 3.36 million acres of land stretching more than 200 miles from the Oregon–Nevada border northward to the base of the Blue Mountains. This wild and rugged country is the place to be if you're seeking wide-open spaces, sunny blue skies, and solitude.

The plants that live in this open landscape vary from sagebrush, bunch grass, and western junipers of the valleys and open plains, to the ponderosa pine forests of the Blue Mountains foothills and the aspen groves of Steens Mountain, Trout Creek, and the Pueblo Mountains. The animals that inhabit this area are equally diverse—Rocky

Mountain elk, California bighorn sheep, pronghorn antelope, and mule deer are some of the larger game. Also found roaming the lower slopes and valleys in the Steens Mountain area are wild horses. These free-spirited equines are thought to be descendents of horses owned by Native Americans, ranchers, miners, and early explorers. A variety of raptors claim the skies of the southeast high desert. One of the more impressive raptors is the golden eagle, identified by its dark-brown plumage with golden-brown highlights. Armed with an impressive wingspan of 7 feet and talons designed for gripping and tearing, these magnificent birds soar on the air currents high above the cliffs and slopes of Steens Mountain, where they scout their prey: jackrabbits, small birds, and other small game.

Your tour of Steens Mountain is along the 66-mile backcountry byway known as Steens Mountain Loop Road. You'll hook up with Steens Mountain Loop just outside of the small town of Frenchglen. As you head up to the summit, you'll pass through multiple ecozones, each with its own unique plants and animals. The historic P Ranch, infamous ranch headquarters of cattle baron Peter French, is along the route, as is the Page Springs Campground. The campground has flush toilets, running water, and hiking trails with interpretive signs. If you camp here, be sure to hike up the trail that parallels the Donner und Blitzen River. There are numerous opportunities to spot deer and other wildlife, and the river affords some excellent fishing.

As you continue on your road tour, approaching elevations of 4,000 to 6,000 feet, you'll pass through the sagebrush-covered Blitzen Valley, dotted with western juniper

Snow on Steens Mountain can be present well into July.

The author and her dogs hike on the Steens Mountain Summit Trail. PHOTO KEN SKEEN

and mountain mahogany. Between 6,000 and 8,000 feet, the landscape transforms to groves of quaking aspen. These shimmering green trees provide food and shelter for bighorn sheep, pronghorn antelope, and mule deer. Those looking to camp will want to keep their eyes open for Fish Lake and Jackman Park Campgrounds. Fish Lake is a high moraine lake stocked with brook, rainbow, and native redband trout. Twenty primitive campsites are available here. Jackman Park Campground has six primitive sites.

Your first stop is the Kiger Gorge Viewpoint, on your left. Notice that the landscape on this part of the mountain resembles treeless, rocky tundra. From this viewpoint you'll be able to see the impressive U-shaped Kiger Gorge. After Kiger Viewpoint continue another 2.7 miles to a three-way junction and turn left to reach the East Rim Viewpoint. This spot rests right on the edge of East Rim, which drops dramatically thousands of feet below you. Here you'll have a commanding view of Mann Lake, an attractive pit stop for migratory waterfowl and a good spot for cutthroat trout. You'll also be able to see the Sheepsheads Mountains, Owyhee Uplands, and one of the oldest settlements in the area, Alvord Ranch, established in 1885. Keep your eye out for bighorn sheep grazing on the ridges below you.

From the East Rim head back to the three-way junction and take the middle fork toward the Wildhorse Lake Trail, where you can descend 1.5 miles to Wildhorse Lake. Nestled in a scenic amphitheater, Wildhorse Lake was carved by a huge Ice Age glacier. The lake bottom is rich in pollens from ancient plants. Scientists study these sediments to help determine the region's climatic changes. From the Wildhorse trailhead parking area, turn right and continue another 0.25 mile to the Steens Summit Trail parking area. You can hike 0.5 mile to the 9,733-foot summit of Steens Mountain, where you'll have grand views of Winter Rim, Summer Lake, Lake Abert, Abert Rim, the Warner Basin, Hart Mountain, and the Alvord Basin.

Before you plan a trip to this area, call ahead to verify that Steens Mountain Loop is open. It can be closed well into mid-July. Also keep in mind that summit temperatures can be as much as forty degrees cooler than those in lower elevations. Be sure to wear (or at least carry) warm clothing if you're planning the summit hike, as the summit has a reputation for high winds and intermittent thunderstorms.

Miles and Directions

A. Kiger Gorge Viewpoint Trail

0.0 Start from the Kiger Point Viewpoint trailhead and turn right on the dirt path.

0.1 Come to a viewpoint and interpretive sign describing how Kiger Gorge was formed. When you're finished reading, continue walking on the faint trail that leads to your right.

0.2 Turn around here.

0.4 Arrive back at the trailhead.

HORSE BUYER'S JARGON

Angel—a greenhorn buyer at an auction who can be depended on to buy unsound horses

Sold to halter—no guarantee whatsoever

Dizzy—a dummy; a horse corresponding to a human imbecile

Goosey—nervous

Indian—a horse completely dangerous to handle

Jibber—a green, untrained horse

Pilgrim—a horse once good, now too old

Plug—a horse of little worth, maybe worn out; no spirit; so poor in conformation that he never was much good

One bum lamp—blind in one eye

Smokes his pipe—lip torn at point where the bit commonly rests

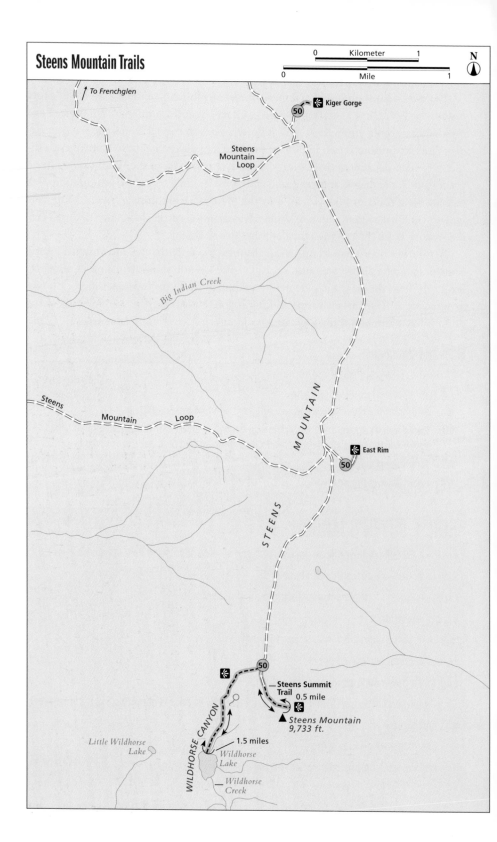

Steens Mountain Trails

To Frenchglen

Kiger Gorge

50

Steens
Mountain
Loop

Big Indian Creek

Steens

Mountain   Loop

MOUNTAIN

East Rim

50

STEENS

50

Steens Summit
Trail 0.5 mile

Steens Mountain
9,733 ft.

Little Wildhorse
Lake

WILDHORSE CANYON

1.5 miles

Wildhorse
Lake

Wildhorse
Creek

B. East Rim Viewpoint

0.0 Start by walking the short trail to the viewpoint and interpretive signs.

0.05 Arrive at the viewpoint. Turn around here.

0.1 Arrive back at the parking area.

C. Wildhorse Lake Trail

0.0 Start from the parking area where a wooden trail sign indicates the start of the Wildhorse Lake Trail. Be sure to sign in at the trail register.

0.2 Reach a scenic overlook of Wildhorse Lake. Continue down the steep, sometimes slippery path to the lake.

1.5 Reach the lake and your turnaround point.

3.0 Arrive back at the parking area.

D. Steens Summit Trail

0.0 Start from the parking area, where the rocky doubletrack road takes you steeply uphill.

0.2 Pass a viewpoint of Wildhorse Lake on your right.

0.5 Reach the summit of Steens Mountain (9,733 feet). Retrace the same route back to the trailhead.

1.0 Arrive back at the parking area.

Hike Information

Local Information

Harney County Chamber of Commerce, 484 N. Broadway, Burns, OR 97720; (541) 573-2636; harneycounty.com

Local Events and Attractions

Malheur Wildlife Refuge, 36391 Sodhouse Lane, Princeton; (541) 493-2612; www.fws.gov/malheur/

Honorable Mentions

Southeast Oregon

AAA Page Springs Campground Hikes

Page Springs Campground has two trails that you'll enjoy exploring. The river trail parallels the meandering Donner und Blitzen River through a rimrock canyon. This short trail begins at the far end of the parking lot and passes through several marshy areas filled with the soft brown cattail plumes that are a favorite perch for red-winged blackbirds. Continue on the trail until it fades out at 0.7 mile. Retrace the route back to the parking area. Once your trail hound has cooled off, get ready to explore the nature trail that is accessed from the same parking area. This loop trail treks through a small juniper and sagebrush canyon to a viewpoint of the campground and surround-

Deer grazing along the Donner und Blitzen River

ing valley. Look for the start of this trail on the left side of the road as you enter the trailhead parking area.

To get there from Frenchglen (about 62 miles south of Burns on OR 205), head south on OR 205 and turn left onto Steens Mountain Loop Road. Continue 3 miles to a T intersection and turn right toward Page Springs Campground. Continue 1 mile to the campground entrance. From there drive to the end of the campground and the trailhead.

For more information contact the Bureau of Land Management, Burns District Office, 28910 Highway 20 W., Hines, OR 97738; (541) 573-4400; blm.gov/or/districts/burns/recreation/steens-mtn.php. *DeLorme: Oregon Atlas & Gazetteer:* Page 74 A1.

BBB Big Indian Gorge Hike

This 6.2-mile out-and-back route explores beautiful Big Indian Gorge. To get there from Burns, travel about 62 miles south on OR 205 to Frenchglen. From Frenchglen continue south 10 miles toward Fields until you arrive at the junction with Steens Mountain Loop Road. Turn left onto Steens Mountain Loop Road and travel 19.5 miles to South Steens Campground, located on the right side of the road. Continue to the second campground entrance. The trailhead is on the left side of the road beyond the group camping area.

Go around a gate and begin hiking on a doubletrack road for 1.9 miles through a sage-scented canyon filled with fragrant juniper trees to the junction with Big Indian Creek. Cross the creek (there is no bridge) and pick up the trail on the other side. Continue up a scenic canyon for 0.2 mile to the junction with Little Indian Creek. Ford the creek and continue on the trail on the other side. Continue another mile upstream through gorgeous canyon country to another crossing of Big Indian Creek. This is your turnaround point. Retrace the route back to the trailhead.

This route is usually not open until July. For more information, contact the Bureau of Land Management, Burns District Office, 28910 Highway 20 W., Hines, OR 97738; (541) 573-4400; blm.gov/or/districts/burns/recreation/steens-mtn.php. *DeLorme: Oregon Atlas & Gazetteer:* Page 74 B1.

CCC Peter French Round Barn

Take a break from the grueling summit hikes to enjoy a short stroll around the historic Peter French Round Barn. The wagon wheel–shaped round barn was built in the 1880s and was used to break horses during the glory days of the Peter French Empire in the Harney Basin.

To get there from Frenchglen (62 miles south of Burns on OR 205), travel 18 miles north on OR 205 to the junction with Diamond Grain Camp Road. Turn right where a sign indicates DIAMOND CRATERS / FRENCH ROUND BARN 17 / DIAMOND 13. Go 7 miles and turn left onto Lava Beds Road where a sign indicates DIAMOND CRATERS 2. Continue 10.1 miles on Lava Beds Road and turn right onto a dirt road where a sign reads Welcome to Pete French Round Barn State Heritage Site. Continue 1 mile on a well-graded dirt road to a parking area at the road's end.

For more information, contact Oregon State Parks Trust, 888 SW Fifth Ave, Suite 1600, Portland, OR 97204; (503) 802-5750; oregonstateparkstrust.org. *DeLorme: Oregon Atlas & Gazetteer:* Page 78 D2.

DDD Coffeepot Crater

This easy 1.1-mile loop takes you on a tour of Coffeepot Crater in the Jordan Craters Lava Beds. Here you'll have a chance to explore layered lava flows, lava tubes, spatter cones, and lava bombs. Additional side trails lead you into an immense lava field. Avoid this area in midsummer, when temperatures can soar above one hundred degrees.

To get there from Jordan Valley on the Oregon–Idaho border (about 140 miles southeast of Burns via OR 78 and US 95), travel north on US 95 for 8.3 miles to a gravel road signed for Jordan Craters. Turn left and drive 11.4 miles; stay right at a junction. Go 6.7 miles to another junction and go left (the road becomes rough here). Continue on this rough road about 8.8 miles (staying left at all junctions) to a parking area at the end of the road.

For more information, contact the Bureau of Land Management, Vale District, 100 Oregon St., Vale, OR 97918-9630; (541) 473-3144; blm.gov/or/districts/vale/index.php. *DeLorme: Oregon Atlas & Gazetteer:* Page 79 D7.

The Art of Hiking

When standing nose to nose with a mountain lion, you're probably not too concerned with the issue of ethical behavior in the wild. No doubt you're just terrified. But let's be honest. How often are you nose to nose with a mountain lion? For most of us, a hike into the "wild" means loading up the SUV with expensive gear and driving to a toileted trailhead. Sure, you can mourn how civilized we've become—how GPS units have replaced natural instinct and Gore-Tex, true grit—but the silly gadgets of civilization aside, we have plenty of reason to take pride in how we've matured. With survival now on the back burner, we've begun to reason—and it's about time—that we have a responsibility to protect, no longer just conquer, our wild places: that they, not we, are at risk. So please, do what you can. The following section will help you understand better what it means to "do what you can" while still making the most of your hiking experience. Anyone can take a hike, but hiking safely and well is an art requiring preparation and proper equipment.

Trail Etiquette

Zero impact. Always leave an area just like you found it—if not better than you found it. Avoid camping in fragile, alpine meadows and along the banks of streams and lakes. Use a camp stove rather than building a wood fire. Pack up all of your trash and extra food. Bury human waste at least 100 feet from water sources under 6 to 8 inches of topsoil. Don't bathe with soap in a lake or stream—use prepackaged moistened towels to wipe off sweat and dirt, or bathe in the water without soap.

Stay on the trail. It's true, a path anywhere leads nowhere new, but purists will just have to get over it. Paths serve an important purpose; they limit impact on natural areas. Straying from a designated trail may seem innocent, but it can cause damage to sensitive areas—damage that may take years to recover, if it can recover at all. Even simple shortcuts can be destructive. So, please, stay on the trail.

Leave no weeds. Noxious weeds tend to overtake other plants, which in turn affects animals and birds that depend on them for food. To minimize the spread of noxious weeds, hikers should regularly clean their boots, tents, packs, and hiking poles of mud and seeds. Also brush your dog to remove any weed seeds before heading off into a new area.

Keep your dog under control. You can buy a flexi-lead that allows your dog to go exploring along the trail while allowing you the ability to reel him in should another hiker approach or should he decide to chase a rabbit. Always obey leash laws and be sure to bury your dog's waste or pack it in resealable plastic bags.

Respect other trail users. Often you're not the only one on the trail. With the rise in popularity of multiuse trails, you'll have to learn a new kind of respect, beyond the nod and "hello" approach you may be used to. First investigate whether you're on a multiuse trail, and assume the appropriate precautions. When you encounter motorized vehicles (ATVs, motorcycles, and 4WDs), be alert. Though they should always yield to the hiker, often they're going too fast or are too lost in the buzz of their engine to react to your presence. If you hear activity ahead, step off the trail, just to be safe. Note that you're not likely to hear a mountain biker coming, so be prepared and know ahead of time whether you share the trail with them. Cyclists should always yield to hikers, but that's little comfort to the hiker. Be aware. When you approach horses or pack animals on the trail, always step quietly off the trail, preferably on the downhill side, and let them pass. If you're wearing a large backpack, it's often a good idea to sit down. To some animals, a hiker wearing a large backpack might appear threatening. Many national forests allow domesticated grazing, usually for sheep and cattle. Make sure your dog doesn't harass these animals, and respect ranchers' rights while you're enjoying yours.

Getting into Shape

Unless you want to be sore—and possibly have to shorten your trip or vacation—be sure to get into shape before a big hike. If you're terribly out of shape, start a walking program early, preferably eight weeks in advance. Start with a 15-minute walk during your lunch hour or after work and gradually increase your walking time to an hour. You should also increase your elevation gain. Walking briskly up hills really strengthens your leg muscles and gets your heart rate up. If you work in a multistory office building, take the stairs instead of the elevator. If you prefer going to a gym, walk the treadmill or use a stair machine. You can further increase your strength and endurance by walking with a loaded backpack. Stationary exercises you might consider are squats, leg lifts, sit-ups, and push-ups. Other good ways to get in shape include biking, running, aerobics, and, of course, short hikes. Stretching before and after a hike keeps muscles flexible and helps avoid injuries.

Preparedness

It's been said that failing to plan means planning to fail. So do take the necessary time to plan your trip. Whether going on a short day hike or an extended backpack trip, always prepare for the worst. Simply remembering to pack a copy of the *U.S. Army Survival Manual* is not preparedness. Although it's not a bad idea if you plan on entering truly wild places, it's merely the tourniquet answer to a problem. You need to do your best to prevent the problem from arising in the first place. In order to survive—and to stay reasonably comfortable—you need to concern yourself with the basics: water, food, and shelter. Don't go on a hike without having these bases covered. And don't go on a hike expecting to find these items in the woods.

Water. Even in frigid conditions, you need at least two quarts of water a day to function efficiently. Add heat and taxing terrain and you can bump that figure up to one gallon. That's simply a base to work from—your metabolism and your level of conditioning can raise or lower that amount. Unless you know your level, assume that you need one gallon of water a day.

A reliable water filter is crucial for multiday backpack trips.

Now, where do you plan on getting the water? Preferably not from natural water sources. These sources can be loaded with intestinal disturbers, such as bacteria, viruses, and fertilizers. *Giardia lamblia,* the most common of these disturbers, is a protozoan parasite that lives part of its life cycle as a cyst in water sources. The parasite spreads when mammals defecate in water sources. Once ingested, giardia can induce cramping, diarrhea, vomiting, and fatigue within two days to two weeks after ingestion. Giardiasis is treatable with prescription drugs. If you believe you've contracted giardiasis, see a doctor immediately.

Treating water. The best and easiest solution to avoid polluted water is to carry your water with you. Yet, depending on the nature of your hike and the duration, this may not be an option—one gallon of water weighs eight and a half pounds. In that case, you'll need to look into treating water. Regardless of which method you

Square Lake with South Sister in the background in the Three Sisters Wilderness

choose, you should always carry some water with you in case of an emergency. Save this reserve until you absolutely need it.

There are three methods of treating water: boiling, chemical treatment, and filtering. If you boil water, it's recommended that you do so for 10 to 15 minutes. This is often impractical because you're forced to exhaust a great deal of your fuel supply. You can opt for chemical treatment, which will kill giardia but will not take care of other chemical pollutants. Another drawback to chemical treatments is the unpleasant taste of the water after it's treated. You can remedy this by adding powdered drink mix to the water. Filters are the preferred method for treating water. Many filters remove giardia, organic and inorganic contaminants, and don't leave an aftertaste. Water filters are far from perfect as they can easily become clogged or leak if a gasket wears out. It's always a good idea to carry a backup supply of chemical treatment tablets in case your filter decides to quit on you.

Food. If we're talking about survival, you can go days without food, as long as you have water. But we're also talking about comfort. Try to avoid foods that are high in sugar and fat like candy bars and potato chips. These food types are harder to digest and are low in nutritional value. Instead, bring along foods that are easy to pack, nutritious, and high in energy (e.g., bagels, nutrition bars, dehydrated fruit, gorp, and jerky). If you are on an overnight trip, easy-to-fix dinners include rice mixes with dehydrated potatoes, corn, pasta with cheese sauce, and soup mixes. For a tasty breakfast, you can fix hot oatmeal with brown sugar and reconstituted milk powder topped off with banana chips. If you like a hot drink in the morning, bring along herbal tea bags or hot chocolate. If you are a coffee junkie, you can purchase coffee that is packaged like tea bags. You can prepackage all of your meals in heavy-duty resealable plastic bags to keep food from spilling in your pack. These bags can be reused to pack out trash.

Shelter. The type of shelter you choose depends less on the conditions than on your tolerance for discomfort. Shelter comes in many forms—tent, tarp, lean-to, bivy sack, cabin, cave, etc. If you're camping in the desert, a bivy sack may suffice, but if you're above the tree line and a storm is approaching, a better choice is a three- or four-season tent. Tents are the logical and most popular choice for most backpackers as they're lightweight and packable—and you can rest assured that you always have shelter from the elements. Before you leave on your trip, anticipate what the weather and terrain will be like and plan for the type of shelter that will work best for your comfort level (see "Equipment" later in this section).

Finding a campsite. If there are established campsites, stick to those. If not, start looking for a campsite early—around 3:30 or 4 p.m. Stop at the first decent site you see. Depending on the area, it could be a long time before you find another suitable location. Pitch your camp in an area that's level. Make sure the area is at least 200 feet from fragile areas like lakeshores, meadows, and stream banks. And try to avoid areas thick in underbrush, as they can harbor insects and provide cover for approaching animals.

If you are camping in stormy, rainy weather, look for a rock outcrop or a shelter in the trees to keep the wind from blowing your tent all night. Be sure that you don't camp under trees with dead limbs that might break off on top of you. Also, try to find an area that has an absorbent surface, such as sandy soil or forest duff. This, in addition to camping on a surface with a slight angle, will provide better drainage. By all means, don't dig trenches to provide drainage around your tent—remember, you're practicing zero-impact camping.

If you're in bear country, steer clear of creek beds or animal paths. If you see any signs of a bear's presence (i.e., scat, footprints), relocate. You'll need to find a campsite near a tall tree where you can hang your food and other items that may attract bears such as deodorant, toothpaste, or soap. Carry a lightweight nylon rope with which to hang your food. As a rule, you should hang your food at least 20 feet from the ground and 5 feet away from the tree trunk. You can put food and other items in a waterproof stuff sack and tie one end of the rope to the stuff sack. To get the other end of the rope over the tree branch, tie a good-size rock to it, and gently toss the rock over the tree branch. Pull the stuff sack up until it reaches the top of the branch and tie it off securely. Don't hang your food near your tent! If possible, hang your food at least 100 feet away from your campsite. Alternatives to hanging your food are bear-proof plastic tubes and metal bear boxes.

Last, think of comfort. Lie down on the ground where you intend to sleep and see if it's a good fit. For morning warmth (and a nice view to wake up to), have your tent face east.

First Aid

I know you're tough, but get 10 miles into the woods and develop a blister and you'll wish you had carried that first-aid kit. Face it, it's just plain good sense. Many companies produce lightweight, compact first-aid kits. Just make sure yours contains at least the following:

- adhesive bandages
- moleskin or duct tape
- various sterile gauze and dressings
- white surgical tape
- an Ace bandage
- antihistamine
- aspirin
- Betadine solution
- a first-aid manual
- antacid tablets
- tweezers
- scissors
- antibacterial wipes
- triple antibiotic ointment
- plastic gloves
- sterile cotton-tip applicators
- syrup of ipecac (to induce vomiting)
- thermometer
- wire splint

Here are a few tips for dealing with and hopefully preventing certain ailments.

Sunburn. Take along sunscreen or sunblock, protective clothing, and a wide-brimmed hat. If you do get a sunburn, treat the area with aloe vera gel, and protect the area from further sun exposure. At higher elevations the sun's radiation can be particularly damaging to skin. Remember that your eyes are vulnerable to this radiation as well. Sunglasses can be a good way to prevent headaches and permanent eye damage from the sun, especially in places where light-colored rock or patches of snow reflect light up in your face.

Blisters. Be prepared to take care of these hike spoilers by carrying moleskin (a lightly padded adhesive), gauze and tape, or adhesive bandages. An effective way to apply moleskin is to cut out a circle of moleskin and remove the center—like a doughnut—and place it over the blistered area. Cutting the center out will reduce the pressure applied to the sensitive skin. Other products can help you combat blisters. Some are applied to suspicious hot spots before a blister forms to help decrease friction to that area, while others are applied to the blister after it has popped to help prevent further irritation.

Insect bites and stings. You can treat most insect bites and stings by applying hydrocortisone 1 percent cream topically and taking a pain medication such as ibuprofen or acetaminophen to reduce swelling. If you forgot to pack these items, a cold compress or a paste of mud and ashes can sometimes assuage the itching and discomfort. Remove any stingers by using tweezers or scraping the area with your fingernail or a knife blade. Don't pinch the area as you'll only spread the venom.

Some hikers are highly sensitive to bites and stings and may have a serious allergic reaction that can be life threatening. Symptoms of a serious allergic reaction can include wheezing, an asthmatic attack, and shock. The treatment for this severe type of reaction is epinephrine. If you know that you are sensitive to bites and stings, carry a prepackaged kit of epinephrine, which can be obtained only by prescription from your doctor.

Ticks. Ticks can carry diseases such as Rocky Mountain spotted fever and Lyme disease. The best defense is, of course, prevention. If you know you're going to be hiking through an area littered with ticks, wear long pants and a long-sleeved shirt. You can apply a permethrin repellent to your clothing and a deet repellent to exposed skin. There are also many natural alternatives for insect protection that do not have deet as an ingredient. These natural repellents work very well—just keep in mind that they need to be reapplied every few hours. At the end of your hike, do a spot-check for ticks (and insects in general). If you do find a tick, coat the insect with petroleum jelly or tree sap to cut off its air supply. The tick should release its hold, but if it doesn't, grab the head of the tick firmly—with a pair of tweezers if you have them—and gently pull it away from the skin with a twisting motion. Sometimes the mouth parts linger, embedded in your skin. If this happens, try to remove them with a disinfected needle. Clean the affected area with an antibacterial cleanser and then apply triple antibiotic ointment. Monitor the area for a few days. If irritation persists or a white spot develops, see a doctor for possible infection.

Poison ivy, oak, and sumac. These skin irritants can be found most anywhere in North America and come in the form of a bush or a vine, having leaflets in groups of three, five, seven, or nine. Learn how to spot the plants. The oil they secrete can cause an allergic reaction in the form of blisters, usually about 12 hours after exposure. The itchy rash can last from ten days to several weeks. The best defense against these irritants is to wear clothing that covers the arms, legs, and torso. For summer, zip-off cargo pants come in handy. There are also nonprescription lotions you can apply to exposed skin that guard against the effects of poison ivy/oak/sumac and can be washed off with soap and water. If you think you were in contact with the plants, after hiking (or even on the trail during longer hikes) wash with soap and water. Taking a hot shower with soap after you return home from your hike will also help to remove any lingering oil from your skin. Should you contract a rash from any of these plants, use an antihistamine to reduce the itching. If the rash is localized, create a light bleach/water wash to dry up the area. If the rash has spread, either tough it out or see your doctor about getting a dose of cortisone (available both orally and by injection).

Snakebites. Snakebites are rare in North America. Unless startled or provoked, the majority of snakes will not bite. If you are wise to their habitats and keep a careful eye on the trail, you should be just fine. When stepping over logs, first step on the log, making sure you can see what's on the other side before stepping down. Though your chances of being struck are slim, it's wise to know what to do in the event you are.

If a nonpoisonous snake bites you, allow the wound to bleed a small amount and then cleanse the wounded area with a Betadine solution (10 percent povidone iodine). Rinse the wound with clean water (preferably) or fresh urine (it might sound ugly, but it's sterile). Once the area is clean, cover it with triple antibiotic ointment and a clean bandage. Remember, most residual damage from snakebites, poisonous or otherwise, comes from infection, not the snake's venom. Keep the area as clean as possible and get medical attention immediately.

If you are bitten by a poisonous snake, remove the toxin with a suctioning device, found in a snakebite kit. If you do not have such a device, squeeze the wound—*do not* use your mouth for suction, as the venom will enter your bloodstream through the vessels under the tongue and head straight for your heart. Then, clean the wound just as you would a nonpoisonous bite. Tie a clean band of cloth snugly around the afflicted appendage, about an inch or so above the bite (or the rim of the swelling). This is *not* a tourniquet—you want to simply slow the blood flow, not cut it off. Loosen the band if numbness ensues. Remove the band for a minute and reapply a little higher every 10 minutes.

If it is your friend who's been bitten, treat him or her for shock—make the person comfortable, have him or her lie down, elevate the legs, and keep him or her warm. Avoid applying anything cold to the bite wound. Immobilize the affected area and remove any constricting items such as rings, watches, or restrictive clothing—swelling may occur. Once your friend is stable and relatively calm, hike out to get help. The victim should get treatment within 12 hours, ideally, which usually consists of a tetanus shot, antivenin, and antibiotics.

If you are alone and struck by a poisonous snake, stay calm. Hysteria will only quicken the venom's spread. Follow the procedure above, and do your best to reach help. When hiking out, don't run—you'll only increase the flow of blood throughout your system. Instead, walk calmly.

Dehydration. Have you ever hiked in hot weather and had a roaring headache and felt fatigued after only a few miles? More than likely you were dehydrated.

Symptoms of dehydration include fatigue, headache, and decreased coordination and judgment. When you are hiking, your body's rate of fluid loss depends on the outside temperature, humidity, altitude, and your activity level. On average, a hiker walking in warm weather will lose four liters of fluid a day. That fluid loss is easily replaced by normal consumption of liquids and food. However, if a hiker is walking briskly in hot, dry weather and hauling a heavy pack, he or she can lose one to three liters of water an hour. It's important to always carry plenty of water and to stop often and drink fluids regularly, even if you aren't thirsty.

Heat exhaustion. The result of a loss of large amounts of electrolytes, heat exhaustion often occurs if a hiker is dehydrated and has been under heavy exertion. Common symptoms of heat exhaustion include cramping, exhaustion, fatigue, light-headedness, and nausea. You can treat heat exhaustion by getting out of the sun and drinking an electrolyte solution made up of one teaspoon of salt and one tablespoon of sugar dissolved in a liter of water. Drink this solution slowly over a period of 1 hour. Drinking plenty of fluids (preferably an electrolyte solution/sports drink) can prevent heat exhaustion. Avoid hiking during the hottest parts of the day, and wear breathable clothing, a wide-brimmed hat, and sunglasses.

Hypothermia. One of the biggest dangers in the backcountry is hypothermia, especially for day hikers in the summertime. That may sound strange, but imagine starting out on a hike in midsummer when it's sunny and eighty degrees out. You're clad in nylon shorts and a cotton T-shirt. About halfway through your hike, the sky begins to cloud up, and in the next hour a light drizzle begins to fall and the wind starts to pick up. Before you know it, you are soaking wet and shivering—the perfect recipe for hypothermia. More advanced signs include decreased coordination, slurred speech, and blurred vision. When a victim's temperature falls below ninety-two degrees, the blood pressure and pulse plummet, possibly leading to coma and death.

To avoid hypothermia, always bring a windproof/rainproof shell, a fleece jacket, tights made of a breathable, synthetic fiber, gloves, and hat when you are hiking in the mountains. Learn to adjust your clothing layers based on the temperature. If you are climbing uphill at a moderate pace, you will stay warm, but when you stop for a break you'll become cold quickly, unless you add more layers of clothing.

If a hiker is showing advanced signs of hypothermia, dress him or her in dry clothes and make sure he or she is wearing a hat and gloves. Place the person in a sleeping bag in a tent or shelter that will protect him or her from the wind and other elements. Give the person warm fluids to drink and keep him awake.

Frostbite. When the mercury dips below thirty-two degrees F, your extremities begin to chill. If a persistent chill attacks a localized area, say, your hands or your toes, the circulatory system reacts by cutting off blood flow to the affected area—the idea being to protect and preserve the body's overall temperature. And so it's death by attrition for the affected area. Ice crystals start to form from the water in the cells of the neglected tissue. Deprived of heat, nourishment, and now water, the tissue literally starves. This is frostbite.

Prevention is your best defense against this situation. Most prone to frostbite are your face, hands, and feet, so protect these areas well. Wool is the material of choice because it provides ample air space for insulation and draws moisture away from the skin. Synthetic fabrics, however, have recently made great strides in the cold weather clothing market. Do your research. A pair of light silk liners under your regular gloves is a good trick for keeping warm. They afford some additional warmth, but more importantly, they'll allow you to remove your mitts for tedious work without exposing the skin.

If your feet or hands start to feel cold or numb due to the elements, warm them as quickly as possible. Place cold hands under your armpits or bury them in your crotch. If your feet are cold, change your socks. If there's plenty of room in your boots, add another pair of socks. Do remember, though, that constricting your feet in tight boots can restrict blood flow and actually make your feet colder more quickly. Your socks need to have breathing room if they're going to be effective. Dead air provides insulation. If your face is cold, place your warm hands over your face, or simply wear a head stocking.

Should your skin go numb and start to appear white and waxy, chances are you've got or are developing frostbite. Don't try to thaw the area unless you can maintain the warmth. In other words, don't stop to warm up your frostbitten feet only to head back on the trail. You'll do more damage than good. Tests have shown that hikers who walked on thawed feet did more harm, and endured more pain, than hikers who left the affected areas alone. Do your best to get out of the cold entirely and seek medical attention—which usually consists of performing a rapid rewarming in water for 20 to 30 minutes.

The overall objective in preventing both hypothermia and frostbite is to keep the body's core warm. Protect key areas where heat escapes, like the top of the head, and maintain the proper nutrition level. Foods that are high in calories aid the body in producing heat. Never smoke or drink when you're in situations where the cold is threatening. By affecting blood flow, these activities ultimately cool the body's core temperature.

Altitude sickness (AMS). High, lofty peaks, clear alpine lakes, and vast mountain views beckon hikers to the high country. But those who like to venture high may become victims of altitude sickness (also known as acute mountain sickness—AMS). Altitude sickness is your body's reaction to insufficient oxygen in the blood due to decreased barometric pressure. While some hikers may feel lightheaded, nauseous, and experience shortness of breath at 7,000 feet, others may not experience these symptoms until they reach 10,000 feet or higher.

Slowing your ascent to high places and giving your body a chance to acclimatize to the higher elevations can prevent altitude sickness. For example, if you live at sea level and are planning a weeklong backpacking trip to elevations between 7,000 and 12,000 feet, start by staying below 7,000 feet for one night, then move to between 7,000 and 10,000 feet for another night or two. Avoid strenuous exertion and alcohol to give your body a chance to adjust to the new altitude. It's also important to eat light food and drink plenty of nonalcoholic fluids, preferably water. Loss of appetite at high altitudes is common, but you must eat!

Most hikers who experience mild to moderate AMS develop a headache and/or nausea, grow lethargic, and have problems sleeping. The treatment for AMS is simple: Stop heading uphill. Keep eating and drinking water and take meds for the headache. You actually need to take more breaths at altitude than at sea level, so breathe a little faster, without hyperventilating. If symptoms don't improve over 24 to 48 hours, descend. Once a victim descends about 2,000 to 3,000 feet, his signs will usually begin to diminish.

Severe AMS comes in two forms: high altitude pulmonary edema (HAPE) and high altitude cerebral edema (HACE). HAPE, an accumulation of fluid in the lungs, can occur above 8,000 feet. Symptoms include rapid heart rate, shortness of breath at rest, AMS symptoms, dry cough developing into a wet cough, gurgling sounds, flulike or bronchitis symptoms, and lack of muscle coordination. HAPE is life threatening, so descend immediately, at least 2,000 to 4,000 feet. HACE usually occurs above 12,000 feet but sometimes occurs above 10,000 feet. Symptoms are similar to HAPE but also include seizures, hallucinations, paralysis, and vision disturbances. Descend immediately—HACE is also life threatening.

Hantavirus pulmonary syndrome (HPS). Deer mice spread the virus that causes HPS, and humans contract it from breathing it in, usually when they've disturbed an area with dust and mice feces from nests or surfaces with mice droppings or urine. Exposure to large numbers of rodents and their feces or urine presents the greatest risk. As hikers, we sometimes enter old buildings, and often deer mice live in these places. We may not be around long enough to be exposed, but do be aware of this disease. About half the people who develop HPS die. Symptoms are flulike and appear about two to three weeks after exposure. After initial symptoms a dry cough and shortness of breath follow. Breathing is difficult. If you even think you might have HPS, see a doctor immediately!

Natural Hazards

Besides tripping over a rock or tree root on the trail, there are some real hazards to be aware of while hiking. Even if where you're hiking doesn't have the plethora of poisonous snakes and plants, insects, and grizzly bears found in other parts of the United States, there are a few weather conditions and predators you may need to take into account.

Lightning. Thunderstorms build over the mountains almost every day during the summer. Lightning is generated by thunderheads and can strike without warning, even several miles away from the nearest overhead cloud. The best rule of thumb is to start leaving exposed peaks, ridges, and canyon rims by about noon. This time can vary a little depending on storm buildup. Keep an eye on cloud formation and don't underestimate how fast a storm can build. The bigger they get, the more likely a thunderstorm will happen. Lightning takes the path of least resistance, so if you're the high point, it might choose you. Ducking under a rock overhang is dangerous as you form the shortest path between the rock and ground. If you dash below tree line, avoid standing under the only or the tallest tree. If you are caught above tree line, stay away from anything metal you might be carrying, Move down off the ridge slightly to a low, treeless point and squat until the storm passes. If you have an insulating pad, squat on it. Avoid having both your hands and feet touching the ground at once and never lay flat. If you hear a buzzing sound or feel your hair standing on end, move quickly as an electrical charge is building up.

Flash floods. On July 31, 1976, a torrential downpour dumped tons of water into the Big Thompson watershed near Estes Park, Colorado. Within hours, a wall of water moved down the narrow canyon killing 139 people and causing more than $30 million in property damage. The spooky thing about flash floods, especially in western canyons, is that they can appear out of nowhere from a storm many miles away. While hiking or driving in canyons, keep an eye on the weather. Always climb to safety if danger threatens. Flash floods usually subside quickly, so be patient and don't cross a swollen stream.

Bears. Most of the United States (outside of the Pacific Northwest and parts of the Northern Rockies) does not have a grizzly bear population, although some rumors exist about sightings where there should be none. Black bears are plentiful, however. Here are some tips in case you and a bear scare each other. Most of all, avoid scaring a bear. Watch for bear tracks (five toes) and droppings (sizable with leaves, partly digested berries, seeds, and/or animal fur). Talk or sing where visibility or hearing are limited. Keep a clean camp, hang food, and don't sleep in the clothes you wore while cooking. Be especially careful in spring to avoid getting between a mother and her cubs. In late summer and fall, bears are busy eating berries and acorns to fatten up for winter, so be extra careful around berry bushes and oakbrush. If you do encounter a bear, move away slowly while facing the bear, talk softly, and avoid direct eye contact. Give the bear room to escape. Since bears are very curious, it might stand upright to get a better whiff of you, and it may even charge you to try to intimidate you. Try to stay calm. If a bear does attack you, fight back with anything you have handy. Unleashed dogs have been known to come running back to their owners with a bear close behind. Keep your dog on a leash or leave it at home.

Mountain lions. Mountain lions appear to be getting more comfortable around humans as long as deer (their favorite prey) are in an area with adequate cover. Usually elusive and quiet, lions rarely attack people. If you meet a lion, give it a chance to escape. Stay calm and talk firmly to it. Back away slowly while facing the lion. If you run, you'll only encourage the curious cat to chase you. Make yourself look large by opening a jacket, if you have one, or waving your hiking poles. If the lion behaves aggressively, throw stones, sticks, or whatever you can while remaining tall. If a lion does attack, fight for your life with anything you can grab.

Moose. Because moose have very few natural predators, they don't fear humans like other animals. You might find moose in sagebrush and wetter areas of willow, aspen, and pine, or in beaver habitats. Mothers with calves, as well as bulls during mating season, can be particularly aggressive. If a moose threatens you, back away slowly and talk calmly to it. Keep your pets away from moose.

Other considerations. Hunting is a popular sport in the United States, especially during rifle season in October and November. Hiking is still enjoyable in those months in many areas, so just take a few precautions. First, learn when the different hunting seasons start and end in the area in which you'll be hiking. During this time frame, be sure to wear at least a blaze orange hat, and possibly put an orange vest over your pack. Don't be surprised to see hunters in camo outfits carrying bows or muzzle-loading rifles around during their season. If you would feel more comfortable without hunters around, hike in national parks and monuments or state and local parks where hunting is not allowed.

Navigation

Whether you are going on a short hike in a familiar area or planning a weeklong backpack trip, you should always be equipped with the proper navigational equipment—at the very least a detailed map and a sturdy compass.

Maps. There are many different types of maps available to help you find your way on the trail. Easiest to find are Forest Service maps and BLM (Bureau of Land Management) maps. These maps tend to cover large areas, so be sure they are detailed enough for your particular trip. You can also obtain national park maps as well as high-quality maps from private companies and trail groups. These maps can be obtained either from outdoor stores or ranger stations.

U.S. Geological Survey topographic maps are particularly popular with hikers—especially serious backcountry hikers. These maps contain the standard map symbols such as roads, lakes, and rivers, as well as contour lines that show the details of the trail terrain like ridges, valleys, passes, and mountain peaks. The 7.5-minute series (1 inch on the map equals approximately 2/5 mile on the ground) provides the closest inspection available. USGS maps are available by mail (U.S. Geological Survey, Map Distribution Branch, P.O. Box 25286, Denver, CO 80225), or at store.usgs.gov.

If you want to check out the high-tech world of maps, you can purchase topographic maps on CD-ROM or download them from the web. These software-mapping programs let you select a route on your computer, print it out, then take it with you on the trail. Some software mapping programs let you insert symbols and labels, download waypoints from a GPS unit, and export the maps to other software programs. If you are interested in learning more about mapping programs, you may want to try Garmin BaseCamp (garmin.com/us/products/onthetrail/basecamp).

Google Earth is a very popular navigation program that you can download from the web by visiting google.com/earth/index.html

The art of map reading is a skill that you can develop by first practicing in an area you are familiar with. To begin, orient the map so the map is lined up in the correct direction (i.e., north on the map is lined up with true north). Next, familiarize

yourself with the map symbols and try and match them up with terrain features around you such as a high ridge, mountain peak, river, or lake. If you are practicing with a USGS map, notice the contour lines. On gentler terrain these contour lines are spaced farther apart, and on steeper terrain they are closer together. Pick a short loop trail, and stop frequently to check your position on the map. As you practice map reading, you'll learn how to anticipate a steep section on the trail or a good place to take a rest break, and so on.

Compasses. First off, the sun is not a substitute for a compass. So, what kind of compass should you have? Here are some characteristics you should look for: a rectangular base with detailed scales, a liquid-filled housing, protective housing, a sighting line on the mirror, luminous alignment and back-bearing arrows, a luminous north-seeking arrow, and a well-defined bezel ring.

You can learn compass basics by reading the detailed instructions included with your compass. If you want to fine-tune your compass skills, sign up for an orienteering class or purchase a book on compass reading. Once you've learned the basic skills of using a compass, remember to practice these skills before you head into the backcountry.

If you are a klutz at using a compass, you may be interested in checking out the technical wizardry of the GPS (Global Positioning System) device. The GPS was developed by the Pentagon and works off twenty-four NAVSTAR satellites, which were designed to guide missiles to their targets. A GPS device is a handheld unit that calculates your latitude and longitude with the easy press of a button. The Department of Defense used to scramble the satellite signals a bit to prevent civilians (and spies!) from getting extremely accurate readings, but that practice was discontinued in May 2000, and GPS units now provide nearly pinpoint accuracy (within 30 to 60 feet).

There are many different types of GPS units available and they range in price from $100 to $400. In general, all GPS units have a display screen and keypad where you input information. In addition to acting as a compass, the unit allows you to plot your route, easily retrace your path, track your travel speed, find the mileage between waypoints, and calculate the total mileage of your route as well as elevation change. Some GPS devices have cameras so you can take photos that are GPS tagged. Later, you can upload them to the web and share them with friends.

Before you purchase a GPS unit, keep in mind that these devices don't pick up signals indoors, in heavily wooded areas, on mountain peaks, or in deep valleys.

Pedometers. A pedometer is a small, clip-on unit with a digital display that calculates your hiking distance in miles or kilometers based on your walking stride. Some units also calculate the calories you burn and your total hiking time. Pedometers are available at most large outdoor stores for less than $50.

◀ *Kathleen and Rowdy and the author with Heidi and Bear backpacking in the Three Sisters Wilderness* PHOTO KEN SKEEN

Trip Planning

Planning your hiking adventure begins with letting a friend or relative know your trip itinerary so they can call for help if you don't return at your scheduled time. Your next task is to make sure you are outfitted to experience the risks and rewards of the trail. This section highlights gear and clothing you may want to take with you to get the most out of your hike.

Equipment

Since most name brands will differ only slightly in quality, it's best to know what you're looking for in terms of function. Buy only what you need. You will, don't forget, be carrying what you've bought on your back. Here are some things to keep in mind before you go shopping.

Clothes. Clothing is your armor against Mother Nature's little surprises. Hikers should be prepared for any possibility, especially when hiking in mountainous areas. Adequate rain protection and extra layers of clothing are a good idea. In summer a wide-brimmed hat can help keep the sun at bay. In the winter months the first layer you'll want to wear is a "wicking" layer of long underwear that keeps perspiration away from your skin. Wear long underwear made from synthetic fibers that wick moisture away from the skin and draw it toward the next layer of clothing, where it then evaporates. Avoid wearing long underwear made of cotton as it is slow to dry and keeps moisture next to your skin.

The second layer you'll wear is the "insulating" layer. Aside from keeping you warm, this layer needs to "breathe" so you stay dry while hiking. A fabric that provides insulation and dries quickly is fleece. It's interesting to note that this one-of-a-kind fabric is made out of recycled plastic. Purchasing a zip-up jacket made of this material is highly recommended.

DAY HIKES

- camera/film
- compass/GPS unit
- cell phone
- pedometer
- daypack
- first-aid kit
- food
- guidebook
- headlamp/flashlight with extra batteries and bulbs
- hat
- insect repellent
- knife/multipurpose tool
- map
- matches in waterproof container and fire starter
- fleece jacket
- rain gear
- space blanket
- sunglasses
- sunscreen
- swimsuit
- watch
- water
- water bottles/water hydration system

The last line of layering defense is the "shell" layer. You'll need some type of waterproof, windproof, breathable jacket that will fit over all of your other layers. It should have a large hood that fits over a hat. You'll also need a good pair of rain pants made from a similar waterproof, breathable fabric. Some Gore-Tex jackets cost as much as $500, but you should know that there are more affordable fabrics out there that work just as well.

Now that you've learned the basics of layering, you can't forget to protect your hands and face. In cold, windy, or rainy weather, you'll need a hat made of wool or fleece and insulated, waterproof gloves that will keep your hands warm and toasty. As mentioned earlier, buying an additional pair of light silk liners to wear under your regular gloves is a good idea.

Footwear. If you have any extra money to spend on your trip, put that money into boots or trail shoes. Poor shoes will bring a hike to a halt faster than anything else. To avoid this annoyance, buy shoes that provide support and are lightweight and flexible. A lightweight hiking boot is better than a heavy, leather mountaineering boot for most day hikes and backpacking. Trail running shoes provide a little extra cushion and are made in a high-top style that many people wear for hiking. These running shoes are lighter, more flexible, and more breathable than hiking boots.

OVERNIGHT TRIP

- backpack and waterproof rain cover
- backpacker's trowel
- bandanna
- bear repellent spray
- bear bell
- biodegradable soap
- pot scrubber
- collapsible water container (2-3 gallon capacity)
- clothing—extra wool socks, shirt, and shorts
- cook set/utensils
- ditty bags to store gear
- extra plastic resealable bags
- gaiters
- garbage bag
- ground cloth
- journal/pen
- nylon rope to hang food
- long underwear
- permit (if required)
- rain jacket and pants
- sandals to wear around camp and to ford streams
- sleeping bag
- waterproof stuff sack
- sleeping pad
- small bath towel
- stove and fuel
- tent
- toiletry items
- water filter
- whistle

If you know you'll be hiking in wet weather often, purchase boots or shoes with a Gore-Tex liner, which will help keep your feet dry.

When buying your boots, be sure to wear the same type of socks you'll be wearing on the trail. If the boots you're buying are for cold-weather hiking, try the boots on while wearing two pairs of socks. Speaking of socks, a good cold weather sock combination is to wear a thinner sock made of wool or polypropylene covered by a heavier outer sock made of wool. The inner sock protects the foot from the rubbing effects of the outer sock and prevents blisters. Many outdoor stores have some type of ramp to simulate hiking uphill and downhill. Be sure to take advantage of this test, as toe-jamming boot fronts can be very painful and debilitating on the downhill trek.

Once you've purchased your footwear, be sure to break them in before you hit the trail. New footwear is often stiff and needs to be stretched and molded to your foot.

Hiking poles. Hiking poles help with balance and, more importantly, take pressure off your knees. The ones with shock absorbers are easier on your elbows and knees. Some poles even come with a camera attachment to be used as a monopod. And heaven forbid you meet a mountain lion, bear, or unfriendly dog, the poles can make you look a lot bigger.

Backpacks. No matter what type of hiking you do, you'll need a pack of some sort to carry the basic trail essentials. There are a variety of backpacks on the market, but let's first discuss what you intend to use it for. Day hikes or overnight trips?

If you plan on doing a day hike, a daypack should have some of the following characteristics: a padded hip belt that's at least 2 inches in diameter (avoid packs with only a small nylon piece of webbing for a hip belt); a chest strap (the chest strap helps stabilize the pack against your body); external pockets to carry water and other items that you want easy access to; an internal pocket to hold keys, a knife, a wallet, and other miscellaneous items; an external lashing system to hold a jacket; and a hydration pocket for carrying a hydration system (which consists of a water bladder with an attachable drinking hose).

For short hikes, some hikers like to use a fanny pack to store just a camera, food, a compass, a map, and other trail essentials. Most fanny packs have pockets for two water bottles and a padded hip belt.

If you intend to do an extended, overnight trip, there are multiple considerations. First off, you need to decide what kind of framed pack you want. There are two backpack types for backpacking: the internal frame and the external frame. An internal frame pack rests closer to your body, making it more stable and easier to balance when hiking over rough terrain. An external frame pack is just that, an aluminum frame attached to the exterior of the pack. An external frame pack is better for long backpack trips because it distributes the pack weight better and you can carry heavier loads. It's easier to pack, and your gear is more accessible. It also offers better back ventilation in hot weather.

The most critical measurement for fitting a pack is torso length. The pack needs to rest evenly on your hips without sagging. A good pack will come in two or three

Kathleen taking a break at Hunts Cove in the Mount Jefferson Wilderness

sizes and have straps and hip belts that are adjustable according to your body size and characteristics.

When you purchase a backpack, go to an outdoor store with salespeople who are knowledgeable in how to properly fit a pack. Once the pack is fitted for you, load the pack with the amount of weight you plan on taking on the trail. The weight of the pack should be distributed evenly and you should be able to swing your arms and walk briskly without feeling out of balance. Another good technique for evaluating a pack is to walk up and down stairs and make quick turns to the right and to the left to be sure the pack doesn't feel out of balance. Other features that are nice to have on a backpack include a removable daypack or fanny pack, external pockets for extra water, and extra lash points to attach a jacket or other items.

Sleeping bags and pads. Sleeping bags are rated by temperature. You can purchase a bag made of synthetic fiber, or you can buy a goose-down bag. Goose-down bags are more expensive, but they have a higher insulating capacity by weight and will keep their loft longer. You'll want to purchase a bag with a temperature rating that fits the time of year and conditions you are most likely to camp in. One caveat: The techno-standard for temperature ratings is far from perfect. Ratings vary from manufacturer to manufacturer, so to protect yourself, you should purchase a bag rated ten to fifteen degrees below the temperature you expect to be camping in. Synthetic bags are more resistant to water than down bags, but many down bags are now made with a Gore-Tex shell that helps to repel water. Down bags are also more compressible than synthetic bags and take up less room in your pack, which is an important consideration if you are planning a multiday backpack trip. Features to look for in a sleeping bag include a mummy-style bag, a hood you can cinch down around your head in cold weather, and draft tubes along the zippers that help keep heat in and drafts out.

You'll also want a sleeping pad to provide insulation and padding from the cold ground. There are different types of sleeping pads available, from the more expensive self-inflating air mattresses to the less expensive closed-cell foam pads. Self-inflating air mattresses are usually heavier than closed-cell foam mattresses and are prone to punctures.

Tents. The tent is your home away from home while on the trail. It provides protection from wind, snow, rain, and insects. A three-season tent is a good choice for backpacking and can range in price from $100 to $500. These lightweight and versatile tents provide protection in all types of weather, except heavy snowstorms or high winds, and range in weight from four to eight pounds. Look for a tent that's easy to set up and will easily fit two people with gear. Dome-type tents usually offer more headroom and places to store gear. Other tent designs include a vestibule where you can store wet boots and backpacks. Some nice-to-have items in a tent include interior pockets to store small items and lashing points to hang a clothesline. Most three-season tents also come with stakes so you can secure the tent in high winds. Before you purchase a tent, set it up and take it down a few times to be sure it is easy to handle. Also, sit inside the tent and make sure it has enough room for you and your gear.

Cell phones. Many hikers are carrying their cell phones into the backcountry these days in case of emergency. That's fine and good, but please know that cell phone coverage is often poor to nonexistent in valleys, canyons, and thick forest. More importantly, people have started to call for help because they're tired or lost. Let's go back to being prepared. You are responsible for yourself in the backcountry. Use your brain to avoid problems, and if you do encounter one, first use your brain to try to correct the situation. Only use your cell phone, if it works, in true emergencies.

Hiking with Children

Hiking with children isn't a matter of how many miles you can cover or how much elevation gain you make in a day. It's about seeing and experiencing nature through their eyes.

Kids like to explore and have fun. They like to stop and point out bugs and plants, look under rocks, jump in puddles, and throw sticks. If you're taking a toddler or young child on a hike, start with a trail that you're familiar with. Trails that have interesting things for kids, like piles of leaves to play in or a small stream to wade through during the summer, will make the hike much more enjoyable for them and will keep them from getting bored.

You can keep your child's attention if you have a strategy before starting on the trail. Using games is not only an effective way to keep a child's attention, it's also a great way to teach him or her about nature. Play hide-and-seek, where your child is the mouse and you are the hawk. Quiz children on the names of plants and animals. If your children are old enough, let them carry their own daypack filled with snacks and water. So that you are sure to go at their pace and not yours, let them lead the way. Playing follow-the-leader works particularly well when you have a group of children. Have each child take a turn at being the leader.

With children, a lot of clothing is key. The only thing predictable about weather is that it will change. Especially in mountainous areas, weather can change dramatically in a very short time. Always bring extra clothing for children, regardless of the season. In the winter have your children wear wool socks and warm layers such as long underwear, a fleece jacket and hat, wool mittens, and good rain gear. It's not a bad idea to have these along in late fall and early spring as well. Good footwear is also important. A sturdy pair of high-top tennis shoes or lightweight hiking boots are the best bet for little ones. If you're hiking in the summer near a lake or stream, bring along a pair of old sneakers that your child can put on when he wants to go exploring in the water. Remember when you're near any type of water, always watch your child at all times. Also, keep a close eye on teething toddlers who may decide a rock or leaf of poison oak is an interesting item to put in their mouth.

From spring through fall you'll want your kids to wear a wide-brimmed hat to keep their face, head, and ears protected from the hot sun. Also, make sure your children wear sunscreen at all times. If you are hiking with a child younger than 6 months, don't use sunscreen or insect repellent. Instead, be sure that his or her head, face, neck, and ears are protected from the sun with a wide-brimmed hat, and that all other skin exposed to the sun is protected with the appropriate clothing.

Remember that food is fun. Kids like snacks so it's important to bring a lot of munchies for the trail. Stopping often for snack breaks is a fun way to keep the trail interesting. Raisins, apples, granola bars, crackers and cheese, cereal, and trail mix all make great snacks. If your child is old enough to carry her own backpack, fill it with treats before you leave. If your kids don't like drinking water, you can bring boxes of fruit juice.

Avoid poorly designed child-carrying packs—you don't want to break your back carrying your child. Most child-carrying backpacks designed to hold a forty-pound child will contain a large carrying pocket to hold diapers and other items. Some have an optional rain/sun hood.

Hiking with Your Dog

Bringing your furry friend with you is always more fun than leaving him behind. Our canine pals make great trail buddies because they never complain and always make good company. Hiking with your dog can be a rewarding experience, especially if you plan ahead.

Getting your dog in shape. Before you plan outdoor adventures with your dog, make sure he's in shape for the trail. Getting your dog into shape takes the same discipline as getting yourself into shape, but luckily, your dog can get in shape with you. Take your dog with you on your daily runs or walks. If there is a park near your house, hit a tennis ball or play Frisbee with your dog.

Swimming is also an excellent way to get your dog into shape. If there is a lake or river near where you live and your dog likes the water, have him retrieve a tennis ball or stick. Gradually build your dog's stamina up over a two- to three-month period. A good rule of thumb is to assume that your dog will travel twice as far as you will on the trail. If you plan on doing a 5-mile hike, be sure your dog is in shape for a 10-mile hike.

Training your dog for the trail. Before you go on your first hiking adventure with your dog, be sure he has a firm grasp on the basics of canine etiquette and behavior. Make sure he can sit, lie down, stay, and come. One of the most important commands you can teach your canine pal is to "come" under any situation. It's easy for your friend's nose to lead him astray or possibly get lost. Another helpful command is the "get behind" command. When you're on a hiking trail that's narrow, you can have your dog follow behind you when other trail users approach. Nothing is more bothersome than an enthusiastic dog that runs back and forth on the trail and disrupts the peace of the trail for others. When you see other trail users approaching you on the trail, give them the right of way by quietly stepping off the trail and making your dog lie down and stay until they pass.

Equipment. The most critical pieces of equipment you can invest in for your dog are proper identification and a sturdy leash. Flexi-leads work well for hiking because they give your dog more freedom to explore but still leave you in control. Make sure your dog has identification that includes your name and address and a number for your veterinarian. Other forms of identification for your dog include a tattoo or a microchip. You should consult your veterinarian for more information on these last two options.

The next piece of equipment you'll want to consider is a pack for your dog. By no means should you hold all of your dog's essentials in your pack—let him carry his own gear! Dogs that are in good shape can carry 30 to 40 percent of their own weight.

Most packs are fitted by a dog's weight and girth measurement. Companies that make dog packs generally include guidelines to help you pick out the size that's right for your dog. Some characteristics to look for when purchasing a pack for your dog include a harness that contains two padded girth straps, a padded chest strap, leash attachments, removable saddle bags, internal water bladders, and external gear cords.

You can introduce your dog to the pack by first placing the empty pack on his back and letting him wear it around the yard. Keep an eye on him during this first introduction. He may decide to chew through the straps if you aren't watching him closely. Once he learns to treat the pack as an object of fun and not a foreign enemy, fill the pack evenly on both sides with a few ounces of dog food in resealable plastic bags. Have your dog wear his pack on your daily walks for a period of two to three weeks. Each week add a little more weight to the pack until your dog will accept carrying the maximum amount of weight he can carry.

You can also purchase collapsible water and dog food bowls for your dog. These bowls are lightweight and can easily be stashed into your pack or your dog's. If you are hiking on rocky terrain or in the snow, you can purchase footwear for your dog that will protect his feet from cuts and bruises.

Always carry plastic bags to remove feces from the trail. It is a courtesy to other trail users and helps protect local wildlife.

The following is a list of items to bring when you take your dog hiking: collapsible water bowls, a comb, a collar and a leash, dog food, plastic bags for feces, a dog pack, flea/tick powder, paw protection, water, and a first-aid kit that contains eye ointment, tweezers, scissors, stretchy foot wrap, gauze, antibacterial wash, sterile cotton-tip applicators, antibiotic ointment, and cotton wrap.

First aid for your dog. Your dog is just as prone—if not more prone—to getting in trouble on the trail as you are, so be prepared. Here's a rundown of the more likely misfortunes that might befall your canine friend.

Bees and wasps. If a bee or wasp stings your dog, remove the stinger with a pair of tweezers and place a mudpack or a cloth dipped in cold water over the affected area.

Porcupines. One good reason to keep your dog on a leash is to prevent it from getting a nose full of porcupine quills. You may be able to remove the quills with pliers, but a veterinarian is the best person to do this nasty job because most dogs need to be sedated.

Heatstroke. Avoid hiking with your dog in really hot weather. Dogs with heatstroke will pant excessively, lie down and refuse to get up, and become lethargic and disoriented. If your dog shows any of these signs on the trail, have him lie down in the shade. If you are near a stream, pour cool water over your dog's entire body to help bring his body temperature back to normal.

Heartworm. Dogs get heartworms from mosquitoes, which carry the disease in the prime mosquito months of July and August. Giving your dog a monthly pill prescribed by your veterinarian easily prevents this condition.

Plant pitfalls. One of the biggest plant hazards for dogs on the trail are foxtails. Foxtails are pointed grass seed heads that bury themselves in your friend's fur, between his toes, and even get in his ear canal. If left unattended, these nasty seeds can work their way under the skin and cause abscesses and other problems. If you have a long-haired dog, consider trimming the hair between his toes and giving him a summer haircut to help prevent foxtails from attaching to his fur. After every hike always look over your dog for these seeds—especially between his toes and his ears.

Other plant hazards include burrs, thorns, thistles, and poison oak. If you find any burrs or thistles on your dog, remove them as soon as possible before they become an unmanageable mat. Thorns can pierce a dog's foot and cause a great deal of pain. If you see that your dog is lame, stop and check his feet for thorns. Dogs are immune to poison oak but they can pick up the sticky, oily substance from the plant and transfer it to you.

Protect those paws. Be sure to keep your dog's nails trimmed so he avoids getting soft tissue or joint injuries. If your dog slows and refuses to go on, check to see that his paws aren't torn or worn. You can protect your dog's paws from trail hazards such as sharp gravel, foxtails, lava scree, and thorns by purchasing dog boots.

Sunburn. If your dog has light skin, he is an easy target for sunburn on his nose and other exposed skin areas. You can apply a nontoxic sunscreen to exposed skin areas that will help protect him from overexposure to the sun.

Ticks and fleas. Ticks can easily give your dog Lyme disease, as well as other diseases. Before you hit the trail, treat your dog with a flea and tick spray or powder. You can also ask your veterinarian about a once-a-month pour-on treatment that repels fleas and ticks.

Mosquitoes and deer flies. These little flying machines can do a job on your dog's snout and ears. Best bet is to spray your dog with fly repellent for horses to discourage both pests.

Giardia. Dogs can get giardia, which results in diarrhea. It is usually not debilitating, but it's definitely messy. A vaccine against giardia is available.

Mushrooms. Make sure your dog doesn't sample mushrooms along the trail. They could be poisonous to him, but he doesn't know that.

When you are finally ready to hit the trail with your dog, keep in mind that national parks and many wilderness areas do not allow dogs on trails. Your best bet is to hike in national forests, BLM lands, and state parks. Always call ahead to see what the restrictions are.

Index

About the Author

Lizann Dunegan is a freelance writer and photographer who specializes in writing outdoor guidebooks and travel articles about the Northwest. Her other books include *Best Easy Day Hikes Bend, Best Easy Day Hikes Portland, Best Easy Day Hikes Oregon's North Coast, Hiking the Oregon Coast, Trail Running Oregon, Mountain Biking Oregon: Northwest and Central Oregon, Road Biking Oregon,* and *Canine Oregon.* Lizann has been hiking trails in the Northwest for more than twenty-five years and is often accompanied by her partner, Ken Skeen, and two dogs, Bear and Tiz. Lizann also loves trail running, trail riding with her horse Miguel, backpacking, and camping.

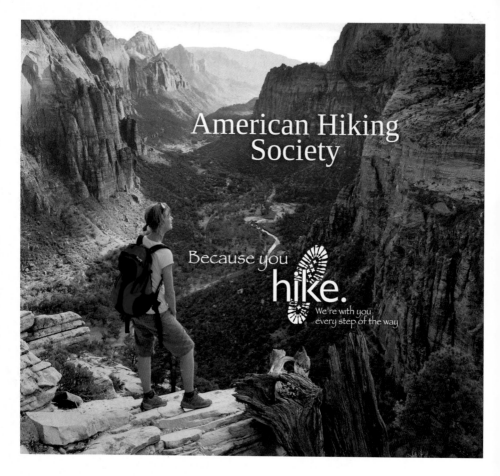

American Hiking
Society

Because you
hike.
We're with you
every step of the way

As a national voice for hikers, **American Hiking Society** works every day:

- Building and maintaining hiking trails
- Educating and supporting hikers by providing information and resources
- Supporting hiking and trail organizations nationwide
- Speaking for hikers in the halls of Congress and with federal land managers

Whether you're a casual hiker or a seasoned backpacker, become a member of American Hiking Society and join the national hiking community! You'll enjoy great member benefits and help preserve the nation's hiking trails, so tomorrow's hike is even better than today's. We invite you to join us now!

American
Hiking
Society